The Irish Catholic
Diaspora in America

The Irish Catholic Diaspora in America

Lawrence J. McCaffrey

The Catholic University of America Press
Washington, D.C.

Published originally in 1976 as *The Irish Diaspora in America* by Indiana University Press. Reprinted in 1984 by The Catholic University of America Press. This edition is revised.

Copyright © 1976, 1984, 1997
The Catholic University of America Press
All rights reserved
Printed in the United States of America

LIBRARY OF CONGRESS CATALOGING-IN-PUBLICATION DATA
McCaffrey, Lawrence John, 1925–
    The Irish Catholic diaspora in America / Lawrence J. McCaffrey.
       p. cm.
    Rev. ed. of: The Irish diaspora in America, 1984.
    Includes bibliographical references and index.
       1. Irish Americans—History.   2. Catholics—United States—
    History.   3. Immigrants—United States—History.   I. McCaffrey,
    Lawrence John, 1925–   Irish diaspora in America.   II. Title.
    E184.I6M345   1997
    973'.049162—dc21
    97-9720
       ISBN 0-8132-0896-3 (alk. paper)

To my father and mother: John Thomas and
Alma Ellen McCaffrey, in gratitude; and my
children: Kevin, Sheila, and Patricia McCaffrey,
in hope

Contents

Preface

Since *The Irish Diaspora in America* first appeared in 1976, university and commercial presses and scholarly journals have published a number of quality books and articles on Irish America in national and regional contexts. These and continuing changes in the Irish-American situation have persuaded me to take a fresh look at an ethnic experience that I began to research and write about more than twenty years ago. Although I am not necessarily pleased with all of its current aspects, I am considerably more optimistic about the preservation of an Irish-American identity than I was in 1976. I am still convinced that Catholic culture and values largely shaped that identity, but I am also aware that a majority of people in the United States who now define themselves as Irish or partly Irish are not Catholic. Because I write about the Irish who trace their lineage to Catholic immigrants, I have changed the title of this revision to *The Irish Catholic Diaspora in America*. Although my knowledge and interpretation of Irish-American Catholics comes from the contributions of many scholars, for the sake of readability I have been economical in the use of notes and have paid tribute to the people I have learned from in an extended "Recommended Reading" section.

Introduction: Irish Pioneers of the American Ghetto

From 1820 to 1920, about five million people born in Ireland entered the United States; about 75 percent were Catholic. Before and during the Great Famine of the 1840s, a number of families crossed the Atlantic. After 1850 most people leaving Ireland were young and single. In the early and middle stages of Irish emigration, males slightly outnumbered females. By the close of the nineteenth century, more women than men went to America.

For the most part, members of the Irish Catholic Diaspora came from rural backgrounds. Among those who settled in Canada, Australia, or New Zealand, quite a few decided to farm. But most of those selecting the United States as their destination, like those who chose Britain, settled in industrial and transportation centers. As pioneers of the American urban ghetto, they previewed the experiences of almost every other ethnic, religious, and racial minority that followed their trail.[1]

As the first large group of non–Anglo Protestants to arrive in American cities, they became targets for hate and violence. Nativism in the United States, a cultural child of English parents, defined itself in terms of the centuries-old conflict between Anglo-Saxon Protestants and their Irish Catholic enemies. Nativists in Britain and the United States despised Irish Catholics as cultural and political subversives, treacherous agents of authoritarianism, ignorance, and superstition, the key ingredients of popery. Obnoxious Irish Catholic social behavior, largely the result of a psychologically traumatic shift from rural to urban environments, reinforced prejudices that were essentially religious but also contained racist elements.

In his well-written, diligently researched, award-winning *Emigrants and Exiles: Ireland and the Irish Exodus to North America* (1985), Kerby A. Miller attributes Irish social and adjustment problems to pre-modern Gaelic and Catholic features of their culture that rendered them dysfunctional in urban-industrial settings. Miller's "social misfit" interpretation is largely based on immigrant letters. It argues that for a considerable period of time, Irish-American Catholics thought of themselves as exiles rather than immigrants, constantly dreaming of home and wishing to return there, and refusing to come to terms with their new situation. But immigrant letters are a shaky foundation for such a strongly stated thesis. There is always the question: who writes home and who does not? Are those least successful in the United States more likely to express alienation and homesickness than those making progress in the New World? Is it not likely that most people writing to fathers, mothers, sisters, brothers, and friends in the Old Country would reveal longings to see familiar faces and landscapes and to hear friendly sounds and voices from the past? Sentimentality is almost a social obligation in this type of correspondence.

Of course Miller is correct in describing the loneliness of Irish "immigrants or exiles" in the United States. But country boys and girls who left New England or Midwest farms for the cities were probably as unhappy in their new surroundings as were Irish immigrants. In many ways, urban life in the United States represents a wide variety of alienation experienced by newcomers who are frightened by a strange, new, competitive environment, and original inhabitants who resent being displaced by louts from rural America and immigrants from foreign countries. There is strong evidence that of all the European ethnics who arrived in the United States, the Irish felt most adjusted and comfortable. In his latest publication, *Out of Ireland* (1994), co-authored with Paul Wagner, Miller points out that they were the least likely to reverse the Atlantic crossing: "Among Italian immigrants to America, more than 40 percent returned to live in their homeland. Among Poles and Hungarians, more than 50 percent returned. And among Greek immigrants, more than 60 percent went back to their native land. But fewer than 10 percent of Irish immigrants to the New World ever returned to 'Mother Ireland.'"[2] These figures seem to contradict the "exile" and "sociologically and psychologically dysfunctional" Irish Catholic immigrant themes of *Emigrants and Exiles*.

In *The Irish Diaspora: A Primer* (1993), Donald Harmon Akenson disputes Miller's contention that Gaelic and Catholic cultural values were a significant barrier to social and economic mobility for Irish immigrants. He presents convincing evidence that Irish Catholics in Canada, Australia, New Zealand, and South Africa were as successful as English and Irish Protestants and other immigrant groups. Historian Malcolm Campbell supports Akenson's findings in his research on the Irish in Australia.[3] With the possible exception of Britain, where economic and social mobility continued to be slow, the Irish Catholic Diaspora throughout the English-speaking world has equaled and sometimes surpassed the income and status levels of Anglo and Irish Protestants. The fact that twentieth-century descendents of nineteenth-century tenant farmers and agricultural laborers have become university professors; elementary and secondary school teachers; distinguished novelists, playwrights, and poets; important figures on stage and screen; physicians; political leaders; and corporation executive officers classifies the Irish-American Catholic experience as a tremendous success story. Although the exile theme haunts the book and video version of *Out of Ireland,* Miller and the Wagners, Ellen Casey and Paul, concede examples of Irish Catholic achievement and prosperity in various regions of the United States.

In *The Irish Diaspora: A Primer* and a number of other works, Akenson criticizes me and others who equate Irish with Catholic, going so far as to accuse us of racism. He argues that anyone who has a personal or ancestral geographic connection with Ireland is Irish. And he points to the fact that among the forty million or so Americans who identify themselves as Irish in a 1970s National Opinion Research Center study, a 1980s Gallup poll, and a 1989–90 *National Survey of Religious Identification* conducted by the Graduate Center of the City University of New York, a substantial majority were Protestant.[4]

It seems to me that place of birth is a flimsy criterion for ethnic identity. When someone referred to the duke of Wellington as Irish because he was born in Ireland, he replied that if someone was born in a stable it would not make him a horse.[5] Ethnicity involves an interest in and commitment to the culture and history of your people, and usually a patriotic desire for your country's sovereignty. But very few Protestants, either Anglicans or Nonconformists, have had the same kind of Irish identity as Catholics. In Ireland, Protestant patriotism retreated before the advance of Irish nationalism linked with Irish Catholicism. Ideologically Irish nationalism has been inclusive, rejecting Catholic ascendancy, and there have been important Protestant political and literary figures who have espoused the cause of Irish independence, but the overwhelming majority of their coreligionists have refused invitations to participate in Irish freedom movements and, instead, have functioned as a British colonial garrison. Unfortunately, in Ireland, as in Bosnia and other trouble spots around the globe, religion has symbolized national and cultural identities.

One of Ireland's leading intellectuals, whom Akenson has described in a recent biography (*Conor: A Biography of Conor Cruise O'Brien,* 1994) as "the greatest living Irishman," insisted in his 1972 *States of Ireland* that the boundary separating Northern Ireland and the Republic delineates two distinct cultural nations occupying the island. In his important and successful venture into Irish intellectual history, *Culture and Anarchy in Ireland, 1890–1939* (1979), F. S. L. Lyons identified three cultural nations in Ireland, all flowing from religious identities: Irish Catholic, Anglo-Irish Protestant, and Ulster Nonconformist. To give credence to the O'Brien and Lyons theses and to invalidate Akenson's interpretation of Irishness as geographic rather than cultural, in December 1993 John Taylor, MP, a prominent Northern Ireland Unionist politician, insisted on a British and rejected an Irish identity for Ulster Protestants, insisting that Ireland consisted of two nations and two people: "Much as I enjoy the Irish and admire many of their cultural pursuits, I have to remind them that we in Northern Ireland are not Irish."[6]

In late eighteenth- and early nineteenth-century America, there was some community of feeling and interests between Irish Catholics and Protestants. But after 1820, when conflicts between nationalism and unionism fostered sectarian enmity in Ireland, and when American nativists, frightened by waves of Irish immigration, focused on Irish Catholics as the main target of their anxieties, Irish Protestants disassociated themselves from Irish Catholics. Presbyterians with Ulster backgrounds took on a Scots-Irish identity. Clashes between Orangemen and Catholics in late nineteenth-century America indicated that religious animosities also emigrated.

In the United States as in Ireland, to be Irish was to be Catholic. Negative Irish stereotypes in fiction and public entertainments were Catholic. And the Irish wore their religion as a badge of honor and embraced it as their nationality and culture. When stage and screen portraits of Irish Catholics shifted from unfavorable to favorable, when they acquired acceptability and respectability, and when John F. Kennedy won the hearts of the nation and the world, then Americans with Protestant roots in Ireland decided they were Irish after all.

Irish-American Catholics were more than just passive victims of nativism. In their efforts to overcome hate and discrimination and to achieve respectability in the United States, they cultivated ethnic pride, fostered self-sufficiency, and exploited political talents to achieve power. Irish Catholic responses to the challenges of Anglo-American prejudice established precedents for identity-seeking and survival politics that have influenced the conduct of other minorities.

Catholic Irish America is also a fascinating case study of the relationship between European and American experiences. Before the recent interest in minority-group studies, examinations of non-Anglo-American Protestant Whites in the United States tended to accent accommodation, acculturation, and assimilation, de-emphasizing the European components of their personalities. Contemporary studies focus more on the European roots of American ethnicity, but not enough. For example, many examinations of the American Irish give little attention to both the cultural and psychological luggage they transported across the Atlantic and the continuing links between Ireland and America.

It is true, of course, that Irish Catholic immigrants were probably the least sophisticated Europeans entering the United States in the first half of the nineteenth century. But they did have a culture, meager as it was, and a history—a painful record as victims of conquest, colonialism, tyranny, prejudice, poverty, and famine. Most Irish Catholics arriving in the United States between 1820 and 1850 came as refugees from disaster; they were running away from destitution and oppression rather than rushing toward freedom and opportunity.

While these nineteenth-century Irish immigrants landed culturally and technologically limited on the American shore, seeking survival in the New World as an alternative to extinction in the Old, their unfortunate experience in Ireland positively influenced adjustments to life in the United States. Perhaps the most important thesis of this book is the assertion that the American Irish Catholic Diaspora remained part of the totality of Irish history, linking Ireland, Britain, and the United States as participants in the Irish Question. For example, the close associations between Irish and Catholic identities that generated Anglo-Protestant prejudice in Britain and the United States provided its victims with a means to bridge Old and New Worlds and ease the problems of adaptations to strange urban environments. Catholicism also provided a focus for unity in the Irish ghettos, creating an Irish-American community out of a people who arrived in the United States with diverse loyalties to parish, townland, and county. Through Catholicism, they developed a solidarity that was expressed in Irish-American nationalism and political power.

The famous Irish political style was shaped by Irish history, Catholic communal values, and confrontations with British imperialism and colonialism. In their efforts to free themselves from anti-Catholic Penal Laws and to achieve national independence, the Irish learned to compete within the context of the Anglo-Saxon Protestant political system. They became particularly adroit in the techniques of mass agitation, political organization and confrontation, and liberal-democratic politics. They expressed their nationalist ambitions in the rhetoric of British liberalism, and the words and values of liberal democracy became essential elements of Irish political and nationalist theory. Such politicization meant that, although the Irish arrived in this country culturally unpolished and technologically impoverished, they were politically sophisticated and prepared to challenge Anglo Americans for a share of political power and influence. In time they took control of most of the large cities in the East and Midwest, San Francisco in the West, and New Orleans in the South. Irish political machines were often guilty of corrupt practices, but employing Catholic values, they moved the Democratic party away from individual toward communal liberalism.

While the Irish historical experience prepared Irish Catholics to function in Anglo-Protestant America, in time the educational process was geographically reversed. In the second half of the nineteenth century, the American Irish influenced the nationalist agenda. Their hatred of British rule that had degraded them in Ireland and their search for respectability in America through the establishment of an independent European homeland made them in the United States more passionately committed to a sovereign Ireland than those who remained at home. Irish-American money and commitment to liberal-democratic republicanism sustained and colored Irish nationalism, contributing significantly to the final success of the liberation movement. And in their efforts on behalf of Ireland's independence, Irish Catholics set precedents for the use of ethnic power to manipulate American foreign policy.

Irish Nationalism persisted in the United States longer than it did in Canada, Australia, or New Zealand, where Irish Catholics eventually decided that it was an impediment to assimilation. But the American population mix, as well as memories and myths about Ireland and reactions to Anglo-Protestant nativism perpetuated commitments to the Irish freedom cause. With the exception of segregated, non-White native populations, and the French, who were mostly confined to the province of Quebec, until recently Irish Catholics in Britain and Commonwealth countries only mixed with British and Irish Protestants. In the United States they have had to interact not only with Anglo and Irish Protestants but also with a plethora of ethnic, religious, and racial groups. In this mosaic, identity issues that discouraged assimilation and fostered ethnic nationalisms were more crucial than in more homogeneous environments.

Frequently this book argues that liberal intellectuals, in criticizing the conservativeness of American Catholicism and its Irish leadership, have libeled both an institution and a nationality. Despite the charges of opponents both within and outside the Catholic Church, the influence of the Irish on American Catholicism has been, for the most part, progressive rather than reactionary. The European and American traditions of the Irish, their familiarity with two contrasting cultures—Anglo-Saxon Protestant and Roman Catholic—and their domination over American Catholicism and urban politics placed them in a position to solidify Catholic ethnics into a larger religious community. And because of their essentially democratic political commitment, the Irish were the only Catholic group that could have led an American Catholic Church, with its diverse European immigrant constituency, into an accommodation with the dominant, Anglo-American Protestant culture. Irish leadership of Catholic America has politically and socially if not theologically liberalized the American Church and prevented the construction and maintenance of permanent walls of hostility and suspicion between Catholics and most other Americans. Irish influences in Catholic America have also made possible that unique quality of American life—political consensus existing side by side with cultural pluralism—preventing a suffocating dullness and conformity while sustaining an essential unity.

The Irish Catholic journey in America from ghetto to suburbs, from despised aliens to valued members of the community has been arduous, but in historical time relatively brief. Less than three generations after the Famine washed hundreds of thousands of unwanted human refuse onto the American shore, Irish Catholics controlled the Catholic Church, most of the major cities, and a large portion of the organized labor movement in the United States. Their social and economic mobility and twentieth-century absorption into the middle-class mainstream, qualifies rather than eliminates them as objects of ethnic study. Are the same people who pioneered the American urban ghetto now establishing precedents for the future "progress" of other ethnics, both Black and White? Does the present degree of assimilation of Irish America indicate that the melting-pot myth has become a suburban reality? If so, is the change from unwelcome alien to respectable, middle-class suburbanite a progressive or retrogressive move?

In evaluating the late twentieth-century Irish Catholic community where many of its values approximate those of Anglo-American Protestants, the historian and social scientist can begin to ask some fundamental questions about the future of ethnic America. Have the many Irish who have shed their ethnicity in a successful quest for respectability been adequately compensated for abandoning their cultural identity? Has their trip from Irish Catholic, urban neighborhoods to suburban melting pots been a journey to achievement and contentment or a trip from someplace to noplace? Is the history of Irish America an inspiring ethnic success story or a warning to other groups that they should be wary of surrendering cultural distinctiveness for the sake of assimilation? Will the effort of many Irish-American Catholics to base their identity on history and culture rather than religion succeed in improving the quality if not the quantity of a self-conscious Irish ethnicity, thus preserving it as a significant portion of the American ethnic mosaic? These questions are complex, the answers cannot be simple, and they will be a long time in coming.

PART I

The Irish Cultural, Political,
Social, and Religious Heritages

1. Ireland: English Conquest and Protestant Ascendancy, 1170–1801

Ireland's long and turbulent association with England began in May 1170 when Richard fitz Gilbert de Clare, earl of Pembroke, known as Strongbow, a vassal of Henry II, led a small contingent of Norman knights across the Irish Sea from Wales to the southwestern tip of Wexford. Dermot MacMurrough, deposed king of Leinster, invited these freebooters to help him regain the throne he had lost in a civil war in 1166. MacMurrough persuaded Strongbow to join forces by promising him the hand of his daughter in marriage and succession to the kingship of Leinster.[1] After the Normans landed in Ireland they quickly made it clear that they intended to stay and that their territorial ambitions extended beyond Leinster. The invaders began a military sweep through the country, winning victories with superior weapons, armor, and horses, and securing conquered territory with castle fortresses. The Irish, divided by clan and regional loyalties and factionalism, could not muster a united, defensive front.

Worried that Norman victories might mean that his vassals would establish an independent, rival state in the neighboring island, Henry II in 1171 traveled to Ireland and received the homage of Norman barons and a few clan chiefs as lord of Ireland, a title Adrian IV had first conferred by papal grant. The pope, an Englishman, blessed and ratified the Norman conquest, not as a gesture of ethnic loyalty but as a means of forcing individualistic Irish Christians and their anarchistic church to accept the authority of Rome. Adrian's actions indicated that Ireland was a victim of religious as well as political imperialism.

In the struggle between Normans and Celts, Irish disunity was a more decisive factor than English military superiority. England represented a new and dynamic Europe, Ireland the old and static. While other parts of Western civilization were in the process of evolving through feudalism into centralized nation states, Ireland had remained a clan society where major chiefs reigned as monarchs over seven petty kingdoms. When the Normans arrived, Rory O'Connor was Ard Rhi (high king) at Tara, but since clan and territorial interests took precedence over any concept of nation, his title was more nominal than real.

Although Gaelic Ireland lacked the institutional framework and loyalties essential for political nationhood, a common language and literary tradition, laws reflecting the customs and values of the entire population, and Celtic Christianity—more Eastern than Western in spirit and practice—welded the Irish into a distinct cultural community.[2]

Following the collapse of the Roman Empire in the West, Irish monks played a major role in re-Christianizing and re-civilizing Europe. Artistic genius, an emphasis on learning, and zealous missionary activity exhibited the dynamic intensity of Celtic Christianity. But with the development of the papal monarchy and Roman religious imperialism, it slowly retreated from the Continent to Britain and finally back to its original

Irish base. Eighth- and ninth-century Viking raids, which concentrated on monastic centers of wealth and learning, seriously damaged Celtic Christianity, initiating a long period of corruption and decay, draining much of Irish cultural vitality. Although Irish Christianity and culture had slipped from golden peaks, outside criticism, an apologia for foreign intervention, was exaggerated. Even before the Norman arrival, Irish society was already affected by European trends. Feudalism had modified the clan system. Petty kings had become vassals of provincial monarchs whose powers were so evenly balanced that none were able to politically unify the country. Irish Christianity also experienced a reformation. Diocesan structures challenged monastic dominance, and Benedictine communalism was replacing the individualism of Celtic monasticism. No doubt Viking invasions damaged the quality of Irish learning, but there was a cultural renaissance of some significance in the eleventh and twelfth centuries. Despite the evolving character of Irish life, from Continental and English perspectives, Ireland appeared a primitive, even savage place, with an archaic clan system and a decadent, disorganized, and immoral brand of Christianity remote from Roman authority. Normans came to "civilize" and modernize the country by Anglicizing and Romanizing it. Their superiority complex in regard to conquered natives remained a permanent feature of Anglo–Irish relations.

Exploiting the chaos and jealousies within the Irish clan system, English invaders enjoyed a century and a half of territorial conquest, in many areas substituting Continental and English feudal and manorial practices for Gaelic political and economic institutions. But early in the fourteenth century, the Irish launched a counter offensive, forcing the English into a defensive posture. This reversal was due to a number of factors, including the Irish adoption of Norman military tactics and their alliance with the Scots against the common English enemy. From 1315 to 1318, Scottish liberator Edward Bruce and his

Irish allies almost drove the English out of Ireland. But the anarchy at the core of the clan system reasserted itself at the moment of victory, preventing the sustained unity and cooperation necessary to purge the English presence. Clan chiefs fought to recapture or retain local power rather than restore Irish sovereignty. Once secure in their little bailiwicks, they were as likely to battle one another as to fight the foreigner.

Probably more than improved Irish military skills and the Scottish alliance, assimilation retarded a complete English victory. While Irish clan chiefs were adopting Norman military practices as well as feudalism and manorialism, Norman barons were embracing the values, customs, and language of Gaelic Ireland. Geography and marriage encouraged the assimilation process. Isolated in predominantly Irish areas, Normans wed native women and, after several generations, not much more than their names was left of their English origins. Far from the Leinster core of English rule in Ireland, Normans in Munster, Connacht, and southern fringes of Ulster cultivated an Irish life style, resembling clan chiefs in their manners and resentment of outside interference.

From the early fourteenth until the early sixteenth century, the unassimilated English were more concerned with holding on to what they had than in expansion, confining their energies to a garrison region in Leinster called the Pale. In 1366 their Parliament expressed this defensive mentality in the Statutes of Kilkenny. They were an early example of cultural segregation in Western civilization, an attempt to protect minority values and institutions from the threat of a majority native culture. According to the Statutes, the English in Ireland could not associate with the Irish, marry their women, wear their costumes, speak their language, adopt their children, or utilize the services of their priests.

In 1509, when Henry VIII ascended the English throne, he was actually lord of three Irelands: the Pale or Anglo-Ireland, Gaelic Ireland, and the ambiguous in between. Covering the present counties of Dublin, Louth, Meath, Westmeath, Kildare, and Kilkenny, the Pale was a miniature England in language, cultural loyalties, and institutions.

Although the relationships between Irish minor chiefs in their tribal enclaves and the major chiefs who dominated vast areas, and between tenants and landowners in Gaelic Ireland beyond the Pale, were often similar to those between vassals and lords in feudalism and lords and serfs in a manorial system, the native Irish still lived within the borders of a separate cultural nation. Their laws reflected Irish values, and their judges (Brehons) arbitrated legal disputes between contending parties, punishing with fines rather than with physical retribution. Church influences, the weight of public opinion, and the scorching satire of bardic poets helped enforce judicial decisions. And since in the Irish tradition the family was a corporate whole, the complete tribe bore the responsibility for the crimes, debts, and penal obligations of its members.

Differing attitudes toward primogeniture formed a major distinction between the natives and the English in Ireland, one with both property and political implications. Unlike the English in their own country and in Ireland, who passed on land and political authority associated with it to the eldest male heir, the Irish elected their chiefs (taoiseachs) among the leading male members of each clan, and successors (tanistes) were chosen before the death of chiefs. All sons received a portion of their fathers' lands (gavelkind). Theoretically, the election of chiefs was supposed to guarantee the succession of talent; often it encouraged civil wars among taniste candidates, intensifying the anarchy of the clan system. Becoming a clan chief involved the ability to survive civil war and assassination attempts—requiring as much luck as skill—but at least it meant the victory of strength and cunning if not virtue.

Religion in Gaelic Ireland also differed from that of the Pale. The Irish wore their religion more lightly than the English, and continued to have little respect for or contact with

Rome. Bishops and abbots came from clan chief families, married or kept concubines, and passed on dioceses or monasteries to sons, sometimes listed as nephews. Clan chiefs usually married in civil ceremonies, divorced easily and frequently, and often were involved in polygamous relationships. The Irish were not hypocritical about their casual sexual encounters; bastardy did not even exist as a concept in their legal system. Men freely acknowledged their paternity on a mother's claim, and sons of both wife and paramour shared equally in their father's inheritance and in the right to be considered as candidates for clan chief. Among the clergy, mendicant friars—Franciscans, Dominicans, Augustinians, and Carmelites—best represented orthodox Western Christian values and practices. They endeavored to live and teach the austerity of the Christian ideal to the wild and exuberant Irish.

While the Pale represented the core of the English colony, Ulster in the North was the essence of Gaelic Ireland, an area barely touched by the invading culture. On the fringes of the Pale and in parts of Connacht in the West and Munster in the South, institutions, language, dress, and religious practices represented a fusion of Anglo- and native-Irish cultures. The feudal aristocracy in these areas drifted toward Irishness, but they tried to maintain close relationships with the English colony in the Pale as well as with clan-chief neighbors.

In an effort to enhance the national and international prestige of the Tudor monarchy and to improve England's security, both Thomas Cardinal Wolsey and Thomas Cromwell, his successor as the king's minister, advised Henry VIII to jettison a defensive strategy in Ireland and to convert his authority there from shadow to substance. Taking their advice, in the 1530s, the king crushed the power of the Kildare Fitzgeralds, the most influential family in the Pale, and in 1540, he persuaded leading clan chiefs in other sections of the country to surrender their lands to him, receiving them back as his vassals along with feudal titles—O'Neill became earl of Tyrone, O'Donnell, earl of Tyrconnell, and O'Brien, earl of Thomond. In 1541 an Irish parliament dominated by Anglo barons, with a sprinkling of clan chiefs, recognized Henry as king rather than lord of Ireland.

Henry's new title and the feudal policy of surrender and regrant theoretically violated the Gaelic institutional structure, but they were more symbolic of English domination than actual indications of any significant change in the reality of Irish life. Distracted by English and Continental affairs, tight-fisted Henry refused to fund a bureaucracy adequate to control Ireland. Beyond the Pale, much of Ireland remained culturally Gaelic and politically chaotic and tribal. Henry's real impact on the course of Irish history was the introduction of the Reformation rather than the superficial paraphernalia of English feudalism.

Desirous for a male heir and frustrated in his efforts to obtain an annulment of his marriage with Catherine of Aragon, aunt of Charles V, the Holy Roman Emperor, Henry in 1534 broke with Rome, declaring English religious independence and his own leadership over the church in England and Ireland. English and Irish Parliaments passed Acts of Supremacy confirming the king's religious claims. Irish bishops, Anglo Ireland's leaders, and Gaelic clan chiefs all accepted the new state religion.

Tudor quarrels with the pope had little relevance for the Irish, who were Catholics rather than papists. And Irish lords and chiefs, like representatives of the aristocracy all over Europe, accepted the principle "cuius regio, eius religio"—the religion of the prince should determine the faith of the people—because union of church and state was a valid method of securing public order and tranquility. In addition, the change of religious leaders from pope to king did not interfere with the devotional life of the people. Although Henry confiscated the wealth and property of Irish monastic establishments, keeping much of the spoils for the royal treasury and distributing the rest to loyal vassals and clan chiefs, his rejection of papal supremacy did not affect theology or liturgy. The Irish continued to attend Mass and receive the sacraments, remaining essentially Catholic.

Full implications of the Reformation became apparent during the reigns of Henry's son, Edward VI (1547–1553), and his younger daughter, Elizabeth I (1558–1603), when the state church adopted a Protestant theology and a less Catholic liturgy. The native Irish and the Old English, descendents of the Norman conquerors, viewed the effort to make them conform to Protestantism as cultural imperialism, more pernicious than English political and military adventures in Ireland. Their leaders negotiated with Continental Catholic powers to obtain allies in their resistance to England. And the religious dimension of Ireland's struggle to thwart English power altered the character of Irish Catholicism, transforming it into the main component of Irish identity, the nucleus of an incipient nationalism. Counter-Reformation agents, Jesuits and Franciscans, poured into Ireland, beginning a process of Romanizing Irish Catholicism not fully completed until the second half of the nineteenth century. Leaders of Catholic Ireland began to scorn Oxford and Cambridge educations for their sons, sending them instead to Continental Catholic universities. Candidates for the priesthood studied in Spain, France, Belgium, and Italy. Although the English had employed Protestantism as a crusading instrument to achieve effective control of Ireland, the results were far different from those they had anticipated. Anglo-Saxon Protestant imperialism worked politically but created stubborn cultural pockets of resistance in the Irish mind.

Protestantism destroyed the mechanism of cultural assimilation that for centuries had protected Ireland from complete conquest by her stronger neighbor. Religious differences erected an impassable barrier between English and Irish identities. Catholicism symbolized a besieged Irish culture: Protestantism represented Anglo-Saxon aggression. While the native Irish and Old English rallied behind the standard of Catholicism to defend their cultural and political autonomy, the English justified their effort to conquer, subdue, and dominate Ireland as a Protestant crusade against the alien, tyrannical, and subversive forces of popery.

While most Irish and English historians have emphasized the significance to the British Isles of the conflict between English Protestants and Irish Catholics, the struggle also had European aspects. During the sixteenth and seventeenth centuries, England was engaged in a series of wars against Spain and France to achieve and maintain status as a major power. Since its enemies were Catholic nations, the English government cultivated Protestant nativism as an ideological weapon. England's numerous wars against Continental Catholics and the religious propaganda aspects of those conflicts prompted arguments for total subjugation of Ireland. English leaders feared that the Spanish or the French would exploit Irish Catholic animosity toward Protestant England by providing troops to aid Irish liberation movements. And an Ireland occupied by either the Spanish or the French would place England geographically in a papist pincer, diminishing the effect of its sea power. So from the mid-sixteenth well into the twentieth century, militant, Protestant, anti-Catholic, English nativism coupled with British imperialism and national security needs provided the foundations for England's Irish policy.

Elizabeth I's armies conquered Munster and Connacht and pushed stubborn Ulster to the point of surrender. In her effort to permanently suppress the potential for rebellion in Ireland, the queen employed a plantation policy first tried by her Catholic sister Mary in Laoise and Offaly. She seized large amounts of Munster rebel property and colonized it with Protestant loyalists from England. After Ulster Chief Hugh O'Neill submitted to Mountjoy, Elizabeth's deputy in Ireland, on March 30, 1603, six days after her death, he and other Gaelic clan chiefs left Ireland in fear that they had been marked for assassination by English enemies. In 1607, James I, the first Stuart king, took advantage of "the flight of the earls" by branding them traitors, confiscating their vast estates, and "planting" them with English Protestants and Presbyterians from the Scottish lowlands. They joined other Scots who had moved into northeastern Ulster in the late fifteenth and early sixteenth centuries. Unlike the earlier southern plantations, where the major change was from Catholic to Protestant landowners, the Ulster project involved density, settling a variety of classes and occupations to create the only sizable Protestant community in Ireland, sowing the seeds of today's political-religious-cultural crisis in Northern Ireland.

In the seventeenth century, Stuart adherence to Divine Right of Kings political theories, their arbitrary governing styles, Catholic marriages, and sometimes sympathies for Catholic subjects antagonized the English Parliament, setting the stage for civil war. Taking advantage of division and conflict in England in the 1640s, Gaelic and Old English Catholics joined forces in the Confederation of Kilkenny, and recaptured a considerable portion of the country previously lost to English conquest. But the Gaelic–Old English alliance was fragile. The latter group still considered themselves more English than Irish and wanted to recover the property and political and social influence that they had lost to New English Protestants. The former wanted a complete revolution, one that would restore the Gaelic order. Giovanni Battista Rinuccini, papal legate, and James Butler, earl of Ormond and King Charles I's deputy in Ireland, exploited and manipulated divisions within the Confederation. Rinuccini encouraged the Gaelic faction to function as a sword of the Counter-Reformation. Butler concentrated on luring the Old English into the Stuart camp in the war with Parliament.

Oliver Cromwell took advantage of the lack of solidarity in Catholic Ireland. After defeating Stuart forces in England and

Scotland, in 1649 he crossed over to Ireland and crushed Irish rebels, confiscated their property, transferring it to English Protestant loyalists, and proceeded to drive Catholic leaders and their followers west of the Shannon river into Connacht.

Despite the plantations by Mary and Elizabeth in Leinster and Munster and the massive resettlement under James, before the rebellion of the 1640s Catholics still owned two-thirds of Irish property. After Cromwell's confiscations and resettlements, however, a small Protestant minority controlled three-fourths of Irish soil. Nine years of struggle against British authority and Cromwell's vengeance had diminished the Irish population by a third and massively reduced the property, social standing, and political influence of Catholics. Many were transported to the West Indies as slaves.

After the Restoration in 1660, Irish Catholics supported the Stuarts because they believed that Charles II (1660–1685) and his brother, James II (1685–1688), were empathetic to their religious convictions and might even restore some of the property lost to the Tudors and to Cromwell. Aware of the loyalty of Catholic Ireland, James II, following his deposition by the English Parliament in 1688 (the Glorious Revolution), decided to fight for his throne in Ireland rather than in England. As before, war in Ireland was part of a wider European conflict. Led by the new English King William III, a European alliance was trying to restrain the territorial ambitions of France's Louis XIV. Popes Innocent XI and Alexander VIII were also hostile to Louis, and thus supportive of the alliance.

On the banks of the Boyne on July 12, 1690, William's Dutch, German, English, Danish, and Irish Protestant army defeated James's French, German, Walloon, and Irish Catholic troops. When Protestant victory became inevitable, James fled the battlefield and then Ireland, leaving his Irish supporters with a few French allies to struggle on against superior forces. Under the brilliant leadership of Patrick Sarsfield, Old English and Gaelic Catholics made a brave fight in an impossible situation, gradually falling back on Limerick where they held out against a long and large-scale Protestant siege.

Because he had to cope with other problems, such as maintaining the alliance against Louis XIV and securing the English throne, William offered the leaders of Catholic Ireland honorable terms of surrender. According to the 1691 Treaty of Limerick, they were permitted to leave their country and to serve under Continental Catholic monarchs with a guarantee that co-religionists left behind would not suffer either persecution or property loss. When they sailed off to France, their dependents were protected by only a piece of paper that relied on the integrity of England and its Tudor-, Cromwellian-, and Williamite-planter colony in Ireland.

William was anything but a Protestant fanatic. His own country, the Dutch Republic, had experimented with a policy of religious tolerance as an alternative to civil war between Catholics and Calvinists. He was prepared to apply this same flexibility to religious divisions in England and Ireland. To William, stability and unity were more important political objectives than Protestant Ascendancy or Catholic humiliation. But British and Irish Protestants demanded a harsh reckoning with "seditious" Catholic enemies. In the last decade of the seventeenth and the first two decades of the eighteenth centuries, British and Irish Parliaments, purged of Catholic representation, enacted laws abolishing the civil rights of papists and outlawing Catholic worship. Carefully considering the intensity of English and Irish Protestant no-popery fanaticism, William and his successors decided that it would be impolitic to resist popular passions and reluctantly assented to anti-Catholic legislation.

Resulting Penal Laws in Ireland were more comprehensive and severe than those in Britain (England, Scotland, and Wales), covering all aspects of the political, social, economic, and religious lives of Catholics. They exiled Catholic bishops, forbade the entry of priests into the country, outlawed religious orders, and restricted the movements of resident secular clergy. If rigidly enforced, the exile of bishops and restrictions against priests would have eventually eliminated the Catholic clergy. In addition to assailing Catholic institutions and curtailing Catholic worship, the Irish Penal Laws also relegated Catholics to subcitizen status. They could not vote, sit in Parliament, hold commissions in the armed forces, serve as government employees, establish schools, practice law, possess weapons, or purchase property. If the son of a Catholic landowner became a Protestant he could seize his father's land, reducing his parent to the status of life tenant.

Defeat and the revenge policies of their common enemy welded the Old English and the native Irish into one oppressed Irish Catholic community. Penal legislation polarized Ireland into conquerors and conquered. A Protestant minority possessed over 90 percent of the country's property and enjoyed a complete monopoly of political power. The 75 percent Catholic majority held less than 10 percent of the property and paid tithes to support the Protestant religious establishment. Of course not all Protestants were members of the aristocracy and gentry. Some were merchants, tradesmen, clerics, even tenant farmers and agricultural laborers. And many non-Catholic Christians did not belong to the Established Church. A substantial number, perhaps 12 percent, were Nonconformists, mostly Ulster Presbyterians. A Sacramental Test Clause attached to the 1704 Popery Act excluded them from civil and military office. Toleration and Indemnity Acts eased their legal burdens, but they were less than first-class citizens. Resenting their inferior status, during the eighteenth century several hundred thousand Nonconformists emigrated and became the first Irish diaspora in America.

English conquest and Protestant Ascendancy reduced most Catholics to illiterate, poverty-stricken agricultural laborers, or small tenant farmers working for alien masters. But not all Catholics were members of the rural or urban lower classes. A minority of the landed aristocracy and gentry, often with the connivance of Protestant neighbors, managed to retain property. They were quiet and humble, hoping to avoid notice and trouble by proclaiming loyalty to the crown. Restrictions on Catholic property ownership encouraged the growth of a substantial Catholic middle class, particularly in the provisions trade. Upper- and middle-class Catholics had to send children abroad for advanced schooling, and significant numbers of the Catholic aristocracy and gentry continued to serve as officers in Bourbon and Hapsburg armies.

Some Protestants who wrote, supported, and enforced the Penal Laws said that they were endeavoring to root out the "evils" of popery, expecting that persecution would force many Catholics to convert to the "true faith." Terror, however, rather than proselytism was the essential purpose of anti-Catholic legislation. Protestants in Ireland were an outnumbered English garrison constantly fearing a slave revolt that might cost them their property and perhaps their lives. The Penal Laws expressed this paranoia and were designed to guarantee a permanent minority Protestant Ascendancy by demoralizing and dehumanizing the native Catholic majority. Penal Law psychology was flawless: conquered, debased, humiliated, and frightened people, more concerned with survival than human rights, do not make good revolutionary material.

Because Protestant politicians and officials did not invest much money or energy in enforcing the religious clauses of the Penal Laws, Catholicism continued to flourish. In fact, by the end of the eighteenth century the Catholic Church in Ireland was a much healthier and dynamic institution than it had been in 1691. Repression inspired reform, and persecution improved the quality of the hierarchy and clergy, reinforcing ties between Irish and Continental Catholicism and increasing the influence of Rome in Irish Catholic affairs. To hold on to property and to retain social status and political influence, most members of the Catholic aristocracy and gentry did defect to

Protestantism. With few exceptions, middle-class, agricultural-laboring, tenant-farming, city and town working-class Catholics remained loyal to the old religion.

Despite the continued commitment of the overwhelming majority of the Irish people to a Catholic Church revitalized under the lash of persecution, the Penal Laws accomplished their main purpose. Physical and psychological terror did demoralize Irish Catholics, and their fear and insecurity strengthened Protestant Ascendancy.

There were of course some exceptions to Catholic timidity. Not all quietly submitted to poverty and oppression. During the eighteenth and early nineteenth centuries, Catholic associations and committees, representing the aristocracy, gentry, and middle class, frequently petitioned the crown and the Irish Parliament for the repeal of laws depriving them of civil, religious, and property rights. And many Catholic rural folk joined secret societies to protest high rents, tithes to the Protestant Church, the low wages that tenant farmers paid agricultural laborers, and excessive dues that their own priests demanded for baptisms, weddings, and funerals. In the border counties of Ulster, Catholic Defenders fought Protestant Peep O'Day Boys over land. After one such County Armagh brawl, the so-called Battle of the Diamond, in September 1795 victorious Protestants founded the Orange Order; it remains the most extreme voice of Protestant opinion in Ulster. Secret societies—White boys, Captain Moonlight, Molly Maguires, Defenders, Ribbonmen—used violent methods of intimidation: burning hayricks, destroying buildings, maiming cattle, and assaulting landlord agents, tithe collectors, and other farmers who dared occupy farms of evicted members of their own class. Through much of the eighteenth and into the early years of the nineteenth century, a guerrilla war raged in parts of rural Ireland between secret societies and forces of law and order. Though often cruel and capricious, terrorism did serve to enforce a minimal moral economy in agrarian Ireland by limiting financial pressures exerted by the Protestant Church and by landlords on the native population.

Some historians have taken tremendous liberties with reality by referring to agrarian secret societies as the embryo of Irish nationalism. These societies were concerned with local tenant farmer and agricultural labor grievances and, in the case of the Ulster border counties, with sectarian defense. They did not wage war on landlordism as such or articulate a comprehensive nationalist ideology.

The English Protestant colony rather than Irish Catholics first delineated an Irish political nation. In the course of the eighteenth century, with Catholics demoralized by physical and psychological terror, Protestant planters began to relax and assumed an Anglo-Irish patriot identity in defiance of British restrictions on Irish commerce and the sovereignty of the Irish Parliament.[3] Anglo-Irish Protestant patriotism grew concurrently with and shared the same principles as Anglo-American patriotism. Both protested British political and economic imperialisms, insisting on the role of new adults no longer dependent on mother England's protection. Anglo-Irish and Anglo-American patriots both expressed principles and goals in British Whiggery rhetoric, exalting the Glorious Revolution and John Locke's *Two Treatises on Government* as the sources of their ideals. They borrowed the English myth that in the 1640s and in 1688 Parliament contested the Stuarts to preserve the individual liberty and popular sovereignty premises of the Social Contract, rather than the reality that its main objective was to protect the interests of the landed oligarchy.

Anglo-Irish and Anglo-American patriots affirmed allegiances to British culture and institutions. At the same time they argued that British tyranny denied them natural rights as human beings and constitutional privileges that could best be protected and nourished in local legislatures freely discussing and deciding local issues.

During the late 1770s and early 1780s, the courses of Irish

and American history were linked when the Americans resorted to a war of liberation to emancipate themselves from the British empire. With most Irish soldiers serving in North America and the combined French and Spanish fleets in control of Atlantic sea-lanes, Ireland was left virtually defenseless against a possible Bourbon invasion. When neither the Irish nor the British governments could muster an Irish home army, Anglo-Irish patriots organized a Volunteer force and then used it to intimidate Britain. Responding to Volunteer threats and the pressures of Anglo-Irish Protestant opinion, the British Parliament in 1779–1780 removed restrictions on Irish commerce and finally in 1782 surrendered its claim to legislate for Ireland.

From 1782 until the end of 1800 there was an Irish nation, but it was exclusively Protestant. Although Henry Grattan, the most prominent and talented champion of the patriot cause, argued for a nonsectarian Ireland and warned his fellow Protestants that they could never really be free as long as the Catholic majority remained slaves, most Anglo-Irish Protestants were convinced that total repeal of the Penal Laws would lead to Catholic power at the expense of Protestant property and political influence. They refused to admit Catholics to first-class citizenship in the Irish nation, insisting on the permanence of Protestant Ascendancy.

The threatened invasion by the armies of the French Revolution compelled the British government to court support from English and Scottish Catholics and the goodwill of its Catholic Hapsburg ally by repealing many of the Penal Laws in Britain and urging similar concessions from the Irish Parliament. Such pressures did persuade the Anglo Irish to lift some burdens of prejudice from Catholics, permitting them to operate schools, practice law, hold commissions in the army below the rank of colonel, lease property on a long term basis, and vote in parliamentary elections if the property they occupied was rated at 40 shillings for tax purposes. The Irish

Parliament even endowed a Roman Catholic seminary at Maynooth, County Kildare, to prevent exposing young seminarians to the ideology of the French Revolution permeating the Continent. Despite improvements in their situation, Catholics remained pariahs, excluded from Parliament and political office. Since landlords could control tenant farmer votes with the threat of eviction, even the 40s franchise seemed meaningless without a secret ballot.

Anglo-Irish Protestants as well as Irish Catholics were dissatisfied with the political and religious exclusiveness of the Protestant nation. Complaining that the Dublin Parliament, like its Westminster counterpart, represented the interests and opinion of the landed aristocracy and gentry, middle-class radicals, inspired by events in France, agitated for popular sovereignty. In the 1790s, Protestant radicals in Belfast and Dublin organized the Society of United Irishmen to express their liberal, democratic ideology. Instructed by their Jacobin cousins in France and exasperated by government repression in Ireland, United Irishmen demands ranged beyond parliamentary reform, finally insisting on establishing a democratic republic through a French-supported revolution. In order to achieve a united front as a prelude to insurrection, Theobald Wolfe Tone, a United Irishmen leader, appealed to the Catholic population for support, strongly endorsing its claim to equal citizenship and pledging a nonsectarian Irish republic.

Anticipating an uprising, the Irish government arrested a number of United Irishmen and moved mostly Catholic militia companies into Ulster to seize arms and frighten potential rebels. When revolution came in 1798, it was a badly coordinated fiasco and, contrary to a myth perpetuated by many Irish nationalists to this day, Protestants and Catholics did not unite to free Ireland from tyranny. Catholic peasants in Wexford fought a bloody religious and class war against Protestant landlords, and Orange yeomen brutally punished them. Revolution in Ulster was as sectarian as it was in Wexford. More influenced by Orange bigotry than United Irishmen idealism, Protestant rebels in Antrim and Down were unenthusiastic about cooperating with Catholics in a struggle to create an ecumenical Irish republic. When General Jean Humbert finally landed with a small French Army in August 1798, confused Catholic peasants met him on the shores of Killala Bay in County Mayo and promised to help him defend the pope and the Blessed Virgin. The combined French and Irish forces, short on numbers and provisions, fought well and won some impressive victories, but Lord Charles Cornwallis's army, containing many Catholics, outnumbered and eventually defeated them. After the surrender, Humbert's soldiers were returned to France; Irish rebels were executed.

While the rebellion of 1798 created martyred heroes to spice the legends and ballads of Irish nationalism, the immediate result was the reduction rather than the expansion of Irish liberty. British politicians and frightened Irish Protestants viewed the events of '98 as an effective argument against Irish sovereignty. For some time, British leaders, primarily prime minister William Pitt, were apprehensive about the Irish situation, fearing that Protestant, middle-class radicalism and Catholic discontent were open invitations to French intervention. Again the prospect of Ireland in enemy hands threatened British security. Since Pitt and his cabinet colleagues doubted that the Irish Parliament could preserve law and order in that troubled land, they decided that the final solution to the Irish Question was a political union of the two islands.

Pitt instructed Cornwallis, the lord lieutenant, and Lord Robert Castlereagh, the chief secretary, to persuade the Irish that union with Britain would serve the interests of both countries. Cornwallis and Castlereagh told Irish Protestants that a British connection would guarantee stability in Ireland, and assured Catholics that it would result in their emancipation. Pitt and his agents in Ireland were sincere in their promise to relieve Catholics from the remaining restrictions of the Penal

Laws, realizing that the Union could never work unless the Irish Catholic majority entered a United Kingdom as first-class citizens.

Irish Protestant opinion divided on the Union. Invoking Locke and his Irish disciple, William Molyneux, as authorities, some Anglo-Irish patriots insisted that the British connection would endanger Irish political and economic interests. Irish Protestant patriot Henry Grattan emerged from retirement to protect the victory of 1782. Orange Protestants also opposed the Union, but for more selfish, sectarian reasons. They warned that a Westminster parliament might destroy Protestant Ascendancy in Ireland by submitting to the pressures of Catholic agitation. Anti-Catholicism also motivated Protestants who favored the British connection. They were convinced that Protestant, middle-class radicalism allied with Catholic agitation and the ideology of the French Revolution was a more dangerous threat to Protestant Ascendancy than the risks involved in the Union. Protestant advocates of the Union argued that British power would defend their interests in Ireland, claiming that British anti-Catholicism would frustrate Pitt's effort to merge the issues of Catholic Emancipation and the Union.

In 1799, the British Parliament approved the principle of Union with Ireland, but a majority of the Irish House of Commons remained either opposed or uncommitted on the subject. A year later, after vigorous debate in Ireland, considerable pressure from the British government, and a generous application of funds and Crown patronage, the Irish Parliament by a narrow majority finally agreed to its extinction. On January 1, 1801, Ireland officially became part of the United Kingdom of Great Britain and Ireland.

2. Ireland: The Rise of Irish Nationalism, 1801–1850

For Britain, the Union altered the Irish Question from one of external security into a perennial internal crisis. Irish problems and protests and British responses transformed economic and political institutions and changed the shape of the empire. They also destroyed governments and political careers. The presence of Ireland within the United Kingdom intensified rather than diminished ethnic and cultural tensions between Anglo-Saxon Protestants and Irish Catholics. Recent events in Northern Ireland indicate that Britain still has not escaped the implications of the Irish connection.

From the Union's beginning, the Westminster Parliament fulfilled the pessimistic prophecy of its Anglo-Irish patriot and Irish Catholic nationalist foes; it governed in the interest of increasingly industrial Britain at the expense of agrarian Ireland. A hundred Irish MPs in a 658-member House of Commons (this number was increased to 105 after the 1832 Reform Bill) and twenty-eight Irish peers and four bishops in a 360-

member House of Lords had little impact on government policy. And with few exceptions, Protestants representing Ireland at Westminster spoke for a British colony in that country dependent on the Union to maintain its ascendancy.

Religious differences magnified the contrasts between British and Irish points of view. When Westminster politicians refused to concede Catholic Emancipation in concert with the Act of Union, they sealed its doom. Since Irish Catholics entered the United Kingdom as less than equal citizens, they were unable to develop a sense of Britishness similar to Protestant Celts in Wales and Scotland. When Pitt attempted to fulfill his Catholic Emancipation pledge, George III flew into a rage, insisting that he would never violate his coronation oath or Protestant conscience by consenting to equality for papists. George IV shared his father's antipathy to Catholics and his determination to preserve the last vestiges of the Penal Laws. On several occasions a practical and enlightened House of Commons majority indicated a willingness to scuttle seventeenth-century bigotry, but the House of Lords and no-popery British public opinion reinforced the crown's insistence that Catholics remain outside the perimeters of British life and politics.

Poverty and religion were inseparable aspects of the Irish Question. For the most part, Irish Catholic tenant farmers and agricultural laborers were victims of an inefficient, reactionary agrarian economy. Anti-Catholic prejudices played a role in persuading British politicians to preserve unrestricted property rights for Irish landlords who were usually Protestant. Reflecting general British attitudes, they perceived the Irish as savages, innately inferior to Anglo-Saxons, and their Catholicism as a manifestation of ignorance, irrationality, and a subversive temperament.

Despite its prominent role, anti-Catholicism was not the only obstacle to social and economic reforms in Ireland. Right-wing Tories, the Whig center, and the radical left all insisted on free exercise of property rights as unassailable economic dogma.

They argued that any significant change in the Irish land system or modification of landlord rights in favor of tenant-farmer security would establish precedents endangering property throughout the United Kingdom.

Irish nationalism emerged from the failure of the Union to confirm Catholic civil rights and alleviate Irish poverty. In the first half of the nineteenth century, three men—Robert Emmet (1778–1803), Daniel O'Connell (1775–1847), and Thomas Osborne Davis (1814–1845)—respectively represented the myth, reality, and ideology of the Irish struggle for freedom.

Emmet, a younger brother of Thomas Addis Emmet, one of the cofounders of the Society of United Irishmen, who later had a brilliant career in New York state politics, was a Trinity College Protestant. With his brother and other veterans of '98 in exile and Wolfe Tone dead, a suicide victim after his captors insisted on a hanging rather than the honorable death of a firing squad, young Emmet was left to carry on the revolutionary republican cause in post-Union Ireland. But in 1803, a revolution that he planned degenerated into a Dublin street brawl and the government arrested Emmet, convicted him of treason, and sentenced him to death.

Emmet did not possess the necessary skills for a successful revolutionary leader. He failed to obtain French support for his enterprise, and was unaware that informers had penetrated his organization; even his defense attorney was a British agent. But Emmet was a man of passion and sincerity, inspired more by words than by deeds. After his conviction but before receiving the death sentence, he made a speech from the dock that transformed him into a glorious legend. In his statement to Judge Lord Norbury, the jury, and the people of Ireland, Emmet defended his revolutionary ideals, condemned British oppression, and called on future generations of Irishmen to take up his cause. He concluded by asking the Irish people to postpone memorials to his memory until Ireland was free: "When my country takes her place among the nations of the earth, then and not until then, let my epitaph be written."

With his death on the gallows, Robert Emmet joined Tone at the top of what would become a long list of martyred Irish republicans. More talented men would serve Ireland, and many would accomplish significantly more for their fellow countrymen, but none would match Emmet as a popular hero. His youth, idealism, zeal, and words captured the imagination of the Irish masses. Emmet's portrait decorated the walls of numerous Irish homes; parents memorized his speech from the dock and recited it to their children. Many fathers and mothers, particularly in Irish America, named their sons Robert Emmet or just Emmet. Thomas Moore, the first bard of nineteenth-century romantic Irish nationalism, contributed to the Emmet legend. In a poem entitled "Oh, Breathe Not His Name" he reminded readers of his hero's final request:

> Oh, breathe not his name! let it sleep
>   in the shade,
> Where cold and unhonored his relics are
>   laid;
> Sad, silent, and dark be the tears that
>   he shed,
> As the night-dew that falls on the grass
>   o'er his head.

If Emmet contributed to the inspirational myths and legends of Irish nationalism, Daniel O'Connell created its reality. His reputation traveled far beyond the shores of his own country. As tribune of the Catholic masses, he joined America's Andrew Jackson as a successful, democratic politician in the conservative Metternich era. During the first half of the nineteenth century, British and European liberals and radicals respected and took inspiration from his achievements.

Coming from a prominent Catholic landed family in Kerry, O'Connell took advantage of modifications in the Penal Laws to study law at Lincoln's Inn, London, and the King's Inn, Dublin. He became the most successful young barrister in Ireland. In 1815 he took charge of the Catholic Committee, which at the time was a preserve of the upper and middle classes. Annually it petitioned Parliament to extend political equality to Catholics. Henry Grattan, MP, the hero of 1782 and champion of Catholic equality, presented them to the House of Commons.

Intellectually, O'Connell was a philosophical radical, a disciple of William Godwin, Thomas Paine, and Jeremy Bentham, and his nationalism was an extension of a liberal concern for human rights. As a young man, influenced by the religious views of the Enlightenment and the philosophers he admired, O'Connell had been an agnostic. Later the cause he espoused and the influence of his devout wife, Mary, converted him into a pious Catholic. Still he remained a liberal democrat, committed to freedom of conscience and separation of church and state, completely opposed to the reactionary politics of Rome. O'Connell never intellectually reconciled his political and Catholic loyalties, but he was too powerful for the papacy to condemn as it had French Catholic leftists Charles de Montalembert, Jean Lacordaire, and Hugues de Lamennais.

Although he admired the American founding fathers and financially and vocally supported Simon Bolivar's effort to liberate Latin America from Spain, O'Connell rejected revolution as an effective tactic for Irish nationalism. He pointed out that pike-armed peasants could not compete on the battlefield with well equipped and trained British soldiers. He said that insurrection in Ireland had led to the loss of life and property, and the expansion of British authority. To prove his point, he blamed the ill-fated rebellion of 1798 for the demise of the Irish Parliament and the Act of Union. In 1803 he expressed the opinion that Robert Emmet deserved to suffer for the violence he unleashed. Borrowing from Godwin, O'Connell insisted that organized, moral-force public opinion was the best means to the desired end of Irish sovereignty. To create such a weapon, he decided to mobilize the Irish masses for political action around the issue of Catholic Emancipation. Although O'Connell opposed physical force and told his followers to obey the law and rely on moral persuasion, he did not hesitate to warn British politicians that if they refused to come to terms with him, an advocate of constitutional methods, they would disappoint the expectations of Irish Catholics who would then have no choice but to turn to men of violence.

While agitating for Catholic Emancipation, O'Connell constantly emphasized that his ultimate goal was the repeal of the Union and the restoration of the Irish Parliament in College Green, Dublin. In appealing for Irish independence, he considered himself an intellectual descendent of John Locke, Thomas Molyneux, and Jonathan Swift, and a spokesman for the eighteenth-century patriotic tradition. Anything but a narrow sectarian, O'Connell rejected a Catholic Ireland as an alternative to Protestant Ascendancy, but the realities of the Irish situation forced him to couple Catholic Emancipation with Irish nationalism. He realized that most Protestants were committed to the Union and that the future of Irish self-government depended on the activities of the oppressed Catholic majority. And he knew that Catholic Emancipation was the only issue that could overcome the torpor that pervaded that community. To Catholics, religion was also their cultural identity, the only proud possession salvaged from a humiliating historical experience. But there were influential Catholics who opposed combining Catholic and nationalist objectives. This division was a major factor in the destruction of the Catholic Committee.

In 1815 Grattan worked out a compromise with important British Whigs. In exchange for Catholic Emancipation, Rome would assure the British government that it would not appoint objectionable bishops to United Kingdom sees. Most Catholic countries already enjoyed such a prerogative, so the selection of prelates by a committee of loyalist Catholic laymen or a rejection of Roman choices by the British government, even though Protestant, was not a radical innovation. The veto compromise stood a good chance of parliamentary acceptance, and powerful voices in Rome were willing to forfeit some control over the hierarchy in Britain and Ireland to establish friendly relations with the world's leading power. Many members of the British and Irish Catholic upper and middle classes also were delighted with prospects for economic and professional mobility and a voice in politics.

O'Connell quickly dashed these hopes by refusing to endorse Grattan's compromise arrangement, and carried the Catholic hierarchy with him. In arguing against the veto, he insisted that it would give the British government control over the Catholic Church in the United Kingdom and that such a prospect violated his convictions concerning the separation of church and state. What he did not say—and most obviously meant—was that British interference with Catholicism in Ireland would destroy links between religion and nationality. O'Connell thought it more important to cultivate Irish self-consciousness as a basis for nationalism than to promote the political, social, economic, and professional ambitions of the British and Irish Catholic upper and middle classes or to facilitate friendly relations between London and Rome.

O'Connell's rejection of Grattan's compromise divided and then demolished the Catholic Committee, and Emancipation languished in Ireland and in Parliament for nearly ten years. In collaboration with two leaders of the veto faction, Richard Lalor Sheil and Sir Thomas Wyse, he reignited its spark in 1823 by creating the Catholic Association. In its early days the Association failed to overcome Irish Catholic lethargy, but in 1825 O'Connell devised a tactic which invigorated the Association, making it the most powerful instrument of public opinion in the United Kingdom. Dues of one pound a year restricted Catholic Association membership to the prosperous. In order to broaden its base, O'Connell created an associate membership for only a shilling, which could be paid in a lump sum or more slowly at a penny a month or a weekly farthing. He asked priests to promote associate memberships and appointed rent collectors to harvest the shillings, pennies, and farthings outside Catholic chapels. In Sunday sermons, priests blessed Emancipation as holy and patriotic, and tenant farmers and urban workers flocked to the Association. Its burgeoning membership exhibited the extent of Catholic discontent as well as O'Connell's hold on the masses. And the rapid increase in the Association's treasury provided it with the financial resources to escalate the agitation.

Joining the Association had a powerful psychological impact on lower-class Catholics. A shilling a year was not much money, but to the average tenant farmer or urban worker it represented a considerable sacrifice. Paying the "Catholic rent" often meant giving up alcohol and tobacco, two popular compensations for the miseries of poverty. But in agitating for Catholic Emancipation, people found identity and dignity and hope for the future, liberating them from pessimism and despair, the marks of a slave mentality.

In the general election of 1826, the Catholic Association tested its strength against the Protestant Ascendancy. O'Connell and his associates endorsed and worked for Protestant candidates who favored Emancipation. Waterford was the crucial contest; there, the Association challenged the mighty Beresford family, which had a monopoly on the Commons seat. Clerical influence clashed with landlord power as tenant farmers marched to the polls accompanied by their priests. And to the consternation of British and Irish Tories, the 40s franchise peasant voters dealt landlordism and Protestant Ascendancy a weakening blow. Waterford inspired victories in other constituencies: Louth, Westmeath, Armagh, Galway, and Cork City.

Two years later, the Catholic Association decided on a bolder challenge to the British government, and again Irish tenant farmers rallied to the cause. In a County Clare by-election, voters chose O'Connell over the incumbent, C. E. Vesy Fitzgerald, a member of the duke of Wellington's cabinet, forcing the British government to make a difficult choice. The prime minister and Sir Robert Peel, the home secretary and leader of Tory forces in the House of Commons, could either accept the reality of Catholic strength or ignore election results in Ireland and maintain Protestant Ascendancy. The latter involved a serious risk of civil strife because it might incite Irish Catholics to abandon constitutional for violent instruments of change. Since they expected some kind of victory, government efforts to suppress them by force would endanger life and property. And British military intervention would be an admission of moral and political failure by conceding that the Union did not work and that Irish Catholics were a subject people, not an integral part of the United Kingdom.

During the crisis of decision, O'Connell reminded Wellington and Peel that they could select either reform or revolution. They finally decided that their Protestant consciences and Tory principles took second place to a well-functioning, law-and-order United Kingdom. At their urging, Parliament in 1829 passed a Catholic Relief Bill, and George IV reluctantly signed it. Unfortunately, the government's concessions to Catholic demands contained vindictiveness as well as generosity. Since the 40s freeholders could no longer be counted on to follow landlord political direction, the Catholic Relief Bill stripped them of the franchise. In addition, the government forced O'Connell to recontest Clare before taking his seat in the Commons; it also outlawed the Catholic Association and insisted that Catholic MPs take an insulting oath of allegiance.

Many O'Connell critics have used the 40s disfranchisement issue to attack his reputation as a true liberal and sincere Irish nationalist. But he never was enthusiastic about the 40s vote because without a secret ballot it was open to intimidation. Of course, in 1826 and again in 1828, tenant farmers had resisted landlord pressure at the polls, but there was no guarantee that they would continue to do so. O'Connell had another reason not to oppose the end of the 40s franchise. Many upper- and middle-class Catholics active in the emancipation movement were not friends of political democracy. If O'Connell had fought to retain the tenant-farmer vote, he might have alienated this powerful block and sabotaged the Catholic cause on the brink of victory.

Immediate benefits of the 1829 Relief Bill were less than revolutionary: upper- and middle-class Catholics achieved increased political, social, and professional opportunities, but the lives of agricultural laborers, tenant farmers, and urban workers remained harsh and insecure. Although the Relief Bill did not really alter the existence of the vast majority of Irish Catholics, it was the beginning of a long process that would lead to extensive economic and social change, and eventually national independence.

The Emancipation agitation initiated modern Irish nationalism and the Catholic Association served as a model for other United Kingdom reform movements. In his effort to achieve Catholic civil rights in the United Kingdom, O'Connell instructed the Irish masses in the art of democratic politics. They learned and acquired the confidence to manipulate the British system, providing those who emigrated to North America, where the political environment was similar, with the tools to compete for power.

In addition to encouraging further reform efforts in Ireland, O'Connell's success against Protestant Ascendancy inspired other champions of liberal democracy to challenge Tory rule in Britain and the reactionary mood of Metternich's Europe. Catholic Emancipation in Ireland paved the way for a similar liberation of Jews and Blacks throughout the Western world. But there was also a negative aspect to O'Connell's victory. It intensified Anglo-Saxon and Anglo-Irish Protestant anti-Catholicism. Fearing an eventual triumph of Catholic democracy and defeat for the Union, Protestant Ireland became an even more defensive garrison bound to Britain as the defender of its religion, property, and political influence.

During the early 1830s, O'Connell sat in the British House of Commons in a dual capacity—leader of an Irish nationalist movement dedicated to repeal of the Union and a prominent Benthamite Radical advocating prison and legal reforms, Black and Jewish emancipation, a secret ballot, curbing the power of the House of Lords, parliamentary reform, and political democracy. O'Connell injected his commitment to liberal democracy into the veins of Irish nationalism, profoundly influencing both British and American history.

Although serving with energy and skill in the Commons, O'Connell had little confidence in the British Parliament as a vehicle for Irish freedom and/or reform. He wrote in 1840:

> It is vain to expect any relief from England. All parties there concur in hatred to Ireland and Catholicity; and it is also founded in human nature that they should, for they have injured us too much to forgive us.[1]

Despite this profound insight into the psychology of British anti-Irish Catholic nativism, O'Connell was prepared to go to any lengths—even cooperation with British politicians—to achieve some improvement in the Irish situation. In the 1834 Lichfield House Compact, he verbally agreed to an alliance with the Whigs. In exchange for a promise of good government and remedial legislation for Ireland, O'Connell pledged to provide the Union with an opportunity to work and to stop agitating its repeal.

In 1831, even before the Lichfield House Compact, a Whig government gave Ireland a primary school system. In an effort to avoid sectarian controversy, national schools took a nondenominational approach to secular subjects but allowed various sects to offer supplemental religious instruction. At first, Protestant leaders protested "Godless education" while Catholic counterparts welcomed the national schools as a means of raising the cultural level of their people. Later, nationalists branded the schools as agents of British cultural imperialism; Catholic bishops described them as vehicles of Protestant proselytism. Protestants then turned around and defended the national school system as a barrier against Catholic empowerment. By the mid-nineteenth century, however, the schools had become denominational in practice if not in theory. In Catholic areas, priests controlled the school board and the hiring of teachers. In Protestant districts their clergy exercised the same power. Still, the Catholic hierarchy continued to insist on state financed denominational education.

No doubt Catholic Emancipation figured in the inauguration of the national school system. Now that Irish Catholics had the vote, British politicians decided that they should be culturally Anglicized. The schools did teach English history, literature, and language, and undermined the use of Irish, but teachers often presented nationalist perspectives, and advancing literacy provided an audience for nationalist newspaper propaganda.

To fulfill their promise to do justice to Ireland, Whigs sent Thomas Drummond to serve as undersecretary at Dublin Castle. He reduced Protestant Ascendancy by appointing a number of Catholics to government positions. But O'Connell was not satisfied. He pointed to the Irish Poor Law as an example of the inability of Westminster politicians to understand the nuances of the Irish situation, and to the recently enacted Irish Municipal Reform Bill as evidence that they were not prepared to trust Irish Catholics with political power. O'Connell considered the Irish measure a pale imitation of the more expansive British bill. He focused most of his anger and scorn on the Poor Law. He said that the workhouse system was totally inappropriate for a country where a third of the population qualified as paupers, and where taxes to support those confined in workhouses would doom another third to penury.

Although his opposition to the Irish Municipal Reform and

Poor Law Bills was vehement, O'Connell and his parliamentary followers continued to keep Lord Melbourne's cynical and lethargic administration in office. But he began to send out signals that he had become impatient with Whig inaction on the Irish front, and that he was preparing to resume agitating for a return of the Irish Parliament.

When O'Connell's old enemy, Sir Robert Peel, became prime minister in 1841, the Irish leader decided it was time to abandon efforts to work within the parliamentary system and to return to the tactics of mass agitation. He organized the Loyal National Repeal Association, modeled after its Catholic Association precursor. By 1843 O'Connell had managed to weave the strands of widespread reaction against the Irish Poor Law, resentment against continued British misgovernment, and the enthusiasm and organization of Father Theobald Mathew's massive temperance crusade into a repeal movement that exceeded in members and wealth the Catholic Emancipation effort of the 1820s. A major factor in the success of the Repeal Association was the contribution of Young Ireland; bright young men who helped formulate and effectively propagandize Irish cultural nationalism.

Thomas Davis—like Robert Emmet, a Protestant product of Trinity College—seemed to epitomize the intelligence, idealism, and romanticism of Young Ireland. In the autumn of 1842, he and two friends, John Blake Dillon and Charles Gavan Duffy, began to publish a weekly newspaper, the *Nation*. Dillon was a middle-class Catholic from Mayo who had attended Trinity with Davis, while Duffy, an Ulster Catholic from Monaghan, had acquired considerable experience as a Belfast journalist. During breaks, while studying law at the King's Inn, they would walk in the Phoenix Park and discuss the need to enrich Irish nationalism with a cultural dimension. The *Nation* was the product of these conversations.

O'Connell's nationalism was a logical extension of Enlightenment political thought. He believed that a Dublin and not a

Westminster Parliament could best protect the rights and promote the dignity of the Irish people and stimulate the prosperity of their country. While he admired British constitutionalism, O'Connell doubted the possibility of complete Irish assimilation into the United Kingdom because Britons and their parliamentary representatives did not understand or respect Ireland or its people, especially Catholics. O'Connell's nationalism was more pragmatic than ideological, essentially pro-Irish rather than anti-British. Since his mind was shaped by eighteenth-century rationalism rather than by the romanticism of the early nineteenth century, he had little sympathy for or understanding of the cultural nationalism that flowed out of Germany to the rest of Europe. Unlike Young Irelanders, who were fanatic advocates of the Irish language, O'Connell was fluent in it but urged the Irish to learn English as a more utilitarian form of communication that would further their progress.

In contrast, young men in the office of the *Nation* were enemies of all things British, insisting that Ireland must be independent culturally as well as politically. They represented an Irish version of the general European Romantic movement, which was at least partially inspired by a reaction against the ugliness, materialism, and urbanization of the Industrial Revolution. To Young Irelanders, Britain was the essence of urban industrialism, and its domination of Ireland subverted a more spiritual, agrarian way of life. They wanted to de-Anglicize Ireland, to purge the Irish mind and soul of alien materialism. Young Irelanders believed that the dogmas of political economy so dear to O'Connell embodied the coarseness of British urban, industrial culture. They based their advocacy of preserving the native language where it existed and restoring it where it had vanished on the premise that it was the true expression of the Irish mind and soul.

In the *Nation*'s columns, editorials, essays, and ballad poetry, Duffy, Dillon, Davis, and their associates encouraged the Irish to be aware of their history, literature, and traditions as well as their language. In addition to their own contributions, editors invited readers to submit articles, poems, stories, and ballads on Irish subjects. Unlike so many romantic, cultural nationalists in other parts of Europe, most Young Irelanders publicly rejected ethnic and religious prejudices, refusing to pit Gael against Anglo Irish. They emphasized an inclusive nationalism, embracing the entire Irish historical experience, insisting that descendents of Celts, Danes, Normans, Elizabethans, Cromwellians, and Williamites could all claim Irish nationality. This cosmopolitan attitude was expressed in Thomas Davis's poem, "Anglo-Saxon and Celt":

> What matters that at different shrines
>   We pray unto one God?
> What matters that at different times
>   Our fathers won this sod?
>
> In fortune and in name we're bound
>   By stronger links than steel;
> And neither can be safe nor sound
>   But in the other's weal.

Unfortunately, reality contradicted Young Ireland's hope for an ecumenical future. It did matter to Anglo-Irish Protestants at what shrines they worshipped and when their fathers occupied Irish sod. They rejected O'Connell's and Young Ireland's invitations to participate in Irish nationalism, insisting that the Union sheltered them from the property lusts and political schemes of a dangerous Catholic democracy manipulated by Rome's priestly agents.

Although Young Ireland's message failed to penetrate the defensiveness of Protestant Ireland, it won Catholic allegiances. Eight thousand subscribers were only a portion of the *Nation*'s readers. Repeal and temperance reading rooms placed it on their shelves, and local "scholars" trained in national schools read it to illiterate relatives and friends in cottages throughout the Irish countryside.

Despite his organizational genius, the appeal of Young Ireland's cultural nationalism, and the repeal enthusiasm of Catholic Ireland, O'Connell could not honor his pledge that 1843 would be "the Repeal Year." Psychologically a victim of past successes, he falsely assumed that confronted by a massive and well-disciplined Irish public opinion, Peel and Wellington would repeat their surrender of 1829. He thought they would concede repeal or major reforms rather than risk the Irish masses abandoning constitutional for physical force methods. Obviously, O'Connell did not understand that the British leaders granted Catholic Emancipation to save the Union. Therefore, they would never submit to an agitation designed to destroy it. Whigs and Radicals, although they criticized Peel's Irish policy, declared that they supported his resistance to repeal and his defense of the Union.

When O'Connell finally realized that British politicians viewed Catholic Emancipation and repeal of the Union as issues demanding different responses, he slowed down agitation, pleading with followers to avoid violence. In October 1843, O'Connell decided to abide by a government proclamation banning a large repeal meeting scheduled for Clontarf, a Dublin suburb. There were hotheads who welcomed a showdown with British authorities, but the Irish leader would not permit repealers to be slaughtered by trained soldiers. His decision was sensible but it ended repeal as a significant expression of Irish nationalism. Shortly after the aborted Clontarf meeting, the government arrested, prosecuted, and convicted O'Connell along with a few of his lieutenants, including Duffy, for sedition. A judge fined and sentenced them to a year in prison, but after they spent only a few months in Richmond Jail, the British Law Lords in a three-to-two decision (three Whigs and two Tories) decided that they were victims of an improper indictment and a packed, exclusively Protestant jury, and ordered them freed. Irish nationalists interpreted O'Connell's release as a great victory over British tyranny and injustice. All over the country they lit bonfires on the hills and a large crowd cheered O'Connell's carriage as it moved from Richmond to his home in Dublin's Merrion Square. Unfortunately, the nearly seventy-year-old O'Connell was too elderly and fatigued by his prison experience to muster enthusiasm for another large-scale agitation. Speechifying replaced action on the Repeal Association agenda.

1843 was not a total defeat for O'Connell. His success in mobilizing Catholic Ireland forced Peel to reconsider the government's Irish policy and the implications of Protestant Ascendancy. In 1845 and 1846, after he was certain that law and order was restored in Ireland and that insurrection was no longer a possibility, the prime minister ordered the lord lieutenant and chief secretary to appoint Catholics to public office in Ireland as a sign that the government intended to treat them fairly, and to encourage their loyalty to the British connection. He also introduced a comprehensive program of reform in an effort to subvert Irish nationalism. His strategy involved fragmenting it into component parts of priest, peasant, and middle class, and giving to each a separate identity superseding loyalty to any abstract concept of an Irish nation. For example, Peel provided the Catholic hierarchy and clergy with a Charitable Bequests Act facilitating the inheritance of property by their church and a permanent rather than an annual endowment with an increased income for the Catholic seminary at Maynooth. He intended these concessions as initial steps on the road to a possible dual religious establishment in Ireland.

While Peel's main intent was to remove the Catholic clergy from the vortex of Irish agitation by nurturing a financial dependence on the generosity of the government rather than the emotionally anti-British Irish masses, he also wanted members of the Catholic middle class in Ireland to share the attitudes of Protestant counterparts in Britain and Ireland. To achieve this goal, he provided them with opportunities for higher education in the newly constructed and staffed Queen's Colleges in

Cork and Galway. To satisfy Ulster Nonconformists, he also established a Queen's College in Belfast. Peel responded to tenant-farmer discontent by appointing a commission chaired by Lord Devon, an Englishman who owned an Irish estate and sympathized with Irish farmers, to investigate landlord-tenant relations as a prelude to legislation that would increase the social and economic security of the latter.

O'Connell hampered Peel's effort to separate and isolate Irish and Catholic identities by frightening nationalists with a warning that an alliance between Britain and Rome, another element in Peel's strategy, would endanger the possibility of Ireland's legislative independence by removing Catholic bishops and priests, agents of the Repeal Association, from the center of agitation. The prime minister's overtures to Irish Catholicism, particularly the permanent endowment to Maynooth, "the classroom of papist treason," incensed Irish and British Protestants. And Catholic bishops, who praised Peel for the Maynooth grant, opposed the Queen's Colleges Bill because it was based on the principle of nondenominational education. They refused Catholics permission to attend the colleges or to hold faculty or administrative positions in them. Land reform as envisioned in the appointment of the Devon Commission encountered the intractable resistance of British Tory, Conservative, Whig, and Radical opposition to any interference with property rights. But Peel's attempt to weaken the fabric of Irish nationalism by concessions to a variety of Irish grievances did improve the condition of Irish Catholicism and established precedents for future changes in Britain's Irish policy.

After O'Connell slowed down the tempo of repeal, his alliance with Young Ireland deteriorated. Temperament, personality, and ideological differences all figured in the animosity. Romantic, uncompromising Young Irelanders scorned O'Connell's pragmatism, evidenced by his renewed collaboration with Whigs to achieve change in Ireland. They argued that such strategy shifts demoralized Irish nationalism. O'Connell often expressed petty jealousies old leaders often display toward bright, ambitious, young challengers. And people around him, mainly his favorite son, John, who envied the talents of Davis, Duffy, and Dillon, distorted the *Nation*'s message, feeding O'Connell's fears and suspicions.

O'Connell believed that Young Ireland's effort to diminish Irish sectarianism was motivated by religious indifference rather than tolerance. And he feared that the *Nation*'s constant tributes to 1798 and the United Irishmen tempted the people to abandon constitutional for physical-force nationalism, particularly while Famine stalked the land. In 1846 O'Connell decided on a showdown with Young Ireland, insisting they formally reject revolution or leave the Repeal Association. Refusing to comply with this ultimatum, Young Irelanders walked out of Conciliation Hall, the Association's headquarters, and organized the Irish Confederation, dedicated to repeal of the Union, cultural nationalism, and reconciliation between Catholics and Protestants.

With O'Connell's death in May 1847 and the inept leadership of his son, John, at the Repeal Association, the Confederation became the focal point of Irish nationalism. But soon after its start, ideological and tactical quarrels, provoked by the fiery zeal of John Mitchel, divided the new organization. After Davis died of scarlet fever in 1845, and while Dillon was recuperating from tuberculosis, Duffy bore most of the responsibility of editing the *Nation*. In managing the Confederation he did have the assistance of William Smith O'Brien, MP, a County Clare Protestant landlord. Reacting against Britain's Irish policy, O'Brien withdrew from the Whig party in 1843 and joined the Repeal Association. While O'Connell was in prison, he presided in Conciliation Hall, but chose the Young Ireland side in 1846. The previous year, Duffy had recruited Mitchel, an Ulster Unitarian with a brilliant and passionate style of journalism, to take Davis's place at the *Nation*.

Mitchel, who despised everything British even more than he loved Ireland, was impressed with the ideas of James Fintan Lalor, a sometime contributor to the *Nation*. Lalor insisted that the land question should have priority over repeal. He argued that Irish property belonged to the Irish people, and urged a rent strike to destroy landlordism. Building on Lalor's premise, Mitchel recommended nonpayment of taxes in addition to rents to paralyze British rule in Ireland as well as ruin its landlord agents.

Since O'Brien and Duffy were confident that nationalism could enlist Protestants, they rejected Lalor's and Mitchel's no-rent recommendation as an incitement to class and sectarian conflict. They also reminded Confederation members that nonpayment of rates would reduce funds necessary for Famine relief. Duffy and O'Brien offered an alternative strategy: the formation of an Irish parliamentary party as a voice of Irish opinion at Westminster. If the British refused the party's demand for repeal, nationalist MPs would withdraw from the Commons, return to Dublin, and establish a Parliament with the backing of Irish public opinion and local government agencies. When the Confederation majority accepted the Duffy–O'Brien proposal and rejected Mitchel's, he left the organization and the *Nation* and launched his own paper, *The United Irishman*. It preached revolution and instructed readers on guerrilla-style street fighting.

Early in 1848, shortly after the split in the Confederation, French rebels replaced the monarchy with a liberal republic. Quickly the spirit of revolution spread to Germany, the Hapsburg empire, Italy, and Poland, taking on often contradictory liberal and nationalist dimensions. Inspired by events on the Continent, Young Ireland abandoned constitutional for revolutionary nationalism. Mitchel rejoined the Confederation, and O'Brien led a delegation to Paris to seek aid from the new republic for Irish independence. Courteous but cautious, unwilling to antagonize Britain and endanger its recognition of their government, French leaders warmly hosted the Irish but sent them home without a pledge of aid.

Finally, in June 1848, British coercion laws and the arrest of Confederation leaders, including O'Brien, Mitchel, and Thomas Francis Meagher, pressured Young Ireland into a premature rebellion. After juries freed O'Brien and Meagher, emergency legislation enabled the government to convict Mitchel for treason and to transport him to Van Dieman's Land, now Tasmania. Continued coercion and arrests—Duffy was in prison awaiting trial—convinced Confederation leaders that they must strike a blow for freedom.

While excellent journalists and intelligent idealists, Young Irelanders were hopeless revolutionaries. Middle-class respect for property, in combination with unrealistic efforts to court Protestants, prevented them from devising cold-blooded, destructive guerrilla tactics that might have produced a few victories. And they did not understand that Irish peasants suffering from hunger and disease were pathetic revolutionary material. Carelessly planned, without public support or adequate equipment, O'Brien's insurrection ended in a comic-opera skirmish with the constabulary in Widow McCormick's Ballingarry, County Tipperary cabbage patch. Shortly after their humiliating defeat, O'Brien and many of his colleagues were convicted of treason and subsequently transported to Australia as political prisoners. Other Young Irelanders managed to elude capture and left the country for exile in France or America.

As 1848 came to a close, Young Irelanders seemed pitiful failures. But as time passed, legend transformed a farce into a heroic enterprise, elevating them into the pantheon of Irish martyrs. *Nation* editorials, essays, and ballad poetry became the scriptures of Irish cultural nationalism. Emigrants took this gospel of Young Ireland with them on journeys across the Irish Sea and Atlantic Ocean, cultivating it in the fertile soil of ghetto discontent.[2] As Thomas N. Brown so eloquently observed: "In the alembic of America the parochial peasant was transformed into a passionate Irish nationalist."[3]

🌿

Up to this point the analysis of Irish nationalism has focused on its religious, political, and cultural sources. But most Irish Catholics were more concerned with economic and social security than Emancipation or Repeal. And after the victory of 1829, land emerged as the most important factor in the clash between Irish nationalism and British and Irish unionism.

Mid-eighteenth century Catholics in rural Ireland were the most wretched people in Western Europe with a standard of living probably lower than that of Black slaves in North America. Most were agricultural laborers working for tenant farmers rather than for landlords, and to feed families they rented small potato patches (conacre) from their employers. Sometimes the patch was in lieu of wages. Tenant farmers usually occupied less than fifteen acres—five was the average. The typical agricultural-laborer and small tenant-farmer dwelling was a windowless mud hut, with a dirt floor and a hole in the thatched roof for a chimney. Cottages were dirty and smoky from turf fires, constant rains turned floors into mud holes, and thatched roofs hosted a variety of vermin. Since animals were precious—their sale paid the rent—large families shared their miserable hovels with pigs and chickens. These unsanitary living conditions resulted in heavy infant mortality and high death rates from tuberculosis and diseases associated with malnutrition and diet deficiencies.

Most of the scanty information about the habits and personalities of eighteenth-century Irish peasants came from the pens of English and Continental visitors. Travelers in Ireland were appalled by the poverty in rural areas and criticized the cruelty of the landlord system. They described Irish peasants as happy-go-lucky, shiftless, emotional, courteous, generous, and generally good-natured but easily provoked into violent rages. In summary, the outsider saw the Irish Catholic peasant as childlike, needing guidance and discipline.

There is, of course, some truth in stereotypes. A miserable standard of living and a constant struggle for survival degrades human nature, encouraging personality weaknesses rather than strengths. In Ireland, landlordism did produce lazy and inefficient farmers, and poverty and insecurity encouraged excessive consumption of alcohol, fueling violence. Since humility is a mask that slaves frequently don for survival purposes, Irish peasants were courteous, often to the point of obsequiousness.

Visitors, however, saw only the superficial traits of country people; they could not distinguish between mask and reality. Seething resentments often boiled over into clashes between families and sectarian party fights in Ulster border counties. Previously discussed secret societies revealed the brutalization of Irish farmers and agricultural laborers, their need to express rage in violence because they could not do so through the Protestant Ascendancy political, social, economic, and legal systems.

During the eighteenth century, most of the Irish peasantry outside the province of Leinster still spoke Irish, and wandering bards preserved Gaelic legends and folklore. Aisling poems, a popular form of literary expression, promised a return of the Gaelic order through a restoration of the Stuarts. But actually there was little vitality left in the Gaelic tradition. Songs and stories of a former aristocratic, Gaelic society or hopes of returning Stuart kings had little relevance in the lives of impoverished and oppressed farmers and agricultural laborers. No doubt some Gaelic values survived, but native culture had been transformed into an essentially rural, peasant, Catholic outlook similar to that of other Catholic countries such as Italy, Poland, Portugal, and Spain.

Catholicism, not Gaelicism, had become the core of Irish cultural identity, comforting and adding a touch of beauty to miserable existences, providing an outlet for pent-up emotions, dampening violent tendencies, offering a hope of salvation and justice in another world if not in this one, and serving as a bond of community.

Due to a population explosion, rural standards of living actually declined during the eighteenth and early nineteenth centuries. Irish numbers expanded from about three to eight million, putting tremendous pressure on a static, inefficient agrarian economy. Competition for tenancies increased rents, leading to the subdivision of holdings already too small for efficient cultivation and decent family incomes, demoting many from the tenant farmer to the agricultural laboring class.

Experts have attributed a population increase that affected all of Europe to the improved technology of the Industrial Revolution, citing its effect on an abundance of inexpensive food, pipes that disposed of sewage and carried clean water for drinking and washing, low cost clothing for frequent changing, and the beginning of preventive medicine. This explanation certainly applies to Britain, but as one social historian, Kenneth H. Connell, emphasized in *The Population of Ireland* (1950), in Ireland the most dramatic population increase took place without industrialization's benefits. He attributed it to increased fertility, the product of early marriages and many children. Infant mortality was high, but many youngsters managed to survive the perils of poverty. Since Connell's book was published, a number of historians have challenged his evidence that the Irish married earlier than other Europeans, but they cannot dispute the extremely large size of families.

In explaining marriages that were imprudent if not especially early, and exceptionally large families, Connell pointed to potatoes. They were easy to cultivate, needing little attention; an acre or less could feed a large family. During the last few decades of the eighteenth and the first four of the nineteenth century, Ireland exported rye, wheat, oats, barley and meat to Britain, but tenant-farming and agricultural-laboring families ate potatoes while selling livestock, grain, eggs, and dairy products to pay rents. On average, individuals consumed between ten and twelve pounds of potatoes daily, usually boiled and seasoned with a little salt. They seldom enjoyed meat, cheese, eggs, fish, or bread; for many even milk was a luxury.

Numerous medical experts have hailed the nourishing quality of potatoes, but their almost exclusive use subjected the rural population to famine. From the 1820s on, bad weather and disease frequently destroyed potato crops, resulting in numerous fatalities, convincing many Irish Catholics that it was time to emigrate to North America.

Although famines were frequent and devastating, they usually were of short duration. In 1845, however, a potato fungus spread from North America to Europe, and destroyed almost the entire crop in Ireland. The next year the fungus returned, and a severe winter that made it difficult to forage under the snow for nettles, weeds, and cabbage leaves magnified its effects. 1847 was fungus free but farmers either lacked funds to purchase seed potatoes or ate those they had. Optimism in 1848 encouraged heavy planting, but the blight returned. Although 1849 was the last year for a diseased potato crop, the effects of hunger, scurvy, typhoid, cholera, and low morale survived into 1851.

In 1845 there were almost nine million people in Ireland. During the Famine years, at least a million-and-a-half perished from starvation and related diseases. They died so quickly and in such large numbers that it was difficult to bury the dead. Rats, cats, and dogs fed on human carcasses. Famine also stimulated emigration. Considerably more than a million left Ireland between 1845 and 1851 to seek refuge in Britain and North America, mainly the United States.

Since emigrants often left home without sufficient provisions, sailed in ships short on space, food, or sanitation facilities, and were infected with typhoid, cholera, and dysentery, a large number perished en route to the New World. Voyages were nightmares for terrified refugees sick from rough seas, stench below decks, and hunger and fever; in many cases ship captains and crews brutalized them. Those who did reach their destinations often were cheated by runners who seized their belongings and took them to combination boarding and grog houses that overcharged for lodging and drink, and by sellers of real and counterfeit railroad, canal, or riverboat tickets. Frequently exploiters of naive travelers were also Irish. Sometimes immigrants landed without clothing, stepping literally naked into a new world. Usually they were members of landlord-sponsored emigration projects. Seriously concerned for the welfare of their tenants, some landowners hired ships and sent them off well-provisioned to what they hoped was a better life. But others were not so magnanimous. Without a sense of decency, responsibility, or humanity, they transported people from their estates without adequate food or clothing to avoid paying poor rates to support them in workhouses.

Without a doubt, the Great Famine was the most painful and decisive event in modern Irish history. Mass hunger, disease, death and emigration had a negative impact on Irish personalities. For some it reinforced negative fatalism associated with Gaelic and Catholic traditions. For others, especially emigrants and their descendents, it intensified hatred for Britain. The Famine added fuel to Irish nationalism which posed this question: why did Britain, the richest and most powerful nation, fail to provide food for people starving in Ireland, its partner in the United Kingdom? In answering its own rhetorical question, Irish nationalism charged the British with genocide.

Were nationalists correct in their accusation? Did British politicians attempt to solve the troublesome Irish Question by permitting a large portion of the Irish population to either die or flee the country? This does not seem to be the case. Even without the exportation of agricultural products from Ireland, there still would have been a serious food shortage. And many British politicians, civil servants, religious groups, and ordinary citizens did contribute money to or otherwise participate in relief efforts.[4] Peel's Conservative administration distributed imported Indian maize from the United States, and Whigs spent millions of pounds for public works projects and soup kitchens. British and Irish physicians and civil servants, and both Catholic priests and Protestant ministers contracted fatal diseases while administering food, medicine, and spiritual comfort to Famine victims.

Despite exaggerated rhetoric, there is some validity to the charge that Britain was largely responsible for Famine suffering. Since it was part of the United Kingdom, the Westminster government had a duty to rule Ireland with compassion. Because British politicians tried to administer relief within the guideline of laissez-faire dogma, the Irish were victims of ideological murder and torture.[5] Since policy makers believed economic ideology more important than Irish lives, they did not make an all out effort to save them. They insisted that the Irish must not lose personal initiative by becoming dependent on government largess, and that relief efforts should not disrupt normal trade and commerce. It is interesting to note that from 1845 to 1851, British governments expended only fifteen million pounds on Famine relief, compared to seventy million during the 1854–56 Crimean War.

If enormous numbers of people in England, Scotland, or Wales had been dying of hunger and fever, British governments might have shown more concern. But religious and cultural prejudices as well as laissez-faire commitments influenced British responses to Ireland's misfortune. Charles Trevelyan, head of the Treasury and the person most responsible for Whig Famine relief, considered the potato blight and its consequences a Divine punishment on a wicked and perverse people. Nassau Senior, a prominent economist who advised Whig leaders, viewed the Famine as a remedy for Ireland's surplus population, regretting its limited efficiency.

Some British newspapers and periodicals of the time also

expressed "racial" and religious prejudices. Furious over the 1848 rebellion, they said that Irish ingrates were undeserving of help or sympathy. The influential Tory *Quarterly Review* claimed that Irish misery was a product of their vices:

> all of civilization, arts, comfort, wealth that Ireland enjoys she owes exclusively to England . . . all of her absurdities, errors, misery she owes to herself . . . this unfortunate result is mainly attributable to that confusion of ideas, that instability of purpose, and above all, that reluctance to steady work which are indubitable features of the national character.

Famine refugees carried bitter memories across the sea, and passed them on to their children. Recollections of the Irish experience, and problems of adjustment to unfriendly environments, made the diasporic Catholic Irish even more anti-British than those in Ireland. They would become a decisive factor in Ireland's struggle for freedom, and their encounters with Anglo-Saxon and Anglo-Irish Protestants in the Old World would color their responses to Anglo-American Protestants in the New.

PART II

American Experiences

3. Emigrants and Immigrants

Refugees from Disaster, 1822–1870

In 1790 there were about forty-four thousand people born in Ireland living in the United States; few were Catholic and most of the Protestants were Ulster Presbyterians. During the eighteenth century many American and Canadian ships that delivered flax seed and lumber to Britain and Ireland carried emigrants as ballast on return voyages. An average ten-guinea transatlantic fare guaranteed that most of the Irish entering America were of at least moderate means. Most Presbyterians were artisans or tenant farmers, many of the latter doubling as handloom weavers. They came to America to escape religious discrimination and to seek economic opportunities.

Ulster Calvinists contributed energy along with economic and intellectual skills and democratic commitments to the development of a new nation. Some of the Catholics who had sufficient funds and courage to journey to America also were farmers and artisans with abilities to succeed in a dynamic new environment. But there were Catholics so poor that they could only reach America by becoming indentured servants for seven or fourteen years. And the majority of transported Irish convicts were also Catholics. After serving time in the plantation economy of the South, convicts and indentured servants tended to migrate to the Appalachian frontier. Because they did not leave Ireland as devout or informed Catholics, and the American Church lacked the manpower and resources to minister to those on the geographic or social fringes, ex-convicts and former indentured servants usually abandoned Catholicism and melded into Protestant evangelical or Ulster Presbyterian communities.

Impoverished and not particularly adventurous, most pre-1820s Catholics who left Ireland went to Britain. Some were harvest workers, others supplied unskilled labor to the industrial and transportation revolutions as canal diggers (navvies), track layers (gandy dancers), horse cart drivers (teamsters), and cargo handlers (stevedores). Men and women also worked in factories, and the latter found additional employment as domestic servants. When they earned enough to pay rents to landlords, harvest workers returned to Ireland; those involved with the industrial and transportation economies and domestics tended to remain in Britain. Even before the Great Famine, there were significant Irish Catholic populations in Liverpool, Manchester, Birmingham, Glasgow, London, Cardiff, and other British urban centers.

During the 1820s, several factors speeded the pace of Irish Catholic emigration to the United States. Famines; an economic recession in the United Kingdom following the Napoleonic Wars that promoted a shift in agriculture from tillage to grazing, and the consolidation of estates and the eviction of many tenant farmers; agrarian secret society violence; and the turbulence of Catholic Emancipation and anti-tithe agitations persuaded a number of Catholics that it was time to leave Ireland for a more emotionally and financially secure America.

From 1815 to 1845, more than a million Irish immigrants

entered the United States. Until the 1820s, most newcomers remained Protestant, but then the reasons mentioned above and increasingly lower ship fares converted Irish emigration to a mainly Catholic adventure. Many who abandoned Ireland first sailed to Canada, finally finding refuge in the United States by walking south across the border. Two-boaters started in the Newfoundland fishing industry before earning passages to Boston.

The Famine had a significant influence on the Irish Catholic exodus. From 1845 to the close of 1854, nearly a million and a half Irish sought shelter in the United States, the vast majority Catholic. The Great Hunger not only speeded the pace of Irish Catholic emigration, it institutionalized it as a safety valve to relieve pressure on a static agrarian economy with few industrial employment opportunities.

Famine experiences and memories persuaded the Irish to marry late, reduce the birth rate, and to cease dividing already small farms. Catholicism's rigid sexual morality reinforced economic necessity, helping to emotionally and spiritually sustain people through years of, sometimes permanent, celibacy. But in spite of later marriages and a significant population decline, Ireland's meager resources remained inadequate to care for all of its inhabitants. Only one son could inherit the farm, and few daughters, even with beauty enhanced by dowries, could find men in a financial position to marry. For landless men there were few prospects of employment in cities or towns or in the Royal Irish Constabulary. Outside of servant work in Big Houses or as waitresses in eating establishments, there were even fewer opportunities for young women. Without a farm, a decent job, or a husband, the youth of Ireland followed the emigration trail to the urban centers of Britain and the United States. Some young men and women entered seminaries and convents, but a good portion of nuns, brothers, and priests also left Ireland to serve the spiritual needs of the Diaspora.

Throughout the nineteenth and early twentieth centuries, Irish emigration to Britain remained steady. Fares for the short passages to Liverpool, Glasgow, and Cardiff were within the means of even the poorest tenant farmers and agricultural laborers. And going to Britain seemed a less permanent and traumatic change than did long, uncomfortable, transatlantic voyages to Quebec, Montreal, Boston, New York, and New Orleans. Many of the Irish in Britain were comforted by the knowledge that home was within reach, just across the Irish Sea. Still, America represented extensive opportunities and a clear break with a grim past. To calm parental anxieties and to present an image of success, many of the Irish in the United States wrote letters home exaggerating their good fortune. These messages, in addition to enclosed money or ship tickets for siblings, stimulated emigration. In post-Famine years, Irish parents raised most of their children for export.

Although emigration slowed after the Famine, from 1855 through 1870 more than a million Irish, usually single men and women between the ages of fifteen and thirty-five, left for America. Since they constituted the first large group of Whites who were not Anglo or Irish Protestants to arrive in the United States, Irish Catholics had the painful and dubious distinction of pioneering America's urban ghettos, previewing experiences that Jews, Italians, Poles and other eastern Europeans, Serbs and Croats, Greeks, Blacks migrating from the rural South, Asians, Chicanos, Haitians, Puerto Ricans and other Latinos would later share.

Although physically absent from their parishes and townlands, emigrants influenced events in Ireland. They, particularly women, generously sent hard-earned dollars to the folks back home. In the thirteen-year period, 1848–1861, although the Irish were on the bottom rung of the American socio-economic ladder, they managed to send almost sixty million dollars to Ireland in bank drafts and money orders. Of course letters contained many more unrecorded dollars. At least a quarter of the money that servant girls and manual laborers sent home financed the emigration of brothers and sisters, but most went to improve the standard of living for relatives left behind. And much American currency financed constitutional and physical-force nationalism. Thus, letters from America containing news of loved ones, dollar gifts, and perhaps ship tickets or passage money were most welcome in rural cottages. And leaders of various nationalist movements traveled through urban America collecting funds for their causes.

Portions of the Irish Catholic Diaspora came from cities and towns, but for the most part it was composed of country people. A large number of Irish Catholic emigrants who went to Canada and later Australia and New Zealand did settle in rural areas, but in the United States they collected in cities, scorning the vast, inexpensive, fertile acres of the Midwest. In 1870, 72 percent of the American Irish were concentrated in seven urban, industrial states—Massachusetts, Connecticut, New York, New Jersey, Pennsylvania, Ohio, and Illinois—usually residing in communities exceeding 2,500. About 85 percent of Irish-American Catholics were engaged in the industrial or transportation sections of the American economy, only 15 percent were involved with farming.

According to the distinguished anthropogeographer, E. Estyn Evans, "The whole nature of Gaelic society was opposed to urban living"; cities were associated with foreign invaders and alien cultures.[1] Considering this distrust of cities and towns, and their largely agrarian roots, why did Irish immigrants decide on urban rather than rural America? In *Boston's Immigrants* (1941), Oscar Handlin argued that Irish Famine refugees really had no choice but to settle in eastern seaboard cities because they lacked funds to move inland. This explanation applied to some but not to all. Relatively affluent pre-Famine immigrants also preferred cities, and when the Irish did begin to trek west, more decided to live in Buffalo, Cleveland, Pittsburgh, Detroit, Chicago, St. Louis, Milwaukee, St. Paul, and

San Francisco than in rural communities. Irish Catholics in Canada did not have as many urban employment prospects.

A scarcity of talents more than of money determined Irish Catholic occupational and residential choices. Irish landlordism did not inculcate agrarian skills or encourage farming initiatives. Irish Catholic peasants were among the most inefficient farmers in Europe and, unlike Scandinavians and Germans of their class, unequipped for rural America. In Ireland, agriculture was more a life style than an economy, and most tenant farmers, working small bits of land, used only simple tools—spades, scythes, and hoes. Cultivating, fertilizing, and harvesting eighty acres of wheat or corn in America was far more difficult than ranching sheep in Australia or New Zealand.[2] And Irish Catholic refugees fleeing from hunger and poverty who scurried to the United States were probably less competent farmers than those who participated in planned emigration projects to Canada and Australia.

Adding to skill shortages, Irish Catholics were psychologically unsuited for rural America. Like other members of their faith, they were communal, gregarious by nature, and fond of visiting and talking. In Ireland small farms were so close together that parishes and townlands functioned as peasant villages. During the day there was considerable conversation across hedges and stone walls. In the evenings neighbors visited, talked, sang, and danced in each others' cottages. In rural America, on the other hand, farms were far apart and towns were distant, forcing families to be self-sufficient, seeing neighbors only on Saturday shopping expeditions, Sunday church services, or harvest cooperative endeavors. Cold and snowy winters added to a sense of isolation. Some Irish Catholics who chose to farm in America sent letters home commenting on the depth of their loneliness. American cities were rough, tough, corrupt, dirty, violent, and unhealthy, but extroverted Irish Catholics found them congenial because they were close to relatives and friends.

John Francis Maguire of the *Cork Examiner* and other Irish journalists who visited the United States were appalled by the crime, disease, and social disorder that afflicted the urban Irish. Catholic bishops in Ireland feared urban America endangered emigrant faith and morals. They and journalists encouraged young people crossing the Atlantic to settle in rural areas compatible with their agrarian and Catholic backgrounds.

In the 1850s, Buffalo's bishop, John Timon, and other Catholic leaders made strenuous efforts to preserve the faith of immigrants and improve their conduct by encouraging them to resettle in rural areas or small towns. New York's archbishop, John Hughes, and other eastern prelates disagreed with Timon. They argued that the urban concentration of the Irish permitted the church, with limited financial and human resources, to best minister to their spiritual needs, and to protect them from American secularism and Protestant proselytism. In the 1890s, John Ireland, archbishop of St. Paul, purchased a large tract of fertile Minnesota land and brought over Belgian and Connacht Irish peasants to farm it. Belgians prospered; the Irish quickly abandoned fields to work on the railroad in St. Paul. The archbishop's failed experiment to save the Irish from American urban vice and brutality revealed the shortage of agricultural proficiencies among those he selected and their preference for community living in the city among their own kind.[3]

Unable to cope with large-scale farming and its loneliness, most Irish Catholics in urban America, like those in Britain, started at the bottom of the unskilled labor force. Women took jobs in textile industry sweatshops and shoe factories. Because Anglo Americans looked down on domestic service as degrading, and other Europeans, with the exception of Swedes, would not let daughters work in the homes of strangers, Irish women became servants in upper- and middle-class houses. Considering that it provided room and board, a healthier environment, and exposure to some of the nicer things in life, domestic service was more pleasant and profitable than factory employment.

Irish men labored as stable boys; teamsters; bartenders, bouncers, and pot boys in saloons; street sweepers; stevedores; and gold, silver, copper, and coal miners. Irish Catholics provided most of the muscle that carved out the American canal system. In 1818, three thousand of them were digging the Erie Canal; eight years later there were five thousand Irish navvies working four major canal projects. Following the Civil War, Irish Catholic laborers built railroads east of the Rockies. Canal and railroad work was dangerous, difficult, and unhealthy, tempting tired and demoralized men to drink troubles and salaries away.

Canals and railroads brought the Irish west; military enlistments also scattered them around the country. Joining the British army and navy was an Irish male escape route, substituting travel and adventure, with a steady if small income, for poverty and boredom. In America, military service had the same kind of appeal. During the Mexican and Civil Wars, and later on the western frontier, many Irish Catholics risked life and limb and fought well for their adopted country. Now they had a motive for fighting that was missing back home. They served Britain as mercenaries, they defended America as patriots.

Unskilled Irish labor significantly contributed to American industrialism. But since women found it easier to find employment than men, and so many of the latter's jobs were seasonal or involved traveling on canal or railroad projects, Irish Catholic families often were unstable and dysfunctional. Early and mid-nineteenth-century Irish Catholic social problems resembled those existing in contemporary, minority group, urban neighborhoods. Although some comparisons between early Irish and present day Black ghettoes are valid, in pre-technocratic and automated industrial and transportation economies the Irish did have more employment opportunities than today's African Americans.

To many Americans "ghetto" has unpleasant connotations. They believe that ethnic and racial enclaves frustrate assimilation and social mobility by preserving violent poverty cultures. No doubt exclusive neighborhoods exaggerate and perpetuate ethnic and racial vices and stereotypes. In the case of Irish Catholics, they tended to nurture failure more than success by fertilizing the paranoia, defeatism, and feelings of inferiority planted in their historical experience. But the negative aspects of the physical ghetto were partially balanced by the emotional security they provided. Life in American cities was cold, competitive, and hostile. Anglo Protestants controlling business, commerce, and industry despised Irish Catholics as barbarian interlopers; members of the Anglo Protestant working class hated and feared them as employment competitors. In such an unfriendly atmosphere, Irish neighborhoods, focused around the Catholic parish, served as psychological havens, preserving faith, tradition, and values, perpetuating a sense of community that could have disintegrated in an oppressive situation.

Irish Catholic parish communities also functioned as halfway houses between two cultures. Although the Irish preferred to dwell among their own people, through much of the nineteenth century there was no other alternative. No one else wanted them around. Their ignorance, squalid living habits, and disorderly social behavior offended Anglo America. But despite the disadvantages they arrived with, Irish Catholic immigrants of the 1820s, 1830s, and early 1840s worked hard and experienced a slight degree of economic and social mobility. They bought or rented homes, built churches and schools, and most lived quiet, decent, respectable lives.

Just when Irish Catholics began to overcome handicaps of their own inadequacies and American prejudices, the Famine deposited masses of new refugees on the American shore. Although more economically and culturally sophisticated than many who could not afford to leave Ireland, they nevertheless were poor, ignorant, and unskilled. America's economy could not easily absorb them, and they pulled down the entire Irish-American community from the modest heights of respectability that it had worked so diligently to attain.[4]

Famine refugees increased the number of urban ghettos and expanded those already existing. When Irish Catholics, totally unfamiliar with urban life, moved into sections of New York, Boston, Philadelphia, Chicago, or New Orleans, others fled. For Irish rural folk the transition from agrarian Ireland to urban America was a mental and psychological dislocation, a culture shock that accented their vices and undermined their virtues.

Housing conditions in post-Famine Irish-American ghettos were atrocious. People lived in old mansions and warehouses converted into crowded tenements or in wooden-crate and tar-paper shacks. They also occupied stuffy attics and damp basements, taking turns using the few available beds. Fresh water and toilet facilities were scarce; sewage flowed through streets and alleys, and fleas, lice, mice, and rats shared accommodations with human hosts. Cholera and tuberculosis took many lives, and mental disorders were common. An abundance of filthy grog houses offered the Irish temporary oblivion from the ravages of poverty and disease. On city streets, a few (surprisingly not many) Irish girls sold bodies to provide food and clothing for their families, and Irish boys prowled as muggers and petty thieves.

Dysfunctional, impoverished, socially maladjusted Irish Catholic families imposed a tremendous strain on urban-government resources and the patience of Anglo Americans who labeled Irish immigration a social plague. During the 1840s, 1850s, 1860s, and 1870s, Irish Catholics were urban America's major social and law and order problems. According to Dennis P. Ryan's *Beyond the Ballot Box: A Social History of the Boston Irish, 1845–1917* (1983), in the late 1840s "97 percent of the residents at the Deer Island almshouse, 75 percent of the prisoners in the county jail, 90 percent of Boston truants and vagabonds, and 58 percent of its paupers" were Irish. In *Boston's Immigrants,* Handlin presents figures showing that from 1856 to 1863 at least half of the inmates of the Boston House of Correction, and in 1864 about three-fourths of the people arrested and detained in the city were Irish.[5] The situation he describes was typical rather than extraordinary. Along the East Coast and in New Orleans, Irish Catholics were a majority of those occupying penal, social service, and health institutions at taxpayers' expense.

Loaded with anger and frustration, Irish ghettos were tinderboxes ready to explode. An 1863 Draft Act initiated rioting in a number of cities. Since it permitted men to purchase substitutes for three hundred dollars to satisfy their military obligations, the Irish were justified in believing that conscription imposed an unfair burden on them. Prosperous Anglos could avoid facing the guns of the Confederacy, the Irish poor could not.

On both sides Irish Catholics fought bravely and well during the Civil War. Most wore uniforms of blue to save the Union, not to liberate Blacks. Protests against the draft involved racial prejudice. Irish workers resented free Black labor competition, especially when employers used it for strike breaking. They worried that emancipation would send many ex-slaves into northern cities to swell the job market, lowering wages and reducing employment opportunities. But much Irish Catholic antagonism to Blacks was based on sheer bigotry. Since Anglo Protestants considered them a human subgroup, in Boston they were thought of as inferior to Blacks, Irish Catholics got an ego lift by feeling and acting superior to another despised minority.

Abolitionism also stimulated Irish opposition to the end of Black slavery. Leading abolitionists, notably Protestant clergy, such as the Reverend Lyman Beecher, often were passionate enemies of Irish Catholics. They expressed anguish over the cruelties that plantation owners inflicted on slaves in the South, but seemed totally indifferent to the social injustices suffered by Irish Catholics in the industrial North.

July 1863 riot reactions to the conscription law involved a variety of members of the urban working class, but in eastern cities, Irish Catholics played the most prominent role. In Boston, some priests, themselves eligible for military service, stirred resistance to the law. For three days angry mobs ransacked parts of the city, cheering for Jefferson Davis and assaulting Blacks. Finally the governor called on the state militia to squelch disorder. It did so by firing into the mob, killing six, four of them Irish.

New York was the scene of the most massive anti-conscription riot. Mobs composed of mostly Irish Catholics, many fueled by drink, roamed city streets, destroying or damaging property, tormenting and killing Blacks, and burning down an orphanage for Black children. When the police force, largely Irish, could not control the situation, officials called in soldiers. A New York Irish regiment, the "Fighting 69th" that had distinguished itself on many a Civil War battlefield, most recently at Gettysburg, was part of the army summoned to put down the New York riot. Archbishop Hughes also helped end the turbulence by telling rioters to get off the streets and go home. Five days of arson, pillage, and violence destroyed over two million dollars worth of property; took the lives of three policemen, 105 rioters, eleven lynched Blacks, and an Indian mistaken for one; and injured countless others on both sides of the law.

On July 12 in Ulster cities and towns, Orange lodges celebrate the triumph of Protestant King Billy over Catholic King James at the Battle of the Boyne in 1690. Beating massive lambeg drums till their hands bleed and singing militant Protestant songs, they march through Catholic neighborhoods to intimidate and keep "Teagues" in their proper, subordinate place. On July 12, 1870, an Orange parade through Irish Catholic neighborhoods triggered retaliation in Elm Park on New

York's upper West Side. When the incident ended, eight were dead and many were injured. Responding to Fenian and Ancient Order of Hibernian threats, Mayor A. Oakley Hall banned the scheduled 1871 Orange parade. But Governor John T. Hoffman, another Tammany hack, catering to Anglo and Irish Protestant opinion, and its contention that if Irish Catholics could parade on March 17 their people had an equal right to do so on July 12, reversed Hall's decision. Reacting to stone throwers and snipers, soldiers protecting the parade route fired indiscriminately into a mostly hostile sidewalk crowd, killing sixty and wounding at least a hundred.

Two New York Julys, 1863 and 1871, further convinced Anglo Protestants that Irish Catholics were an inferior, primitive species, a social plague, and that their religion was an alien and subversive threat to the nation's culture and institutions. To Irish Catholics the events of July 1870 and 1871 were additional evidence that they remained strangers in the land and that Anglo Protestants were their enemies. The anti-draft riot and the Orange-parade incidents reinforced both the anti–Irish Catholic dimensions of American nativism and the mental ghetto of Irish-American Catholicism.[6]

Making Their Way in America, 1870–1922

Although never again reaching Famine peaks, emigration from Ireland continued to be heavy and steady throughout the last half of the nineteenth century. From 1870 to 1900 more than one and a half million Irish entered the United States, an annual average of more than fifty thousand. As the century neared its close, women, breaking out from the narrow social and economic confines of rural Ireland, began to outnumber men. The early and mid-1860s and the first few years of the 1880s were particularly heavy periods of emigration. From 1863 through 1866 blight and bad weather damaged crops, raising emigration to more than one hundred thousand a year, and economic distress coupled with agrarian unrest and violence in the early 1880s also propelled many to America. In 1883 more than 105,000 crossed the Atlantic. Government land reform legislation, public works projects, and aid to congested districts significantly reduced emigration after the mid-1880s. As a result, in 1901 only 39,201 Irish arrived in the United States.

Going to and arriving in America was less an ordeal in the late than it was in the early nineteenth century. Relatively comfortable and clean steam ships with courteous crews were a big improvement on the sailing vessels of old, and they reduced travel time to ten or eleven days rather than three to five weeks. In addition, when the Irish landed in American ports, they no longer had to cope with runners and other cheats. In 1855 New York officials opened Castle Garden, once Fort Clinton and then an opera house, at the lower tip of Manhattan to serve immigrant needs. It offered facilities for bathing, cooking, changing money, collecting and sending mail, depositing valuables, purchasing railroad and riverboat tickets, and obtaining counseling from religious and benevolent organizations. Just outside the main building, newcomers to the United States could find employment agencies staffed with translators. Castle Garden also provided luggage carriers and directions to respectable boarding houses. In 1892 Ellis Island replaced Castle Garden as an American entry depot and vastly improved on its services. In addition to Castle Garden, Ellis Island, and immigrant shelters in other cities, the Irish entering the United States usually had relatives to take them in and get them started with a job.

By the 1880s, however, emigration had become a fixed element in Irish life, a rich subject for song and story. Ballads spoke of peasant lads with kit bags loaded with "Cabbage, spuds, and bacon" shipping out to "The Shores of Americay":

Wid my bundle on my shoulder,
Faith there's no man could be boulder;

I'm lavin' dear old Ireland without warnin'
For I lately took the notion,
For to cross the briny ocean,
And I start for Philadelphia in the mornin'.[7]

Despite the quick tempo and jocular lyrics of many of the songs, they also emphasized hardships waiting for those who found jobs "working upon the railway, the railway" or

Sucking up the coal dust into your lungs,
Underneath the hills where there is no sun
Try to make a living on a dollar a day,
Digging bloody coal in Pennsylvania.[8]

And there were songs that lamented the Irish past and promised vengeance on England, most notably the popular folk ballad "Skibereen." In it, a father, originally from Famine-ravaged Skibereen in west Cork, tells his son that they had to leave Ireland after the potato crop failed, and the landlord evicted them when they could not pay the rent. After listening to this woeful tale, the young man promises:

Oh, father dear, the day may come
    when in answer to the call
Each Irishman, with feeling stern,
    will rally one and all
I'll be the man to lead the van beneath
    the flag of green,
When loud and high we'll raise the cry—
    "Remember Skibereen."[9]

While folk and music hall songs about going to America could be exuberant, those about parting Ireland were inevitably sad. In Percy French's "The Mountains of Mourne," an Irish man in London searching and not finding "gold in the streets" is impressed with the sights and sounds of the city but longs for his Mary in south Down "where dark Mourne sweeps down to the sea." And in his "Emigrant's Letter," a "long sort of sigh" came from the passengers on "the grand Allen liner" when "the last bit of waves hid old Donegal."

If young men and women sailing west were depressed about leaving parents and friends, think of the desolation in the hearts and minds of mothers and fathers. Emigrants on their way to the United States or other parts of the English-speaking world could look forward to adventure, new experiences, and perhaps fame and fortune. Parents were left behind with memories of daughters and sons whom they probably would never again see and with the knowledge that most of their remaining children would follow older siblings across the water. A folk custom called the "American Wake" symbolized the finality of emigration. On the evening before the parting of children for the United States, families would host parties with food, drink, and music. On days when ships sailed for America, weeping and keening relatives and friends crowded docks to bid farewell to those leaving. Beyond the devastating effect on families, emigration was a mixed blessing for Ireland. It worked as a safety valve, siphoning off the surplus population from a one-dimensional economy, and lessening social discontent, but it also robbed the country of bright, energetic, and creative talent. This was particularly true in the last third of the nineteenth century when education, a rising standard of living, and a reformed Catholicism improved the quality of those going to America.

Many Irish Catholics who arrived in the United States before, during, and immediately after the Great Famine were illiterate, and perhaps a third were less than fluent in English. But by 1870, the national schools had radically reduced illiteracy and increased proficiency in English. In 1851 nearly 50 percent of Irish people over five years of age could not read or write. Fifty years later that percentage had dropped to less than fourteen, and only six among persons twelve to forty, the main age bracket for emigrants. By 1900 the literacy rate in Ireland was higher than in the United States. Irish arrivals at

Ellis Island may have been technologically unskilled, but they could read and write and express themselves clearly in English, instruments of economic and social mobility. After the Famine, the main focus of Catholic agitation in Ireland shifted from religious to economic grievances. Tenant rights, including secure land holding at fair rents and the right of occupiers to sell their contribution to the value of the farm on leaving, were the main objectives. These demands indicated rising expectations derived from an improved economic situation rather than a response to desolate poverty.

In the late nineteenth century, Ireland was still one of the most economically depressed countries in western Europe. But except for Connacht, where pre-Famine conditions still prevailed—small farms, over-population, a predominantly potato diet—between 1851 and the late 1870s the rural standard of living rose considerably. Famine casualties and emigration were largely responsible for improvements. Instead of the anticipated population of nine million in 1851, only six and a half million survived the Irish "holocaust," lessening pressure on land resources. As a class, agricultural laborers suffered the most from the Famine, and were no longer a rural majority. Small, uneconomical farms of one to five acres declined from 310,436 in 1841 to 88,083 in 1851. Holdings of between five and fifteen acres also fell from 252,799 to 191,854 during the same time span. Larger farms of from fifteen to thirty acres increased from 79,742 to 141,311, and the number of farms with more than thirty acres rose from 49,625 to 149,090. As farms became bigger, dwellings grew larger, cleaner, and more comfortable.

On larger post-Famine holdings, the shift from tillage to grazing that started in the late eighteenth century and escalated after 1815 continued. Farmers purchased cattle, sheep, and pigs, raised chickens, and profited from rising meat, butter, and egg prices throughout the United Kingdom. Food-producing Ireland became a natural economic partner for urban, industrial Britain. And from 1851 to 1878, agricultural prices rose so much faster than rents that evictions became rare. In the twenty-five years between 1855 and 1880, only 17,771 families lost their farms permanently—a rate of less than 3 percent of all tenants—and many left for reasons other than nonpayment of rents. Significant incomes from the sale of agricultural goods, moderate rents, and dollar gifts from America all contributed to a rising standard of living evidenced by savings accounts in banks; a more varied diet—farm families were eating eggs, butter, vegetables, meat (mostly bacon), as well as potatoes; and generous donations to the church, visible in many new Catholic buildings scattered over the Irish landscape.

The increase of chapels, schools, rectories, and convents was a tribute to the organizational genius of Paul Cullen. In 1849 Pius IX appointed Cullen, rector of the Irish College in Rome, archbishop of Armagh, primate of the Irish Church, and apostolic delegate. He dominated Irish Catholicism until his death in 1878 as cardinal archbishop of Dublin. When he visited Ireland in 1835, Alexis de Tocqueville was impressed with the piety of its people. He favorably compared their devotionalism with Continental Catholics, especially those in his own country, France. Nevertheless, before the Famine in many parts of Ireland, particularly the more Gaelicized, impoverished West, the church was afflicted with a number of problems: an ignorant, poorly instructed laity, inadequately educated and unruly priests, a quarreling bench of bishops (usually over Peel's attempt to seduce them from nationalism with government financial favors), and a shortage of clergy and chapels.

By drastically reducing the population, especially among ignorant and superstitious agricultural laborers, and leveling the balance between the church's resources and the laity's needs, the Famine set the stage for a reformed and revitalized Irish Catholicism. But Cullen deserves the credit for taking advantage of a favorable situation. Not only did he build buildings, he also improved clerical education and discipline; significantly enlarged the number of religious vocations; created a public face of harmony among the hierarchy; successfully cultivated attendance at Mass, parish missions, and a variety of devotions (forty-hours, stations of the cross, benediction, and the rosary), and increased reception of the sacraments among the people; and rooted out strains of Gallicanism in the Irish Church. By the end of the nineteenth century, Irish Catholics were the most devout, financially generous, obedient, and loyal members of the Roman fold. Post-Famine Irish emigrants—priests, nuns, and laity—brought what Emmet Larkin has described as a "Devotional Revolution" with them to the New World.

Reformed Catholicism, added to the results of the national schools and the increased energy and expectations that came from a rising standard of living, did much to improve the quality of the post-Famine Irish Diaspora. But Cullen's highly Romanized style of Irish Catholicism had negative as well as positive features. The alliance between Irish Catholicism and Irish nationalism that began in the agitation for Catholic Emancipation politically civilized the former. De Tocqueville not only praised the piety of the Irish laity, he also lauded the popular sovereignty commitments of the hierarchy and clergy. "Devotional Revolution" Catholicism did not renege on its support of nationalism's liberal democratic values and goals, but it was religiously authoritarian, discouraging creative thought or curiosity among the laity. Irish Catholicism's rigid discipline and clericalism, combined with its puritanism, created an oppressive intellectual and social atmosphere that supplemented economic reasons for leaving Ireland.

Irish Catholicism's obsession with sex is not Jansenism or a "Celtic Heresy" as some critics have charged. As previously mentioned, in Ireland the church, reinforcing economic and social pressures for late marriages and long periods of and sometimes permanent celibacy, emphasized sexual morality with more fervor than it did in other countries. There was also a British Protestant flavor to Irish Catholicism. Partial Anglicization exposed the Irish to British middle-class law and order values, including Victorian prudery. While Latin Catholics shrug shoulders at church regulations they consider arbitrary or silly, the Irish have insisted on living by the rules or changing them, making them at the same time the most rigid yet rebellious members of the faith.[10]

Famine memories, increased expectations, and Roman pietism blended with Anglo-Protestant Evangelical influences melded into an Irish puritan personality. There was far more materialism than romance in Irish marriages. Clerical sermons, to the exclusion of probably more serious frailties, hammered away at the horrors of sex, advising single men and women to avoid physical and social contact. Catholic-preached and church-enforced gender segregation not only speeded emigration, it also encouraged the Irish tendency to over-indulge in alcohol. Drinking became a means of sublimating sexual desire, and a male pub culture became an alternative to the company of women on both sides of the Atlantic.

Without a doubt, authoritarian Catholicism combined with puritanism toned down the zip and flamboyance of the Irish personality, but its moral austerity brought immigrants closer to Anglo-Protestant America's notion of respectability. Although drinking remained a serious problem, Irish-American Catholics were not the brawling, happy-go-lucky rogues of old, and their crime rate declined while their family life became more stable. Catholicism was so effective in controlling Irish morals and conduct that even Anglo Americans hostile to Catholicism reluctantly admitted that without their church, the Irish would be even more offensive. In *Poverty and Progress* (1964), Stephan Thernstrom quoted one New England newspaper on the subject:

> There is not a reasonable person in the town (Newburyport, Massachusetts), who employs a Catholic girl in his family, who would not prefer one devoted to her religion, constant at church . . . When

they deny their religion they seldom accept ours, but that class furnish the night walkers, the drunkards and the criminals.[11]

Improving conditions in Ireland did not translate into a miraculous quick cure for the Irish-American Catholic urban social problem. In the waning years of the nineteenth and the early decades of the twentieth century, alcoholism, mental disorders, abusive husbands and fathers, violence, crime, and juvenile delinquency continued to haunt Irish communities. But a lift in the quality of immigrants, the spiritually coercive power of Catholicism, and its social and educational institutions did much to improve the conduct of Irish-American Catholics and set them on the road to respectability.

In terms of behavior, Irish-American Catholics were becoming less offensive to Anglo Protestants, but were they advancing economically and socially? Looking at Newburyport in the 1880s, Thernstrom says No! He discovers that unlike Anglo Americans, they still held down the manual laboring jobs of their fathers and grandfathers instead of moving into the ranks of skilled labor or into management. But they did experience some success: "Through toil and sacrifice they had been able to buy homes, build their church, and obtain a slender margin of economic security."[12] Thernstrom points out the Irish ambition to own property—they purchased far more than working-class Anglos—and their generous contributions to the church. He argues, however, that the money that went to buy homes and to build churches was at the cost of educating children, seriously limiting their mobility prospects.

Thernstrom fails to assess motives driving the Irish appetite for property and their need to display Catholic loyalty in bricks and mortar. Owning a house was a symbol of freedom and dignity to people who had been landless in Ireland. Generosity to the church was a statement of loyalty to an institution that encompassed an ethnic as well as a religious identity. Catholic worship was a bridge of familiarity between rural Ireland and urban America, providing psychological as well as spiritual comfort in a religious taste of home. Catholic parishes functioned much like the peasant villages in the Old Country. They were social as well as religious centers. To Irish Catholics, their churches symbolized a kind of material success as well as community. In addition, they meant profits for Irish contractors and jobs for Irish workers.

Since the New England states of Massachusetts, Connecticut, and Rhode Island contained only 17 percent of Irish America at the close of the nineteenth century, they were not an accurate gauge of its success or failure. Almost as many, 15½ percent, lived in three Midwest states, Illinois, Iowa, and Missouri, while the largest concentration chose the Mid-Atlantic states of New York and Pennsylvania. Its New England representation was as typical of Irish-American Catholicism as Northern-Ireland nationalists are of Catholic Ireland. Similar to present day Six-County Catholics, those in nineteenth-century Massachusetts lived in a Protestant Ascendancy society determined to retain the status quo. They began on the basement of the American class structure and tended to remain there. Failure, defeat, and paranoia saturated their neighborhoods. They resurfaced in the 1930s and 1940s in support for Father Charles Coughlin's isolationism and anti-semitism, in the 1950s in enthusiasm for Senator Joseph McCarthy's communist witchhunt, and in the 1970s and 1980s in sometimes violent resistance to school desegregation and bussing.

While Thernstrom's thesis holds for New England, it does not for other regions. When Irish Catholics moved to areas where the social and economic situations were more fluid, varied, and dynamic, they shared American enthusiasm and optimism, seizing opportunities to advance, rejecting the pessimism and defeatism that plagued them in such places as Boston and Newburyport. Newly arrived immigrants in the Midwest were more likely to succeed than third or fourth generation Irish Catholics in Boston. In the Mid-Atlantic states and in the Midwest and West, they shared cities with Anglo Protestants and other ethnics, and the farther west Irish Catholics went, the more confident and competitive they became.[13]

At the beginning of the twentieth century, Irish Catholics, particularly immigrants, were still engaged in back-breaking labor, but many, mostly second and third generation, had climbed into skilled employment, dominating the building trades. Along with Jews, they had taken control of the trade union movement. In 1879 Terence V. Powderly became the first grand master of the Knights of Labor, the original effort to create a nationwide labor movement. In the first decade of the twentieth century, 50 out of 110 presidents of American Federation of Labor locals were Irish.

Although few Irish Catholics made their way into the country's financial aristocracy, a good number had penetrated the lower middle class, especially on the urban frontiers of the Midwest and West. In investigating the economic and social mobility of Irish Americans, David Doyle discovered that a larger percentage of them belonged to the lower middle class than Germans or Anglo Americans, and that they were nearly as successful in arriving in the upper middle class as the former. He classified almost 6 percent of American Irish in 1900 as upper and more than 14 percent as lower middle class.[14]

Irish women, the daughters and granddaughters of domestic servants, waitresses, and factory workers, led the vanguard of Irish-American occupational progress. Nuns as nurses, teachers, administrators of schools, hospitals, and orphanages were America's first group of professional women. Protective Irish Catholic parents, believing sons were tough enough to endure the hardships of industrial cities, provided more educational opportunities for daughters. Quite a few of these young women, inspired by the example of the nuns who taught them, found careers in teaching and nursing. By the early twentieth century, in many metropolitan areas, Irish-American Catholic women dominated faculties of elementary and sec-

ondary schools, and cared for the hospitalized sick. Technological changes, typewriters and telephones, provided jobs as
secretaries and operators for young women lacking the interest
or financial resources to nurse or teach.

Public service, with its promises of job permanence and pen-
sions, had great appeal for the Irish who had little taste of security in Ireland or in the early stages of their American
experiences. Parents urged sons to join the civil service, and
the danger and thrills, as well as the benefits, of the police force
and the fire department appealed to them. They made good
policemen and fire fighters; they were physically tough, courageous, loved excitement and comradeship and, except in matters of sex, were flexible and tolerant of most forms of human
frailty. Unfortunately, this moral tolerance often led politicians
as well as policemen to make vague and shaky distinctions between honest and dishonest graft.

Athletics offered Irish-American Catholics an opportunity
to work off frustrations in physical exercise and competition.
Like members of other ethnic and racial minorities that followed them into urban America, the Irish have been excellent
athletes. Ghetto life toughened them, and sports offered fame,
fortune, and recognition unavailable to them in other aspects
of American life. In the late nineteenth and early twentieth centuries, Irish Catholics, like today's African Americans, dominated boxing, baseball, and track and field. Later, when more
attended college, they brought their skills to football gridirons.

Although athletics provided the Irish and other minorities
with heroes, diverted physical energies from socially destructive conduct, and made them competitive in a society where it
was necessary for survival, there were negative as well as positive results from sports successes. Winning boxing champion-
ships confirmed a "racist" opinion of many Anglo Protestants
that the ferocious Irish had strong backs but weak minds. But
Irish domination of baseball, America's favorite, pastoral fla-
vored sport, won them considerable respect.

One unfortunate aspect of athletic success was the glorification of wrong values in the Irish Catholic community. From the elementary level through university, Catholic schools tended to concentrate on winning teams more than quality education. This emphasis, along with the authoritarian character of Catholicism, retarded progress in cultural and intellectual areas, delaying the emergence of an American Catholic intellectual class.

Show business as well as sports attracted Irish Catholic ambition and talent and exhibited their extrovert personalities. Irish Catholic and Jewish entertainers of the past, and African Americans and Italians of the present, have revealed a close connection between the ghetto and the stage. Perhaps poverty, persecution, and insecurity encourage the camouflage of suffering and the cultivation of a sense of humor as survival techniques. As singer, dancer, composer, playwright, and actor, George M. Cohan (1878–1942) epitomized the Irish entertainer. His songs expressed ethnic pride ("Harrigan"); American patriotism ("It's a Grand Old Flag," "Yankee Doodle Boy," and "Over There"); and Irish-American energy, ambition, cockiness, and enthusiasm.

At the turn of the century, Irish-American Catholics were doing a variety of things: mining coal and feeding it into steel-mill furnaces; working as engineers, firemen, switchmen, levermen, and gang foremen on the railroad; fighting fires; preserving law and order on city streets; performing on the stage; pitching and hitting curve balls on baseball diamonds; throwing and taking punches in the boxing ring; nursing hospital patients; waiting tables; cleaning houses; teaching school; covering newspaper stories; tending bar; practicing law and medicine; saying Mass; and managing labor unions and a few small businesses. They were slow, however, in contributing to American cultural and intellectual life. Most were too busy caring for large families to think seriously about art, literature, music, and science; few had the kind of liberal arts education that en-

couraged intellectual creativity. Parochial schools concentrated
on making students functional in urban America, culturally
Anglicizing and religiously Romanizing them in the process,
teaching them to read and write, to love God and country, and
to obey the church. Before World War I, not many Irish Catholic youngsters attended secondary school, and before World
War II a number of women intending to nurse or teach went
on to higher education, but men tended to take a job after grad-
uating from secondary school. Catholic secondary and higher,
like its elementary education, concentrated on the practical
rather than the theoretical. Priests, nuns, and brothers teaching in classrooms focused on preserving the faith, and preparing students for decent jobs and productive lives, and they
succeeded in their mission.

Nor did the culture they inherited inspire Irish-American
Catholic intellectual ambitions. National schools in Ireland,
like parochial schools in the United States, tried to "civilize"
rather than intellectualize students, and sophisticated Anglo-
Irish Protestants exported their best creative talent to London,
while landlords, barristers, bankers, clerics, and businessmen
remained in Ireland to promote second-rate imitations of British art and literature rather than original expressions of Irish
culture.

A revival of cultural nationalism in the 1880s transformed
the Irish intellectual landscape. An Anglo-Irish Protestant-led
movement made Dublin a major literary capital. Even though
Irish writers such as William Butler Yeats, John Millington
Synge, and Lady Augusta Gregory exploited themes from Irish
folklore and praised the life of the noble peasant, the quintessential Gael, emigrants from rural Ireland, the core of Irish
America, had no connection with the urban based literary revival. Well-educated Anglo-American Protestants had more
appreciation for Irish literary genius than Irish Americans.
The former crowded theatres in 1911–1912 when Dublin's Abbey Theatre brought Synge's *The Playboy of the Western World* to

American cities. The latter stood outside picketing paganism and slurs on the virtue of Irish Catholic women.

Most Irish Americans considered the ballad poetry of Thomas Moore and Young Ireland and the novels of Charles Kickham, particularly *Knocknagow or the Homes of Tipperary* (1879), to be good and authentic Irish literature. Later, more sophisticated Irish and Irish-American Catholics would ridicule the literary tastes of their peasant parents and grandparents. But it was better for culturally deprived Irish Americans to read second-rate literature than not to read any at all, and Young Ireland romantics, Moore, and Kickham satisfied a need for attractive images of Ireland and Irishness that created ethnic pride and initiated an interest in cultural things as a prelude to better times.

In his comprehensive and perceptive history of Irish-American literature, *The Irish Voice in America: Irish-American Fiction from the 1760s to the 1980s* (1990), Charles Fanning emphasizes the defensiveness of so much of its nineteenth-century content, namely the work of Mary Anne Sadlier (1820–1903). Her widely read fiction exposed a dour, insecure Irish America, and expressed hostility to the general American milieu, urging cultural isolation as protection for Catholic faith and values. Balancing Sadlier, John Boyle O'Reilly (1844–1890), editor of the *Boston Pilot*, attempted to construct bridges of understanding between Irish and Anglo America. O'Reilly, a native of County Louth, as a member of the British army tried to enlist fellow Irish soldiers in the Irish Republican Brotherhood. Exposed by an informer, a British court in 1866 tried, convicted, and sentenced him to death. The sentence was commuted to life imprisonment, and after a failed escape from Dartmoor, the government transported O'Reilly to Australia. In 1869 he fled on a New Bedford whaler to Philadelphia. The next year O'Reilly settled in Boston and began his twenty-year career with the *Pilot*.

O'Reilly gathered an Irish-American literary circle around

him. His protégés included Katherine E. Conway, James Jeffrey Roche, and Louise Imogen Guiney. Their poetry and fiction borrowed the idealism and the genteel respectability of New England's Anglo-American literary school. Unfortunately, this imitation plus the influence of Young Ireland romanticism delayed Irish-American literature's confrontation with the actuality of its subject's urban existence. Conway's fiction, a blend of realism and romanticism, was a bit of an exception. Her *Lalor's Maples* introduced two Irish-American Catholic literary themes, home and mother.

As Fanning indicates, the start of realistic Irish-American writing came out of the *Chicago Evening Post* rather than the *Boston Pilot*. In the 1890s Finley Peter Dunne (1867–1936) introduced Martin Dooley to Chicago newspaper readers. Fictional Dooley, a Famine immigrant from Roscommon, operated a saloon on Archey Road (Archer Avenue in St. Bridget's parish). Every day he and his friends and customers, McKenna and Hennessey, discussed local and national affairs, but mostly they talked about the trials and tribulations of Bridgeport and Canaryville neighbors: hod carriers, housewives, policemen, firemen, priests, criminals, and politicians. Dooley poked fun at Irish clannishness, volubility, patriotic picnics, the ability to wink at political corruption, and thirst for beer and whiskey. He also complimented their generosity, courage, sense of humor, family loyalty, solidarity, and capacity for hard work. Through Dooley's lyrical brogue and clever dialogue, Dunne satirized Anglo Protestants, scourging their racial and ethnic prejudices, militarism, imperialism, and hypocrisy masquerading as reform politics. According to Fanning, Dunne created the first authentic ethnic community in American literature. Beginning with Eugene O'Neill (1888–1953) and James T. Farrell (1904–1979), Irish Americans would start to make major contributions to twentieth-century American literature, but it all began on Archey Road.

4. Communities in Conflict: American Nativists and Irish Catholics

In his interesting and informative *Paddy and the Republic: Ethnicity and Nationality in Antebellum America* (1986), Dale T. Knobel claims that early nineteenth-century Anglo Americans blamed the Irish Catholic social problem more on ethnicity than religion. They believed that exposure to the American environment, its democratic politics, and its Protestant-based culture would eventually transform Catholic immigrants from Ireland into useful and productive citizens. But as their numbers increased and their quality worsened with the Famine, Anglo-American Protestants attributed Irish urban blight to nature rather than nurture. Knobel describes an American public-opinion consensus that Irish Catholics were an inferior species polluting the country, and that they did not have the intelligence or moral character to ever become a positive and productive community. He also argues that nativist organizations actually were more optimistic about Irish Catholic possibilities than the public-opinion consensus. They continued to believe in the healing possibilities of American surroundings.

Since American prejudices sharply focused on the Irish who were Catholic and not those who were Protestant, Knobel underestimates the religious factor. Despite the American Revolution, the War of 1812, and frequent diplomatic tensions between the United States and the United Kingdom, Americans remained British in language, institutions, cultural tastes, and religious preferences. Since anti-Catholicism was the core ingredient in British nativism, it served the same function in the United States. Like the English, Scottish, and Welsh, Anglo Americans interpreted sixteenth-, seventeenth-, and eighteenth-century wars between England and Catholic Spain and France as defensive crusades against ignorance and tyranny, with Irish Catholics existing as a subversive fifth column.

England's conflicts with Spain and France, and her internal purges of real and imaginary Catholic traitors, had American dimensions. Early English immigrants in New England left home believing that popery had infiltrated and corrupted the established Anglican church. Their Nonconformist friends and relatives in England were the elite corps of the parliamentary army that defeated Stuart "despotism" in two seventeenth-century revolutions. And Protestant dissenters on both sides of the Atlantic associated Stuart Jacobites with Catholicism, connecting Rome with oppression and subversion. Irish Catholics played an important role in the British-Protestant interpretation of history; they sided with James II against the forces of freedom and enlightenment.

In championing the causes of liberty and tolerance, British and Irish-Protestant Whigs insisted that the "Glorious Revolution" of 1688 was a human rights victory over authoritarianism, but they excluded Catholics from their freedom of conscience agenda, insisting that they were alien threats to British constitutionalism. Transforming theory into practice, British and Irish Parliaments enacted Penal Laws to extinguish

Catholic power and influence and crush Catholic morale by denying them property rights and basic civil liberties. With the exception of Quaker Pennsylvania, colonial legislatures in British North America also refused Catholics and Catholicism equal citizenship or religious tolerance.

Anti-Catholicism played a role in the American decision to reject British rule. Colonists deeply resented the 1774 Quebec Act that gave the Catholic Church a privileged position in French Canada, and included within Quebec's boundaries land north of the Ohio River—territory claimed by Connecticut, Pennsylvania, and Virginia. And in the early stages of the war against Britain, Americans celebrated Guy Fawkes Day on November 5 by hanging the pope in effigy. In order not to offend America's French ally and Catholics in the revolutionary army, General George Washington ordered his soldiers to cease an anti-Catholic festivity celebrated by British and American Protestants since the early seventeenth century.[1]

Enlightenment rationalism as well as the British Protestant historical heritage encouraged the perception of Catholicism as a superstitious, anti-intellectual, authoritarian monster threatening to devour American values and institutions. Jeffersonian democracy, a product of the Enlightenment, insisted that the nation's liberties could survive only in an agrarian environment that emphasized the ownership of small farms as a symbol of and protection for individual dignity and freedom. From this perspective, poverty-afflicted Irish Catholics contradicted the rural, liberal individualism that Anglo-American Protestants interpreted as the essential spirit of their country. The nativist view that Irish Catholics were an urban social plague and a cultural tumor eating away at America's heart and soul persuaded those with Ulster Presbyterian backgrounds to cultivate a separate Scots-Irish ethnicity. This ensured that the Irish-American image would be Catholic.

In the United States, as in Britain and Ireland, Anglo-Protestant and Scots-Irish Presbyterian prejudices against Irish

Catholics had racial dimensions. They insisted that indigence and disorderly conduct were inherent in the Irish Catholic personality, and that their religious choice of Rome indicated an inferior intellect. They said that Catholicism locked the Irish into ignorance, shiftlessness, superstition and disloyalty to the American nation.

Irish Catholic social misconduct did place a severe strain on the fabric of urban America, and their religious and political allegiances appeared incompatible. The American constitution sponsored and protected individual rights and liberties, freedom of conscience, and the separation of church and state. Rome was an ally of the Old Regime, the advocate of church and state union, a friend of authoritarian, aristocratic governance, and an enemy of independent consciences. Protestants in the United States asked: how could someone be a good citizen and at the same time follow the dictates of Rome?

American Protestants refused to recognize the considerable differences between Irish and American Catholicism and the Continental European variety. Irish and American Catholics were victims, not instigators of oppression, bearing the burden of Anglo-Protestant persecution. They rejected the reactionary political opinions of Rome, drawing distinctions between politics and theology. Daniel O'Connell in Ireland and Charles Carroll in America embraced Lockian social-contract principles in efforts to liberate Irish and American Catholics from Penal-Law liabilities. Difficulties in trying to reconcile loyalties to conflicting absolutist religious and liberal political systems, however, have tortured the Catholic mind and have often produced a dual-personality neurosis, often expressed in superpatriotism. In a desire to demonstrate love of country, Catholics have been quick to volunteer for military service, but they also at times have zealously supported reactionary causes professing to be patriotic. With some justification, American liberals have frequently blasted both Catholic support of foreign fascist regimes, and their fanatic, at times irrational anti-communism—Coughlinism in the 1930s and McCarthyism in the 1940s. But many of these same liberals have also exhibited cloudy political judgment in their benevolent attitudes toward left-wing totalitarianism. Liberals have also criticized Catholic pressures in regard to American mores when they interfere with personal privacy, especially concerning abortion and contraception. No doubt, the views of Rome and the compliant American hierarchy on birth control seem to contradict common sense, but time has yet to judge whether pro-choice liberals or those Catholics who oppose abortion are doing the most to preserve human dignity.

Following the American Revolution, national and state constitutions destroyed remnants of official Protestant Ascendancy represented by established churches and anti-Catholic laws. On the state level, the establishment of religious freedom was slow: New York did not repeal anti-Catholic legislation until 1806, Connecticut waited until 1818, Massachusetts held out until 1833, and in 1835 North Carolina was the last state to recognize Catholics as full-fledged citizens. Repeal of state discriminatory codes did not scuttle nativism, but at that time Catholicism was not the main target of post-revolutionary Americanism. In the early years of the new republic, Catholics were too few in number to seriously frighten Protestants. Members of the ruling Federalist Party were far more concerned about French Revolutionary ideas that Thomas Jefferson and his Democratic-Republican friends seemed to embrace. In 1798 a Federalist Congress passed the Alien and Sedition Acts, intending to isolate the United States from European radicalism. They included Society of United Irishmen members, mostly Anglo-Irish Protestants, in the undesirable alien category. Authors of the Alien and Sedition Acts wanted to protect American values from foreign contamination by insisting on a fourteen-year residency requirement for naturalization. Delegates to the 1812–1814 Hartford Convention even went further by passing resolutions excluding foreign-born citizens from public office.

Post-1830 American nativism, fueled by Irish immigration, became specifically anti-Catholic. Irish Catholics irritated Protestants not only with social misconduct but by also swelling Catholic numbers in the United States. In 1789 only one bishop and thirty priests served about thirty thousand American Catholics, one-tenth Black slaves. By 1860 the Catholic population had expanded to around three million, most of them Irish living in many dioceses and employing a large number of priests, nuns, and brothers, usually Irish as well. Such massive growth exceeded the general American rate of population increase.

Before the impact of Irish immigration, American Catholics were culturally Anglicized and, like their English counterparts, were humble and quiet in religious observances, tiptoeing about so as not to disturb or antagonize the Protestant majority. English and Anglo-American Catholics, wanting to participate in social, economic, and political life, also were intent on demonstrating loyalty to their native countries. John Carroll, in 1784 named "Superior" of the Catholic mission in the United States, was a member of an old and respectable Maryland family and a close personal friend of Benjamin Franklin and George Washington. His cousin, Charles, signed the Declaration of Independence. For some time Carroll kept Rome at arm's length, emphasizing the unique qualities of American Catholicism, advocating an English vernacular rather than a Latin liturgy, and a theology compatible with the American Enlightenment instead of the mysticism and emotionalism of European Catholic worship.

After Rome in 1789 selected Carroll as first bishop and primate of the church in the United States, he wavered in his intention to create an American Catholicism adapted to its political and social environment. In addition to his responsibilities as head of the American Church, a strong conservative incentive, Carroll found other reasons to adopt the liturgical devotionalism demanded by the papacy and its insistence on obedience to spiritual authority, local and Roman. In the atmosphere of the French Revolution, where many of its clerical refugees gained access to his confidence, upper-class Carroll reacted negatively to the spirit of Jeffersonian democracy.

Not all French priests were reactionary opponents of the American liberalism. Many members of the Society of Priests of St. Sulpice, an order dedicated to teaching seminarians, aided the native American clergy in serving the small but widely dispersed Catholic community. Sulpicians were men of culture and dignity who sympathized with Carroll's early desire for a distinctly American Catholicism, one that would flow into the mainstream of Anglo-American culture.

Irish immigration, particularly its post-Famine, devotional-revolution contingent, guaranteed that Romanization would temporarily at least triumph over Americanization. Instead of melding into American society, the religion, social disorder, and clannishness of Irish Catholics alienated Anglo and other Americans, isolating them in ghettos of mind and place. Irish priests lacked the learning and sophistication of the Anglo-American and French Catholic clergy and, like those they served, were aggressive rather than passive Catholics. Irish Catholics came to the United States to escape Anglo-Protestant religious, economic, political, and social oppression. They had no intention of being deferential and humble about their spiritual and cultural values in a nation that professed freedom.

Archbishop Ambrose Maréchal, Carroll's French successor as bishop of Baltimore and primate, tried to curb the power of Irish priests. He considered the crudity of their peasant manners a limitation on their ability to lift the cultural level of turbulent parishioners. And Maréchal feared that the coarse and aggressive Irish would alienate Anglo Americans, instigating anti-Catholic persecution. Maréchal's anxieties were justified. Irish priests on the American mission were almost as unpolished as church-pew immigrants. Bishops in Ireland had exiled many of them for misconduct involving drink or women or disobedience. Frequently they continued to indulge their vices or disruptive attitudes and behavior in the United States. Some Irish priests encouraged lay boards of trustees to declare independence from American bishops. Maréchal complained to Rome that priests from Ireland were unreliable and sources of scandal and discontent. After the Irish finally gained command of the American Church, bishops such as Charleston's John England, a Cork native, took steps to improve the quality of the clergy by founding seminaries to train Irish-American priests and by insisting that bishops in Ireland send only intelligent and spiritual priests on the American mission. The Irish hierarchy complied and, as one aspect of the "Devotional Revolution," Paul Cardinal Cullen established a special seminary to train missionaries.

Irish numbers and demands for priests of their own gave them control of American Catholicism and transformed its profile from rural to urban. Until quite recently, the church in the United States belonged to an Irish spiritual empire extending throughout the English-speaking world and into the British political and economic empire in Africa and Asia. With Hibernian domination of American Catholicism, the ancient conflict between Anglo Protestant and Irish Catholic expanded into a new arena.

Religion in the schools was a persistent, fundamental, and highly emotional issue in an enduring conflict between nativists and Catholics. The former insisted that public schools were essential for assimilating immigrants and that parochial schools were divisive. Pointing to the use of the King James version of the *Bible* as moral and religious guidance, Catholics accused the public schools of proselytism and demanded state subsidies for their own.

During the late 1830s and early 1840s, the State of New York was the scene of intense struggles over the school issue. Concerned about the education of immigrant children, Governor William Seward sympathized with Catholic requests for public funding of parochial schools, but other politicians suggested an alternative. In 1842 the legislature secularized public schools, setting a separation of church and state precedent in regard to education that other states followed and courts upheld.

At the time, neither Catholics nor Protestants were satisfied with secularization as a compromise solution to their conflicting positions. Catholics continued to expand the parochial school system as a defense against proselytism and secularism, and futilely continued to demand state financing; Protestants denounced Catholic opposition to Bible reading in public schools as illustrative of the difference between the high moral tone and truths of scriptural Protestant Christianity and the ignorance, superstitions, and pretensions of popery. They also continued to criticize parochial schools as un-American, tending to divide rather than unite the nation.

Clearly anti-Catholicism was the core of nativism from the 1830s through the 1850s. In the former decade, a vast number of Americans, instructed by such prominent citizens as the Reverend Lyman Beecher and the famous inventor, Samuel F. B. Morse, believed in an international conspiracy, engineered by European despots, mainly the Hapsburgs, to use Catholicism as a wedge to destroy American liberal democracy. Nativists warned that Catholic Europe had selected the Mississippi Valley as the most vulnerable target and planned to flood it with immigrants. They said that Jesuits disguised as farmers, tinkers, and medicine men were scouting the region as a prelude to invasion. Protestant newspapers were obsessed with the alleged Mississippi Valley conspiracy, and people from all over the country contributed large sums of money to a Protestant crusade to rescue the West and eventually the nation from the machinations of popery.

Publishers profited from the nativist binge. Voracious readers devoured anti-Catholic books, pamphlets, and newspapers. Much of the material had originated in Britain during the Catholic Emancipation agitation of the 1820s and Peel's decision to permanently endow the Catholic seminary at Maynooth in the 1840s. Often the propaganda of prejudice has contained pornographic dimensions to entice as well as incite readers. This certainly was the case in regard to anti-Catholicism. Publications and platform speeches titillated Protestants with descriptions of Catholic sexual depravity, particularly among the clergy. Counterfeit and real ex-priests and nuns traveled lecture circuits with graphic stories of orgies behind convent walls and seductions in confessionals. Maria Monk was a heroine of the Protestant, anti-Catholic crusade. Her *Awful Disclosures of the Hotel Dieu in Montreal* (1836) was the no-popery equivalent of the bogus anti-Semitic *Protocols of the Elders of Zion*. In actuality, Maria Monk was a mentally-retarded and deranged Protestant who ended her days as a prostitute. Her only contact with Catholicism was as a Catholic hospital patient, but she claimed to be an escaped nun, and nativists decided to exploit her fable. In her account of convent life in Montreal, Monk told of seductions by priests in the confessional and of frequent sexual encounters between priests and nuns. She described lust tunnels connecting rectories and convents. They also served as burial grounds for infants resulting from clerical orgies. According to Monk, the babies were baptized and then murdered, so that convent secrets would never reach the outside world. Her revelations became an immediate best-seller and led to a number of convent inspections, all disproving her allegations. But the truth was irrelevant to bigots who wanted to believe the most gruesome and lascivious rumors of Catholic depravity. Maria Monk's tale of horror and lechery continued to anger and mobilize nativists. It reappeared as late as the 1960 presidential-election campaign.

No-popery combined violence with pornography. The August 1834 burning of an Ursuline convent in Charlestown, Massachusetts, initiated a wave of shootings, hangings, and burnings that continued to the 1860s. Nativists targeted Irish Catholic neighborhoods and churches. In 1844, when Philadelphia's bishop, Francis Kendrick, requested public funding for parochial schools, a Protestant mob invaded Catholic sections of the city, burning houses and dynamiting churches. Its leaders justified the attack by claiming that the Irish had stored arms in church basements as a prelude to revolution. Events in Philadelphia tempted New York nativists to move against Irish Catholics. While they were planning their offensive, Archbishop John Hughes surrounded his churches with armed Irish guards and warned city officials that if one place of worship was desecrated, his people would torch all of New York, turning it into a copy of the blazing Moscow that transformed Napoleon's Russian foray into a bitter retreat. Politicians and nativists got Hughes's message, and the Philadelphia story did not have a New York addendum. But anti-Irish violence in Boston, New York, Louisville, and New Orleans (French Catholics shared Anglo-Protestant contempt for Irish barbarians) continued to disturb urban America. In the early 1850s, Protestants attacked and burned the Irish area of Lawrence, Massachusetts, and the next year many Boston brahmins dismissed Irish domestic servants after rumors circulated that they were agents of a Catholic plot to poison the Protestant leadership of Massachusetts.

In addition to pornographic propaganda and violence, anti-Catholic nativism had political dimensions. Many politicians campaigned on no-popery platforms and slogans and, to win votes, both Federalists and Whigs were willing to exploit distrust and hatred of Catholics. Local nativist parties enjoyed election successes, and by 1854 an anti-Catholic, secret society, the Order of the Star Spangled Banner, had evolved into the American party. Members took Masonic type oaths and used a variety of countersigns. When asked about their party goals, principles, and symbols, they feigned ignorance, earning the moniker "Know Nothings."

By proposing restrictions on immigration, a long residency qualification for naturalization, and the exclusion of foreign-born citizens from public office, Know Nothings were determined to keep political power in the hands of Anglo Protestants. Although nativism denounced all things foreign, even the British monarchical system, its main enemy was Catholicism with its numerous Irish membership. Nativists were not necessarily political or social reactionaries. Many respectable and sincere reformers joined the American party because they honestly believed that the Irish Catholic presence had a destructive impact on American society.

Know Nothings had spectacular successes in 1854 and 1855 local, state, and national elections, winning in Massachusetts, Delaware, Pennsylvania, Rhode Island, New Hampshire, Connecticut, Maryland, Kentucky, New York, and California, and they lost by only small margins in many other states. Massachusetts, where Know Nothings captured the governor's mansion and both houses of the legislature, was the leading example of nativist success. They immediately formed a state legislative committee to investigate convents and placed a strict residency naturalization requirement on the statute books. Exhilarated by their 1854 and 1855 triumphs, American party leaders fully expected to win the White House in 1856.

In the 1856 presidential election, Americans cast eight hundred thousand ballots for Know-Nothing candidate Millard Fillmore, former Whig president, but he lost the election. By 1856 anti-Catholicism had receded as a public passion, taking a subordinate position to the sectional tensions between North and South that brought the United States to the precipice of civil war.

When the issue of slavery carried the question of states rights versus federal authority beyond debate to the point of violence, Irish Catholics had an opportunity to demonstrate their Americanism. As previously discussed, economic and racial prejudices alienated the Irish from the abolitionist cause. And they strongly resented conscription laws that favored the rich and discriminated against the poor. But Irish Catholics south of the Mason–Dixon Line were loyal to the Confederacy, and those north of it had the same feeling for the Union. At least thirty-eight Union regiments were drawn from Irish Americans. In addition to the many American-born Irish who wore blue uniforms, 144,221 natives of Ireland served the northern cause. At Fredericksburg, the Irish Brigade commanded by a Young Irelander, Thomas Francis Meagher, kept attacking a well-fortified Confederate position until one of the Brigade's regiments lost 550 of its seven hundred men. And after the battle of Chancellorsville only 520 men survived out of the Brigade's entire five regiments.

Irish Catholic chaplains brought spiritual consolation to men in combat, and Irish nuns tended the wounded in hospitals. While Irish-American soldiers acquired reputations for insubordination and sloppy discipline, they also earned compliments for courage. Some Confederate officers considered the Irish their toughest enemy. And Irishmen, including forty thousand born in Ireland, fought bravely and well for the South. After the Irish Catholic contribution to the war effort, nativist journalists, North and South, found it difficult to question their love of country, but they could still complain about their social impact. On September 9, 1868, the *Chicago Evening Post,* noting the large number of Irish in the city's charitable institutions, jails, reform schools, and hospitals, remarked: "Scratch a convict or pauper and the chances are that you tickle the skin of an Irish Catholic made a criminal or a pauper by the priest and politician who have deceived him and kept him in ignorance, in a word, a savage, as he was born."

Although anti-Catholic nativism did not disappear, immediately after the Civil War public attention concentrated on Reconstruction in the South and the expansion of industrialism in the North. Factories, mills, and railroads required a large labor force, and immigrants filled the need. Italians, Poles, and Jews from eastern Europe joined the Irish and Germans as ethnic members of the urban, industrial work force.

Since nativism took a temporary back seat to the nation's economic necessities, American leaders projected a new image of the nation. They replaced the exclusivity of nativism with the melting pot thesis. Oliver Wendell Holmes announced that the United States was the new Rome, a nation that could and would assimilate the vitality and intelligence of many nationalities and religions while maintaining unity and consensus. Emma Lazarus's statement on the Statue of Liberty, erected in New York harbor in 1886, expressed a new American attitude toward European immigrants:

> Give me your tired, your poor,
> Your huddled masses yearning to breathe free,
> The wretched refuse of your teeming shore,
> Send these, the homeless, tempest-tossed to me;
> I lift my lamp beside the golden door.

Although Lazarus's description of immigrants was distorted—they were vital and intelligent members of Europe's peasantry and working class, not its refuse—the sentiment was generous and humane, promising that the United States would be the land of opportunity and tolerance.

With its encouragement of pluralism, the melting pot thesis persuaded liberal-minded members of the Catholic hierarchy to move the church into an accommodation with American life and culture. During the 1880s and 1890s, many prelates, among them James Cardinal Gibbons, primate and archbishop of Baltimore; John Ireland, archbishop of St. Paul; John Lancaster Spalding, bishop of Peoria; John Keane, bishop of Richmond, later rector of The Catholic University of America in Washington, D.C., and finally archbishop of Dubuque; and Denis O'Connell, who served as rector of both the American College in Rome and Catholic University before becoming bishop of Richmond, insisted that the Catholic Church in the United States must adjust to the American political, cultural, and social climate. Spalding came from Anglo-American Catholic stock, but Ireland, Keane, and O'Connell were born in Ireland, while Gibbons as a child lived and attended elementary school there. Spalding and Ireland gave the new movement in the Catholic Church a midwestern tone. The former was the most intellectual of the liberal bishops, the latter the most dynamic and articulate. Catholics in both Europe and the United States considered Ireland to be the leader of progressive American Catholicism.

Ireland and his allies denied any real or theoretical conflict between American liberal democracy and Catholicism. They emphasized that the Roman Catholic Church, like the United States, was a racial and ethnic melting pot, and predicted that American freedom and the principle of a free church in a free state—Daniel O'Connellism—would promote the growth and influence of Catholicism. The Gibbons–Ireland faction in the hierarchy described American democracy as the perfect political system, engaged in ecumenical dialogues with Protestants, and spoke before predominantly non-Catholic audiences. They also praised rather than disparaged public-school education. Archbishop Ireland even launched a shared-time experiment in Faribault, Minnesota. Catholic children attended parochial schools for religious instruction, and public schools for classes in secular subjects.

Although Gibbons, Ireland, Spalding, Keane, and O'Connell had nothing but kind words for American democracy, as champions of social justice they were harsh critics of *laissez faire* capitalism. Because they believed that the church in the United States could make the same mistake that it did in Continental Europe and lose the love and loyalty of the working class, the Gibbons–Ireland wing of the hierarchy encouraged the development of a strong American labor movement. Gibbons went to Rome and persuaded Leo XIII not to condemn the Knights of Labor, as conservative bishops in the United States and Canada urged him to do. Liberal, Americanizing prelates, demanding intellectual excellence, insisted that Catholic education should be more than a defense against Protestantism and secularism. They were instrumental in the founding of the Catholic University in Washington, expecting it to compete with the best of America's institutions of higher learning. They also objected, unsuccessfully, to the appointment of a Papal Nuncio to the United States, fearing that a Vatican representative would be insensitive to the nuances of a church functioning within a liberal democracy.

Convinced that the church in the United States must preserve ethnic cultures as a way of sustaining the faith, midwestern German bishops opposed Irish-American accommodations to the American situation. Led by Archbishop Michael Corrigan of New York and his friend and advisor, Bishop Bernard McQuaid of Rochester, a number of eastern Irish bishops joined the Germans in defending ethnicity as a shield of Catholicism. Corrigan and McQuaid also opposed the economic and social views of the Gibbons–Ireland group. They defended unfettered capitalism, denounced labor unions as socialist fronts and sources of class conflict, preached poverty's redemptive role, and asked the laity to patiently wait for justice in the next world. Corrigan, McQuaid, and other conservative Irish and German prelates shared Rome's antipathy to liberalism and modernism and its support of the union of church and state. They also discouraged lay intellectualism or leadership, emphatically declaring that the main purpose of Catholic education was maintaining faith and instilling morals. This attitude prevented the Catholic University from reaching the academic heights that Keane, Spalding, O'Connell, Gibbons, and Ireland expected.

Religious orders took sides in the controversy between liberal Americanizers and conservative Romanists. Paulists and Holy Cross fathers at Notre Dame, a small college near South Bend, Indiana, argued that Catholicism in the United States must accommodate to the American environment. Founded in 1858 by Isaac Hecker, a New England convert from Transcendentalism to Catholicism, the Paulists may have been the most talented and intellectual body in the late nineteenth-century American Church. In their stylish, intelligent, and articulate periodical, *The Catholic World,* they attempted to explain Catholicism to Protestant America. Jesuits, who operated a number of secondary schools and colleges for the sons of upper-middle-class Catholics, opposed the liberal views of Americanizers, not out of a sense of ethnicity, but because their order was strongly committed to Roman authority and conservatism.

When French liberal Catholics borrowed American ideas in debating conservatives, they distorted them into a modernist theology. Encouraged by Sebastian Messmer, bishop of Green Bay, Wisconsin, and leading spokesman for the midwestern–German position, and by Corrigan and McQuaid, conservative French prelates requested Pope Leo XIII to officially brand Americanization a heresy. In January 1899 the pope wrote Cardinal Gibbons that the following opinions were heretical: action is more important than contemplation, natural take priority over supernatural virtues, and the teachings of the church must yield to private conscience.[2] Although Gibbons and his friends correctly replied that their concept of Americanization was political, social, and economic rather than theological, they had been censured and humiliated, and their opponents were ecstatic and arrogant in victory. Leo's successor, Pius X, waged a spiritual reign of terror, purging liberal clerics, initiating a long period of stunted creativity and intellectualism in American and European Catholicism.

Despite the conservative, midwestern German and eastern Irish victory at Rome and anti-intellectual and anti-modernist attitudes in Rome that survived until John XXIII in the late 1950s, and revived with John Paul II in the 1980s, the socially and politically liberal, midwestern Irish tradition survived in the American Church. Monsignor John Ryan from St. Paul, an Ireland protégé, was an important champion of social justice and the rights of labor. In the 1920s, as head of the National

Catholic Welfare Conference, he authored an agenda for social justice that anticipated the New Deal. He later denounced Father Coughlin's anti-semitism and sympathy with European fascism.

In response to American ethnic and religious diversity, the melting pot thesis survived as an almost-official doctrine, but economic depression and the closing of the western frontier in the 1880s dampened zeal for pluralism and immigrant assimilation. With factories, mines, mills, and banks shutting down and the stock market plummeting, many Americans were sure that their country had achieved its economic potential. They suggested that its resources and opportunities needed rationing, and that there was no more room for strangers competing with the native born for jobs and straining the social fabric to the danger point.

Xenophobia expressed the anxieties of a wide variety of Americans. While workers feared immigrant employment competition, the middle class doubted that capitalism could survive the combined impact of depression and immigration. They suspected that European socialist ideology permeated the expanding labor movement. An increasing number of strikes, some violent, confirmed these anxieties. Chicago was the scene of two sensational confrontations between capital and labor. An 1886 riot in Haymarket Square ended with eight dead and a hundred wounded. Eight years later, President Grover Cleveland summoned troops to crush a strike at the Pullman company. A jury convicted and the state of Illinois executed eleven anarchists for inciting the Haymarket riot. After the Pullman incident, the federal government imprisoned Eugene V. Debs, the railroad workers union's socialist leader.

Frightened by strikes and general labor unrest, wealthy, property-owning Americans demanded immigration restrictions to protect the United States from the importation of Marxism, syndicalism, and anarchism. Although protests against working-class radicalism and foreign influences were largely anti-Semitic, they included the Irish on the list of dangerous aliens. Most Irish Catholic labor leaders were associated with the more conservative collective-bargaining craft unions, but a few leaned farther left. And Molly Maguire violence in the Pennsylvania coal fields encouraged nativists to link Irish Catholics with anticapitalist, antiproperty violence. Folk legend and song have linked the Molly Maguires, who took the name of an agrarian secret society in Ireland, with a revolt of exploited labor against cruel mine owners who paid them too little, and over-charged them in company stores and for renting miserable company shanties. There is some truth to this view of the Mollys, but there was also considerable ethnic hatred of their Welsh and English mine bosses. In addition to fears of radicalism, there was always the old issue of religion, the nativist doubt that Catholicism would ever permit the Irish to be true-blue Americans.

Due to their occupational mobility and improved manners, urban America started to become a friendlier place for Irish Catholics. Their tradesmen, transportation workers, policemen, fire fighters, nurses, schoolteachers, priests, and nuns became familiar figures in the city. Sports fans cheered the feats of Irish baseball players. And people who attended plays, burlesque theatres, and music halls saw and heard different portraits of Irish Catholics than their parents and grandparents. Formerly, the stage and fiction depicted Paddys and Biddys as naive, feckless, ignorant fools blundering through life. Sometimes they were laughable, other times frightening in an alcoholic, belligerent, shillelagh-swinging way. In the 1870s Irish Catholic characters in plays and comedy sketches became more attractive and pleasant. People began to laugh with rather than at them. Dublin-born and American-settled Dion Boucicault's plays attracted and pleased New York audiences. His Irish peasants were witty rather than foolish, courageous without being violent, and clever enough to out-maneuver landlords, members of the Royal Irish Constabulary, and British soldiers and government officials. Sketches by Edward Harrigan and Tony Hart (Anthony J. Cronin) also appealed to New Yorkers. They included songs that Harrigan composed with his father-in-law, David Brahim. The sketches and songs portrayed Irish Catholics as a humorous but vital community, realistically interacting among themselves and with other ethnics. Although they had faults and problems, the Harrigan and Hart Irish were genial, industrious, decent Americans.

Early twentieth-century songs about Ireland and the Irish touched American hearts. John McCormack's concert tours and recordings, particularly his renditions of Thomas Moore's melodies, made Irish music respectable in drawing rooms as well as theatres. Actor-singer Chauncey Olcott wrote as well as sang songs for plays about Ireland. His words were romantic and sentimental, full of Irish icons—home and mother—but they had tremendous appeal for Irish and other Americans. He popularized such enduring favorites as "When Irish Eyes Are Smiling" and "Mother Machree." Historian William H. A. Williams asks "why did hard-working, disciplined, sober, competitive, Protestant America of the early twentieth century buy into the image of the light-hearted, home-loving, quick-tempered but genial, sentimental, loyal, extravagant, hard-drinking, Irish who dared to love Ireland as much as America?" He answers: "Perhaps the clue lies in the timing. In the early decades of the twentieth century, as the culture of the factory and office reshaped the American character, the popular image of the Irish represented an alternative to the white-collar, organization man of the new urban business culture. The Irish of the popular songs had come to embody simple, old-fashioned virtues: simple, romantic love, as opposed to sex; mother love and filial piety; geniality and neighborliness; hard work and hard play; loyalty and patriotism. The more America changed, the more Ireland and Irishness became repositories for the qualities that might be lost."[3]

Cities may have become more welcoming, but most of Anglo

America did not buy into a favorable image of Irish Catholic America. Industrialism had a rural as well as an urban impact, effecting dramatic changes in agricultural technology, forcing farmers to purchase expensive machinery, usually on credit. They felt themselves at the mercy of bankers as well as unpredictable weather, and recessions and depressions determined food prices and the ability to repay loans and interest. Economic insecurities gathered an audience for populist demagogues and journalists, initiating a rural revolt against urban capitalism. Populism, a distinct brand of American radicalism, now has a popular image—many contemporary politicians describe themselves as new populists—but in the 1880s and 1890s it was saturated with anti-Catholic and anti-Semitic bigotry. According to populist mythology, Jews and Catholics represented urban aliens exploiting farm and small-town Protestants.[4]

Although nativism continued to feature an Evangelical Protestant aura, professional and upper-middle-class sophisticates abandoned "crude" religious bigotry for a nativism rationalized in pseudo-scientific terms. It condemned inferior races rather than alien creeds. American racism borrowed ideas and the arguments from English intellectual sources. In British universities, such respected historians as John R. Green, Edward A. Freeman, James A. Froude, Thomas Macaulay, and William Stubbs credited Angles, Saxons, and Jutes with carrying seeds of liberty from fifth-century German forests, and planting them in English soil where they flowered into the liberality of British constitutional government.

Late nineteenth-century English scholars and intellectuals liked to contrast Anglo-Saxon qualities with those of the Celtic or Irish personality, describing the English as masculine, rational, industrious, thrifty with resources, and committed to individual freedom, and the Irish as feminine, emotional, lazy, improvident, and dependent. They concluded that Anglo Saxons were natural masters, Celts congenital slaves, and that the Irish were fortunate to have found benevolent English masters to protect them from their faulty natures. The April 1868 issue of the Whig journal *Edinburgh Review* criticized the Irish from the perspective of Anglo-Saxon racism, reasoning that they functioned best within the controls of the free yet disciplined British political system:

> They possess, no doubt, qualities of a very serviceable kind, but these qualities require the example and power of another race, more highly endowed, to bring them to perfection and turn them to full account . . . The Irish are deficient in that unquiet energy, that talent for accumulation, those indefinite desires which are the mainsprings of successful colonization, and they are deficient too in that faculty of self-government without which free institutions can neither flourish nor be permanently maintained.

Anthropological, ethnological, and biological arguments bolstered historical explanations of Anglo-Saxon superiority and Celtic inferiority which were applied to Irish Catholics but not Irish, Scottish, Welsh, or Cornish Protestants. Scholars measured skulls, jaw bones, and other portions of human anatomies and then constructed a primate scale, placing Anglo Saxons on top, next to God, the Irish just above Blacks and apes on the bottom. Scholarly racial theories were popularized in newspapers and periodicals. *Punch* and *Puck* cartoons depicted simian-featured, hulking Irish stereotypes.

Respectable, well-educated Liberals as well as reactionary Tories entertained Anglo-Saxon superiority attitudes concerning Irish Catholic Celts. For example, an 1881 letter from historian Edward Augustus Freeman, visiting in the United States, contained this observation:

> This would be a grand land if only every Irishman would kill a negro, and be hanged for it. I find this sentiment generally approved—sometimes with the qualification that they want Irish and negroes for servants, not being able to get any other. This looks like the ancient weakness of craving for a subject race.

And in 1892, Sidney and Beatrice Webb, parents of the Fabian Society, the intellectual arm of the Labour Party, visited Ireland where they found the natives charming, "but we detest them, as we should the Hottentots—for their very virtues." Journeying in Ireland convinced the Webbs that Britain must give Ireland Home Rule in order to get rid "of this detestable race."[5] Comparing the Irish with African Blacks was a fashionable English exercise. Lord Salisbury, prime minister and Conservative and Unionist party leader, was an inflexible foe of self-government concessions to Irish nationalism. He insisted that the natives of the sister isle were as incompetent to manage their affairs as Hottentots.

In the late years of the nineteenth and the early part of the twentieth centuries, Anglo-Saxon racism was a chic ideology in American universities, drawing rooms, and private clubs. In the 1870s, 1880s, and 1890s, Thomas Nast, the famous *Harper's Weekly* cartoonist, in his attack on Tammany Hall, portrayed its Irish politicians and supporters as ape-like beasts. Survival of the fittest Social Darwinism, another English import, provided a scientific and sociological framework for Anglo-American nativists. They not only used it against "inferior breeds" in the United States, but as a propaganda weapon justifying military and economic imperialism in Latin America and in the Far East, claiming that America was bringing the advantages of a superior civilization to the benighted savages of the underdeveloped world.

Nativists also employed Anglo-Saxon racism in efforts to restrict immigration and delay naturalization. Historian Henry Adams and Senator Cabot Lodge, both Boston brahmins, were initiators of the Immigrant Restriction League in 1894. Franklin Walker, president of the Massachusetts Institute of Technology, referred to American immigration and naturalization as the "survival of the unfit," and two popular authors, William Z. Ripley, *The Races of Europe* (1899), and Madison Grant,

The Passing of a Great Race (1916), warned that masses of inferior breeds entering the United States endangered its Anglo-Saxon cultural and racial homogeneity.

Since Jews, Italians, Poles, and Blacks presented more discernible physical, cultural, and linguistic contrasts to Anglo Americans, light skinned, usually blue-eyed, English-speaking Irish Catholics were not the main focus of the racial aspect of American nativism, but remained the principal scapegoat for its original and persistent religious dimension. Irish bishops, priests, and nuns were the dominant force in American Catholicism, still the principal irritant to Anglo-American sensibilities; and Irish Catholic laymen had taken control of the urban wing of the Democratic party in industrial states, and played a prominent role in mobilizing and directing the labor movement. In religious, political, and labor leadership positions, the Irish had made all of Catholic America an extension of Irish America. They presented the most significant challenge to Anglo-Protestant power and influence.

With its religious, economic, and racial expressions, nativism's revival in the 1880s led to the formation of a number of organizations designed to preserve and protect the Anglo-Protestant character of the United States. Founded in Clinton, Iowa, in 1887, the American Protective Association enrolled more than a million members throughout the country, and re-circulated old no-popery propaganda—Maria Monk's tale of convent sex and rumors of revolutionary arsenals stored in the basements of Catholic churches. Before it faded in the late 1890s, the APA successfully influenced local politics and discouraged employers from hiring Catholics.

Following the official demise of the APA in 1891, other organizations carried on the Anglo-Protestant crusade against malignant religious, racial, and ideological incursions into American life: the Guardians of Liberty, the American Minute Men, Convenanters, and the Knights of Luther. But none were as powerful as the Ku Klux Klan. It originated in the South during Reconstruction to intimidate recently emancipated African Americans and northern carpetbaggers. After southern state legislatures enacted and the United States Supreme Court accepted Jim Crow segregation laws, in 1871 the KKK, its task accomplished, ceased to operate.

In 1915 William J. Simmons, a Georgia preacher, revived the Klan, and in the 1920s it became so powerful that its membership may have reached four million. The new KKK was a major force in southern and midwestern states, especially Indiana, enlisting politicians, lawyers, doctors, businessmen, and Protestant clergymen. In the 1920s the KKK was more of a nativist organization than its Reconstruction predecessor, concentrating its anger and intimidation on Catholics and Jews as well as African Americans. During the presidential election of 1928, the KKK militantly campaigned against Democratic candidate Al Smith, labeling him a symbol of the urban ethnic threat to the values of Anglo-Protestant America. White-sheeted mobs marched down streets throughout the South, border states, and Midwest and burned crosses on Catholic lawns. In the prosperous, pre-Depression 1920s there was no conceivable way that Smith could have gathered more popular or electoral votes than Herbert Hoover, but his Irish Catholic, urban background fanned the flames of bigotry, significantly reducing the number of Democratic ballots. Smith's nomination filled Irish and other Catholics with expectations that at last they had achieved acceptability and respectability. His defeat, and the prejudice evident in the election campaign, smothered their hopes, and convinced many if not most that they would always be "strangers in the land."

5. Irish-American Politics

Besides their religious faith, skill in politics was another proud possession that Irish Catholics brought with them to the United States. In 1894 American nativist, John Paul Bocock, angrily complained of the Irish "genius for municipal government—at least for getting municipal office."[1] In January 1916, Sir Cecil Spring-Rice, British ambassador to Washington, in a letter to his foreign secretary, Sir Edward Grey, explained that Irish Americans were the most formidable obstacle to the United States joining Britain, France, and Russia in the war against Germany and the Hapsburg empire. He said that they were the "best politicians in the country . . . with unequaled power of political organization."[2] Some of the most fascinating characters in American fiction have been Irish politicians: Joseph Dinneen's Hughie Donnelly, Edwin O'Connor's Frank Skeffington, Thomas J. Fleming's Ben O'Connor, Mary Deasy's Aloyisius O'Shaughnessy, John O'Hara's Mike Slattery, Wilfrid Sheed's Brian Casey, and Ramona Stewart's John Maguire and

Tom Casey.[3] Real life Irish Catholic politicians are as captivating, if not more so, than their fictional shadows.

Many who acknowledge the political talents of Irish-American Catholics do so begrudgingly, indicting them for massive political corruption. Bocock complained: "How has it come about that the system of government so admirably conceived by the fathers has worked out so perfectly in national affairs and so poorly in municipal affairs . . . since from the turbulence of municipal politics the Irish American has plucked both wealth and power."[4] Theodore Roosevelt described average first generation Irish members of the New York State assembly as "low, venal, corrupt and unintelligent brutes."[5] In a 1965 novel, *All Good Men,* one of Thomas J. Fleming's characters, Larry Donahue makes the same point: "This city is a living testimonial to the ineptitude and the rotten morals of the Irish who are running it."[6]

Daniel Patrick Moynihan, a reputable Irish-American Catholic scholar and a distinguished member of the United States Senate, leveled a devastating attack on the Irish Catholic role in urban affairs. In his essay, "The Irish," in *Beyond the Melting Pot: The Negroes, Puerto Ricans, Jews, Italians, and Irish of New York City* (1963), a book that he coauthored with Nathan Glazer, Moynihan argued that Irish Catholics invested considerable political energy and talent in acquiring and holding power, but lacked the vision and social conscience to convert it into meaningful change. Rapid industrialization, massive population growth, and conflicting ethnic cultures fostered American urban problems demanding energetic responses, but Irish Old-Country, rural-parish-pump, static and essentially conservative politics was reluctant to and/or incapable of meeting the challenge, frustrating rather than generating social improvement. Irish Catholics, he said, "never thought of politics as an instrument of social change."[7]

In the 1950s, such historians and social scientists as J. Joseph

Huthmacher, John B. Buenker, Robert Dahl, and Elmer E. Cornwell began to paint a more favorable picture of Irish Catholic politics. They connected it with economic opportunities that resulted in middle-class respectability. They also insisted that Irish political machines not only catered to the interests of their own people but also opened economic and political doors for other ethnics who, like their own people, were previously excluded from the American mainstream by the Anglo-Protestant establishment.[8]

Steven P. Erie's comprehensive study, *Rainbow's End: Irish-Americans and the Dilemmas of Urban Machine Politics, 1840–1885* (1988), revised the revisionists. According to Erie, the economic benefits and the inclusiveness of Irish-American Catholic politics have been romantically exaggerated. Instead of avenues of economic and social mobility, he depicts political jobs as cul-de-sacs trapping the Irish into lower blue and white collar positions. Erie also insists that in most cases Irish political machines saved the most attractive spoils of their political wars for Irish constituents, offering other ethnics charity and minor services.

In his 1983 study, *Beyond the Ballot Box: A Social History of the Boston Irish, 1845–1917,* Dennis P. Ryan was also skeptical concerning the economic and social advantages of political employment: "It was this preoccupation with security that prevented more Irish from becoming moderately successful as businessmen, doctors, and lawyers, who were considered financially and socially superior to city clerks or street inspectors."[9]

For urban America was Irish Catholic politics a blessing or curse? Did it speed or delay the Irish journey to middle-class acceptability and respectability? Did Irish Catholic politicians empower other ethnics as well as their own kind? Did they do things for people out of generous impulses or only as a means of recruiting voters? Were the Irish incapable of applying political power to meet the needs of a rapidly changing urban landscape? Full or partial answers to these questions can only be found in examining Irish-American Catholic politics in action.

Irish-American Catholics sought power and economic opportunities through politics; the only skill that they brought with them from the Old to the New World. In Ireland, nationalism and political agitation were inseparable. Using the existing avenues of the British constitutional system and creating the tactics and techniques of modern, public-opinion, pressure politics, Daniel O'Connell, founder of modern Irish nationalism and the first Irish machine boss, had mobilized his people for political action. Since necessity forced Irish constitutional nationalists to function within the context of the Anglo-Saxon Protestant political system, Irish Catholics arrived in the United States familiar with the rules and techniques of its Anglo-American counterpart. The consolidation of a self-conscious Irish-American community around a strong Catholic identity provided a focal point for politics as well as ethnicity. And the gregariousness of the Irish personality enhanced their political skills. Despite a reputation for aggressiveness and pugnacity, more a product of the stage, newspaper cartoons, and novels than reality, Irish Catholics like, enjoy, and are interested in people. Conversation is one of their most attractive gifts. They prefer to convince by argument than by force.

In addition to the political experience and skills and, for most, a knowledge of English that the Irish brought with them to the United States, there was another factor that explains their political success in urban America. Anglo Protestants were not particularly fascinated with politics. For many it was a necessary evil, a calling for the second and third rate. They invested their best talent in business and the professions. Nativist prejudices excluded Irish Catholics from opportunities open to Anglo Protestants, forcing them into politics, religion, and the labor movement as avenues to influence and power.

Although urban Irish Catholics did not fit the rural ambience of Jeffersonian democracy, since their arrival in the United States until recently they have been so closely associated with the Democratic party that Irish, Catholic, and Democrat composed a trinity of associations, serving mutual interests and needs. While Jeffersonian Democrats in the late 1700s and early 1800s won Irish loyalty with a welcome to America and an egalitarian political philosophy, the Federalist authors of the anti-immigrant Alien and Sedition Acts reminded the Irish of the Tory, Protestant Ascendancy in Ireland. Because Whig successors to the Federalists also identified with wealth, property, and anti-Catholic nativism, Jeffersonian and Jacksonian democracy continued to attract and maintain Irish support. Since Andrew Jackson's parents had emigrated from Ulster and he had humbled the British at New Orleans, Irish Americans were particularly fond and proud of the rough-mannered, outspoken Tennessean. In the 1850s the new Republican party with its abolitionist following and nativist appeal antagonized Irish Catholics who remained loyal to the Democrats.

When Irish Catholics settled in urban America, Democratic politicians, seeking their support at the polls, saw to it that they were quickly naturalized, employed, and registered to vote. They returned the favor by casting Democratic ballots—often more than once—and by forming street gangs to protect party candidates and intimidate their rivals. But the Irish had no intention of remaining buck privates in the Democratic army. Slowly but surely they gained control of their own neighborhoods, building mini-machines within the general party structure, and began to move up the leadership ladder from block captains to district or precinct leaders to aldermen. In their political quest for power, Irish politicians used Catholic solidarity as a voting base, saloons as political clubs, and police and fire department appointments as patronage sources to recruit votes and party workers.

The increase in numbers and the improved quality of post-

Famine Irish immigration aided the expansion of Irish-American Catholic political influence. By 1900, much to nativist anguish, it was in charge of most of the major American cities in the East and Midwest, San Francisco in the West, and New Orleans in the South. Thomas N. Brown has argued that historians, social scientists, novelists, and journalists exaggerate the existence of a unique Irish political style and approach to the American political process.[10] Comparisons and contrasts between Irish politics in New York, Boston, and Chicago support his thesis.

Tammany Hall is often portrayed by scholars and novelists as the prime example of Irish politics and corruption. In the 1790s, Aaron Burr converted the New York branch of the fraternal and charitable Society of St. Tammany, named after a seventeenth-century Delaware Indian chief, into a political club to promote his own ambitions and to oppose his principal enemy, Alexander Hamilton. Tammany took control of local Democratic politics, but barred Irish Catholics from membership until the 1850s, when their numbers made them a significant voting block. Irish Catholics were loyal supporters of William Marcy Tweed, Tammany's Scots-Irish grand sachem, and living proof that it was not they who first polluted American urban politics, even after corrupt practices sent him to prison.

In 1871 "Honest" John Kelly replaced Tweed as Tammany leader. Like his predecessor, he was not interested in applying the Hall's influence to effect constructive social change, but he did reduce its political corruption and significantly remodeled its structure. A strong practicing Catholic with close personal ties to John Cardinal McCloskey (his second wife's uncle), Kelly used the church as a model for organizing Tammany into a centralized monarchy with a pyramid chain of command. Because of its alliance with affluent bankers, businessmen, industrialists, lawyers, and Irving Hall and County Democrats, Tammany during Kelly's reign had a conservative agenda, and beyond boat trips on the Hudson and clambakes (bread and circuses) did little to improve the lot of its Irish Catholic constituency. Relatively, Irish influence in Tammany actually declined as their numbers increased. From 1844 to 1884 the Irish percentage of the city's population had expanded from about 20 to 40 percent, but they held only 14 to the upper-crust's 64 percent of the Hall's leadership positions.[11]

In 1886 Richard Croker, a Kelly protégé, succeeded him as boss. A Famine refugee from Cork, he arrived in New York as a three-year-old. Croker began his political career as a Tammany street gang thug. Although crude and ignorant, he was a shrewd manipulator of political power. Under Croker's command, the Hall continued its conservative approach to social and economic problems and descended to the lowest depths of ruthless power and massive corruption, finally forcing his resignation. In 1903 he retired to Ireland as a multi-millionaire breeder and racer of horses and a verbal and financial backer of Home Rule and the Irish parliamentary party.

Irish working-class disillusionment with Tammany was apparent in the 1886 mayoral election. Patrick Ford and Father Edward McGlynn, pastor of St. Stephens's, endorsed the candidacy of socialist Henry George, advocate of the single tax. Because he supported the Land League and was a close friend of Ford and Michael Davitt, George had a strong base in New York's Irish Catholic community. Archbishop Corrigan, fearing that socialist ideology might attract Catholic workers, ordered McGlynn to withdraw from George's campaign. When the priest refused, the archbishop suspended him, a decision that Rome later reversed. The alliance between Corrigan and Tammany strongly influenced election returns, resulting in a victory for Abram S. Hewett. But sixty-seven thousand George ballots demonstrated significant German and Irish (second generation) working-class approval. In the predominantly Irish lower and midtown assembly districts, he received 34 percent of the vote.

In *The Boston Irish: A Political History* (1995), Thomas H. O'Connor emphasizes that Boston was much less hospitable to the Irish than were New York, Philadelphia, midwestern cities, or San Francisco. In Boston they confronted an Anglo-Protestant, anti-Catholic elite that despised them for the social strain they inflicted on the city, and for their alien and subversive religion. In many ways Yankee bigotry, their long struggle for survival, and a resulting inferiority complex warped the Boston Irish Catholic personality, leading to massive prejudices against rather than empathy with such other victims of nativism as African Americans and Jews. Although they had no sympathy for abolitionism, and voted in 1860 for Stephen Douglas and four years later for George McClellan rather than Abraham Lincoln, Boston Irish Catholics fought gallantly and well for the Union.

Irish Catholics in Boston, like their co-ethnics in other parts of the country (with exceptions in Ohio and Pennsylvania), were loyal Democrats. After playing a subordinate role to Anglo Protestants, in the 1880s they moved into leadership positions. In 1884 Hugh O'Brien became the first Irish Catholic mayor of Boston, and in 1901 Patrick Collins was the second. O'Brien, Collins, Patrick Maguire, Boston's first effective Irish political boss, and John Boyle O'Reilly, editor of the *Pilot*, were born in Ireland, and despite Yankee bigotry, realized that the United States liberated their people from poverty and oppression. They joined with Bishop John B. Fitzpatrick and his successor, Archbishop John Williams, in encouraging the Irish to become Americanized and to adopt a cooperative rather than a confrontational stance toward Anglo Protestants.

Second-generation neighborhood bosses such as Martin Lomasney, John F. "Honey" Fitzgerald, Patrick J. Kennedy, and James Michael Curley succeeded Americanizers O'Brien, Collins, Maguire, and O'Reilly. Lacking personal experience with and possessing little memory of the misery that the Irish suffered in Ireland, they had considerable involvement with and recollection of Anglo-Protestant arrogance and prejudice in Boston. Despite attempts by the Yankee-controlled state legislature to frustrate Irish political power through civil service examination requirements and limitations on city government independence, Irish bosses took charge of the city. But their politics resembled feudalism rather than Tammany's centralized monarchy, with each chief guarding his own fief against rival encroachments. Instead of reaching an accommodation with Anglo Protestants, Irish bosses went to war in what one novelist, Edward R. F. Sheehan, has described as a politics of revenge. In *The Governor* (1970), he describes Francis Xavier Cassidy, commissioner of public works, as one Irish sword of retribution:

> There, in those deep and misty bogs of his mind, he inexorably relived all the nightmares of his race, even the nightmares he never dreamed. There, in the most wretched hovels of his soul, he felt the pangs of potato hunger and the British lash against his back, only to take flight across a hostile sea to meaner hovels still and horrid Yankee mills whose owners paid him pennies and then posted notices at their gates NO IRISH NEED APPLY.[12]

Sheehan portrays James Michael Curley, Boston mayor and local Irish champion in the struggle against Anglo America, as another "tribal hero who squandered his remarkable talents and devoted a lifetime to settling old scores, a crippled warrior egging on an amused mob of shanty Irish in the sacking of the Yankee Troy."[13]

Curley served as a model for Edwin O'Connor's Frank Skeffington in *The Last Hurrah* (1956), one of the most popular of Irish-American political novels. On occasion, Skeffington practiced the politics of revenge. He explained to his nephew and confidant, Adam, that the bitter feud between himself and Amos Force, the Yankee newspaper publisher, started when Amos's father fired Skeffington's immigrant mother from her job as a house servant when she was caught taking food scraps home to her hungry children:

"As for Amos, he's never been able to forget that the son of the servant who committed this crime against his purse became mayor of his city and governor of his state, and in the course of doing so managed to make life just a little more difficult for him. Amos's life hasn't exactly been a bed of pain, but I think I can say with all modesty that it's been considerably more painful than if I hadn't been around. In any case, that's how it all started, and that's why your paper, even today, continues its splendid crusade for better government. Which is to say, government without me. Amos has a long memory, you see. I may add," he said impassively, "that so have I."[14]

In James Carroll's 1976 political novel, *Mortal Friends,* Curley is immensely talented and charismatic, but is flawed by paranoia, narrow vision, and a lust for power. In *The American Irish,* William V. Shannon's evaluation of Curley is more in harmony with Sheehan and Carroll than O'Connor. According to him, Boston's Irish champion

> exploited the sufferings and inexperience, the warm sentiment, the fears, and the prejudices of his own people to perpetuate his personal power. He solved nothing; he moved toward no larger understanding; he opened no new lines of communication . . . For more than thirty years, Curley kept the greater part of Boston's populace half-drunk with fantasies, invective, and showmanship . . . but he nevertheless committed two mortal sins against the public good; his bad example debased the moral tone of political life in a great city for a generation, and his words distorted the people's understanding of reality . . . and to the end of his days he remained a self-crippled giant on a provincial stage.[15]

In his superb 1992 portrait, *The Rascal King: The Life and Times of James Michael Curley (1874–1958),* Jack Beatty acknowledges and criticizes Curley's political malpractices and roguery, but describes the conflicts between Anglo Protestants and Irish Catholics and feuds among the latter that produced the public and private man. He also pays tribute to the wit, political skills, empathy with people, and generosity that put Curley in the Massachusetts legislature, sent him to Congress twice, elected him governor, and returned him to the mayor's office four separate times.

Chicago's Irish politics was closer to Boston's feudalism than New York's centralized monarchy. In 1836 Irish navvies from the Erie Canal came to Chicago to dig the Illinois and Michigan Canal, linking the Great Lakes with New Orleans via the Illinois and Mississippi Rivers. Seven years later natives of Ireland were 10 percent of the city's 7,580 people. By 1850, the 29,963 Irish-born were 20 percent of the population, making them and the Germans Chicago's two largest ethnic groups. Twenty years later Irish immigrants numbered close to forty thousand. Chicago and its Irish population continued to boom as the city became the transportation and industrial center of the Midwest. At the beginning of the twentieth century, Chicago ranked below New York and Philadelphia as the third largest Irish city in the United States. Some 237,479 first and second generation Irish Americans lived in various parts of the city. But unlike eastern metropolises, the Irish in Chicago lived and mixed with other nationalities, usually Germans. In 1884 they were a majority in only eleven out of 303 census districts. Their politicians served multi-ethnic constituencies.

In 1890, twenty-three of Chicago's sixty-eight aldermen had Irish names. Quite a few gave credence to those who argued that the Irish were a corrupting influence on American urban politics. Chicago was rough, tough, and bawdy in the last two decades of the nineteenth and first two of the twentieth century. Politicians and policemen were hand-in-glove with vice lords of drinking, gambling, and prostitution. Aldermen also profited from selling the city's transportation and utility franchises ("boodling"). They also fattened wallets by exchanging contracts for public buildings and roads for cash payoffs. Edward "Foxy Ed" Cullerton, John "Bathhouse" Coughlin, and Michael "Hinky Dink" Kenna were three of Chicago's most notorious Irish boodlers. Connecticut-born, Peoria-reared, Trinity College, Dublin-educated Edward F. Dunne was a notable exception to the shady character of Chicago's Irish politics. He was a reformer hostile to corruption. From 1905 to 1907 he served as mayor, and from 1912 to 1916 as governor of Illinois. In both offices his rectitude offended Chicago's ward bosses.

Although Irish machines were more interested in maintaining power and profiting from the legal and illicit perks of office than in improving the economic and social conditions of constituents, individual politicians such as New York's Big Tim Sullivan in the Bowery and George Washington Plunkitt in Hell's Kitchen; Boston's Martin Lomasney in the West End's ninth ward; and Chicago's Johnny Powers in the nineteenth ward did provide a multitude of services for the poor. Sullivan, lower Manhattan's most powerful politician, a non-smoking, non-gambling teetotaler, used vice protection graft (he denied any association with prostitution) to buy food and clothing and to pay the rent for people in need. The "King of the Bowery" also championed the labor movement and political and social feminism.

Plunkitt's *Diary* provides a schedule of one long day in the life of an Irish Catholic politician:

> 2 A.M. Wakened by a boy with message from bartender to bail him out of jail. 3 A.M. Back to bed. 6 A.M. Fire engines, up and off to the scene to see my election district captains tending the burnt-out tenants. Got names for new homes. 8:30 to police court. Six drunken constituents on hand. Got four released by a timely word to the judge. Paid the other's (sic) fines. Nine o'clock to Municipal court. Told an election district captain to act as lawyer for a widow threatened with dispossession. 11 to 3 P.M. Found jobs for four constituents. 3 P.M. an Italian funeral, sat conspicuously up front. 4 P.M. A Jewish funeral—up front again, in the synagogue. 7 P.M. Meeting of district captains and reviewed the list of all voters, who's for us, who's agin. 8 P.M. Church fair. Bought ice cream for the girls; took fathers for a little something around the corner. 9 P.M.

Back in the club-house. Heard complaints of a dozen push cart pedlars. 10:30 a Jewish wedding. Had sent handsome present to bride. Midnight—to bed.[16]

If Johnny Powers had left a diary, it would have been equally as fascinating and revealing as Plunkitt's. Alderman of the nineteenth ward on Chicago's Irish, Italian, Jewish, and Polish near southwest side from 1888 to 1927, saloonkeeper Powers provided bail and fixed court cases for constituents; paid rents for impoverished tenants; placed thousands on the public payroll; attended weddings, wakes, and funerals, bringing presents to the bride, covering undertaker and burial expenses for poor families of the deceased; provided railroad passes for constituents needing to visit relatives; bought tickets for church bazaars; and one Christmas personally distributed six tons of turkeys and four tons of ducks and geese to families in need. Powers defeated numerous reform efforts, even those to unseat him by Hull House's Jane Addams, bragging that his saloons produced far more votes than the speeches and pamphlets of reformers, social workers, and clergymen. Despite her hostility to Powers and all he stood for, Addams admitted that he and other Irish politicos showed more concern and did more for the poor than most of the reformers attempting to drive them from office.[17]

Lomasney is the inspiration for Hughie Donnelly in Joseph Dinneen's novel, *Ward Eight* (1936). Like the real life Lomasney, Sullivan, Plunkitt, and Powers, Donnelly is totally involved with the people in his ward, finding them jobs and places to live, putting food on their tables, sending doctors to the sick, providing bail and lawyers to those in trouble with the police, and paying for wakes and funerals when families can afford neither. Graft is the source of much of the money that Hughie provides for the poor, but very little reaches his own pocket. Hughie's price for his services is loyalty rather than cash. When he began in politics, ward eight was all Irish. At the end it had become heavily Italian. But like Irish politicians in other cities, Hughie assimilated newcomers into the party structure, creating an effective multi-ethnic coalition.

In the twentieth century, when Irish and other Catholic ethnic voters became more sophisticated and demanding, and when the Protestant middle class departed for the fringes of the city and the suburbs, major and minor Irish political machines adopted the techniques of individual ward bosses, abandoned conservative agendas, and became more socially conscious and responsible. In 1902 American-born, working-class Charles Francis Murphy took charge of Tammany. Murphy, a conscientious, puritanical Catholic who never cursed or smoked and seldom drank, owned four saloons that served as Irish political and social clubs. Anything but a verbal spellbinder, he was a master organizer and a shrewd judge of talent. Alfred E. Smith, multi-term governor of New York, who introduced and pushed through legislation and policies that previewed the New Deal, and Robert F. Wagner, one of New York's most effective and distinguished senators in Washington, were two of Murphy's protégés.

Unlike "Honest" John Kelly and Richard Croker who catered to New York's high and mighty, Murphy's focus was the common good. He exerted more influence in Albany than his predecessors. Friendly governors guaranteed patronage funds for Murphy's machine and vetoed bills sent to them by a legislature hostile to New York City and to Tammany. When middle-class Protestant opponents of increased taxation left the city for the suburbs, Murphy taxed absentee landlords and businesses, and applied such revenue and patronage funds to public-works and social-welfare programs.

In other cities as well as New York, Irish Catholic politicians used public funds to create jobs for their own people and other ethnics. This was particularly true in Pittsburgh and Chicago, where the Irish shared space with a wide variety of other nationalities and races, forcing political bosses to forge coalitions.

In Chicago, Mayor Edward Kelly (1933–1947) and Patrick Nash, president of the Democratic Central Committee, were able to persuade African Americans to shift allegiances from the Republican to the Democratic party. In addition to necessity, Kelly's sincere dedication to civil rights influenced his decision to include Blacks in the patronage and political power structure.

When soliciting votes in their own community, Irish Catholic office seekers strongly endorsed the cause of Ireland's independence, but relationships between Irish-American politics and nationalism were ambiguous. While in certain places— Chicago, for example, where leading politicians were prominent in the 1880s Clan na Gael—it was difficult to separate the two. Purists such as John Devoy did not want to defile nationalism with the stench of politics. They drew a comparison between Irish politics in the United States and parliamentarianism in Ireland, branding both as corrupt and self-serving.

Devoy and other Clan na Gaelers viewed politicians as shifty vote hustlers basically indifferent to Irish nationalism, and they resented the fanatic loyalty of the overwhelming majority of Irish-American Catholics to the Democratic party. Instead of marching to the polls and automatically casting ballots for Democratic candidates, they advised them to offer their votes to the highest bidder, the party and the candidates most willing to move American foreign policy in pro-Irish, anti-British directions. In 1884 Devoy and his associates endorsed Republican James G. Blaine for president rather than Democrat Grover Cleveland. In 1888 and 1892, they backed Benjamin Harrison against Cleveland. When Woodrow Wilson sought a second term in 1916, Irish-American nationalists and some priests asked the American Irish to vote for Charles Evans Hughes. The clergy thought Wilson too friendly toward anti-Catholic rebels in Mexico, nationalists resented his pro-British leanings in World War I. On each of these occasions, the Irish working class ignored nationalist and clerical pleas, voted for what they perceived as their economic concerns and interests, and remained true to the Democratic party. However, Wilson's indifference to Irish nationalism at the Versailles peace conference cost the Democratic party a considerable number of votes in the 1920 presidential election.

It is now time to respond to questions asked earlier in this chapter. Did Irish politicians lower the moral tone of American politics? Did they introduce and promote graft and corruption in urban politics, and cynically exploit acquisitive tendencies in human nature to gain and hold office? Was the politics of revenge a unique Irish aspect of politics in the United States? Did politics speed or impede Irish-American Catholic economic and social mobility? Did Irish politicians work to include other ethnics in the American political process and to improve their economic situations, or did they reserve the spoils of political power for their own people? Were the Irish remarkably successful at acquiring political power but miserable failures at applying it to urban betterment?

Although Irish-American Catholics have not done much to improve the moral tone of American politics, it is a considerable distortion of reality to blame them for all of its seamy aspects. Their political conduct has not varied dramatically from traditional, Anglo-American, Protestant business and political practices. While it is not legitimate to argue that two wrongs make a right, Irish politicians had a point when they branded attacks on their political ethics as jealous hypocrisy, and when they argued that American business profits often resembled political graft. They asked: what right did those who exploited the working class through high prices and low wages have to complain about Irish politics, particularly when it had supplied food, clothing, shelter, and jobs to people made poor by businessmen's greed?

Political machines and party bosses existed in rural and urban America long before the Irish arrived, and the politics of revenge also preceded them to the "shores of Americay." When Irish politicians won elections, appointed their friends to office, and then raided the public treasury for public-works projects that provided both graft and jobs, they were following an old American political tradition: "To the victor belong the spoils." Irish hostility to political reform was not a defense of corruption so much as it was a response to nativism. As a group, reformers were much more interested in driving Irish Catholics from office and/or closing their saloons than they were in improving the economic status of the urban poor. Reformism's emphasis on temperance was one expression of the middle-class, Anglo-Protestant core of the movement and its hostility to Catholic ethnicity. To the Irish and other Catholics, reformism was an attack on their life-styles, threatening the few pleasures enjoyed by the urban poor.

Irish politicians could and did argue with some justice that the difference between theirs and the Anglo-American political machines that they replaced was a higher degree of efficiency and compassion rather than more corruption. The Anglo-American machines took; the Irish took as well, but they also gave, distinguishing between honest and dishonest graft.[18] In addition to enriching some Irish Catholic politicians, income from graft often went to constructive purposes. In Dineen's *Ward Eight,* Hughie Donnelly insisted that Irish political machines produced more contented cities than Anglo reformers who tried to impose business practices on urban governments. He said that graft recipients usually took a small portion for personal use and applied most of it to public-works projects that supplied jobs and beautified the city, while money-cautious reformers limited urban economic expansion. Sociologist Terry N. Clark's analysis of fifty-one cities between 1880 and 1986 gives credence to Donnelly's position. His evidence indicates cities with large numbers of Irish citizens had very little political reform, but did have big increases of public expenditures, improving conditions among lower socio-economic groups.[19]

Irish politicians were there with fuel, food, jobs, and bail money for troubled constituents. They erected mini-welfare states not only to win votes but also to express concern over their people's struggles against a cold, urban environment— "their people" frequently meaning more than just the Irish. Irish politicians formed minority group coalitions, especially in Chicago, Pittsburgh, and (to a lesser degree) in New York, where ethnic patterns have been very complex and varied. They have protected Poles, Jews, and Italians as well as the Irish. As Steven P. Erie points out, they have been more generous to their own kind. But he underestimates the concern and services they provided other ethnics, which were certainly far more than those that Anglo-Protestant reformers offered.

There is some merit in Erie's and Dennis P. Ryan's contention that in investing too much of their attention and energy in politics, Irish Catholics failed to take advantage of many of the economic opportunities that the United States offered. But the strength of this argument depends on time and place. Until recently, in many American cities Anglo Protestants enjoyed a monopoly of economic and social power, and denied Catholics and Jews opportunities in business and limited their access to the professions. In Thomas J. Fleming's *All Good Men,* Ben O'Connor, county commissioner and boss of the thirteenth ward in a New Jersey city, entered politics because it and the church were the only entries to power and influence for bright young Irish men in anti-Catholic America. And it is difficult to blame people who came out of the poverty of rural Ireland and early urban America to seek and stay with political jobs that guaranteed steady employment at a living wage and retirement with a good pension. Police force, fire department, post office, street-and-sanitation department, urban transport, and city government positions were dependable, particularly during depressions and recessions, and served as a base for Irish Catholics to move economically and socially higher in post–World War II America when nativism had faded and the G.I. Bill of Rights opened up higher education prospects to a large number of Irish Catholic males.

Differences in the styles, accomplishments, and failures of Irish Catholic politics in Boston, Chicago, and New York demonstrate that Thomas N. Brown was correct when he emphasized its diversity. There is no Irish political prototype that holds true for every city and region in the country. But despite local variations, Irish politics does have some common as well as distinctive attributes. In fact, the chameleon-like flexibility that Brown stresses is one of its main components, but there are features that are more universal. As previously discussed, Irish Catholics are both the victims and the beneficiaries of two cultural imperialisms, Anglicization and Romanization. This and fading memories of a defeated Gaelic culture fashioned the values of the Irish at home and abroad, and have been apparent in politics as in religion and literature. Political Anglicization was nurtured in the long struggle for Irish freedom, imparting to Irish nationalism an emphasis on the defense of natural and individual rights as the purpose of good government. In the early decades of the nineteenth century, Daniel O'Connell organized the Irish masses for political action and impregnated Irish nationalism with a firm commitment to liberal democracy.

O'Connell did more than just borrow principles and methods of British constitutionalism and pass them on to his Irish followers; he also developed protest tactics that contributed to the advance of liberty throughout the Western world. In his agitations to emancipate Catholics and to repeal the Union, he created the first modern political party in the United Kingdom, one that rested on constituent support as well as on activity in the British House of Commons. O'Connell was the first European politician to achieve significant victories for individual freedom in the oppressive Age of Metternich by applying the "moral force" of disciplined public opinion. As he worked with British Whig and Radical politicians for reform in Irish government, he taught his people that the success of democratic politics depended on compromise, the notion that some improvement was better than none at all.

Later in the nineteenth century, Charles Stewart Parnell built on O'Connell's foundations. While less charismatic than the Kerry Catholic, the Wicklow Protestant also helped Anglicize Irish politics. His obstruction policy in the House of Commons, his energetic leadership of the Land League, and his masterful employment of balance-of-power politics to force Liberals to adopt Home Rule taught the Irish how to manipulate the weaknesses and strength of parliamentary government to achieve power and, through it, change.

While employing British liberal principles, Irish Catholic politics was also colored by a religious experience which gave it a profoundly different perspective from Anglo-Saxon and Anglo-American liberal democracy, one not detected by Moynihan and other critics. Moynihan, in fact, seems to have accepted a rather prejudiced view among historians that American social reform is the achievement of Protestant, middle-class progressivism in the face of conservative Catholic, ethnic opposition. But throughout the nineteenth century, Anglo-Protestant Americans insisted on a self-help social ethic, a *laissez-faire* creed, while Irish politicians tried to improve the standard of living of the urban poor through government intervention. Coal buckets, food baskets, public-works projects, and other forms of patronage employment often amounted to an inefficient and graft-ridden system of social justice, but the Irish approach rather than that of Anglo Protestants was the precursor of communal liberalism in the United States.

Irish Catholic communalism encouraged a collectivist rather than an atomistic approach to the social order. In contrast, Anglo-Saxon and Anglo-American Protestant liberalism draws its sustenance from an individualistic religious and economic ideology which emphasizes the rights of the person against the "oppression" of the community. The Protestant conscience and value system have found it more difficult to deal with urban-industrial social questions than has the Catholic, collectivist point of view.

As advocates of social reform, the Irish have not functioned as liberals in the Anglo-Saxon or Anglo-American Protestant sense of the word. For a long time, Irish and other Catholic ethnics found it emotionally and intellectually impossible to accept the tenets of the eighteenth-century Enlightenment, which comprises the framework of the American value system, one conceived and born in the "Age of Reason." They cannot accept a dogmatic faith in the perfectibility of human nature or in the inevitability of progress. Philosophically, the Irish view of the human condition has been much closer to Burkean conservatism than to Lockean, Jeffersonian, or Benthamite liberalism. It perceives the dark side of human nature, the existence of objective evil, and the influence of irrational forces on the human personality and the historical process.

Paradoxically, this conservative, skeptical, often cynical attitude toward man and his environment has made Irish Catholic politicians more successful practical reformers than their ideologically-liberal Protestant or Jewish counterparts. Irish Catholics have tended to strive for improvement rather than perfection, always conscious of the importance of blending change with tradition.

In the twentieth century, following a major economic depression that shook confidence in *laissez-faire* capitalism, a majority of American citizens concluded that social justice was an essential foundation for human freedom. When they decided that government had an obligation to guarantee it, Irish Catholic politicians in cities, not Anglo-Protestant leaders in suburban or rural America, served as the core of minority-group coalitions that made possible the New Deal, Fair Deal, New Frontier, and the Great Society.[20]

In Ireland and the United States, Irish Catholics have blended the methodology and principles of Anglo-Saxon and Anglo-American Protestant liberal politics, a Catholic sense of community, and their own tolerant and gregarious personalities into a distinct yet regionally varied brand of politics. And because they bridged the gulf between Roman Catholic and Anglo-Protestant cultures, the Irish were the only European ethnics who could have led the American Catholic community into an accommodation with the dominant, Anglo-American Protestant ethos.[21]

While adjusting other Catholic ethnics to America and propelling a reluctant nation along the road to economically and socially interventionist government, Irish Catholic politicians were quietly achieving a successful social revolution in the status and condition of their own people. In little more than a hundred years, they had moved from ghetto basements, attics, and tar-paper shacks in Boston, Philadelphia, New York, Chicago, and New Orleans to the front ranks of American social, political, and intellectual life, including a brief residency in that very famous mansion on Pennsylvania Avenue in Washington, D.C.

6. Irish America and the Course of Irish Nationalism

Religion and politics were the priority concerns and interests for Irish-American Catholics, but nationalism, a passionate determination to free Ireland from British domination, captured the attention and enthusiasm of many. For a significant number, it possessed an idealism they found wanting in their church, and an integrity absent from their politics.

Daniel O'Connell's agitations for Catholic Emancipation and Repeal planted the political seeds of Irish nationalism, and in the *Nation*, Young Ireland gave voice to its cultural dimension. But as Ireland moved into the post-Famine era, nationalism had to compete with other loyalties and preoccupations. It took time for Catholicism and Irishness to meld into one identity and for a sense of nationality to transcend local allegiances. Although small, about the size of Indiana, Ireland is divided by a number of mountain ranges, and in the early nineteenth century, primitive transportation preserved and strengthened regionalism. To many of its people if not most, "Ireland" meant less than attachments to provinces, counties, parishes, and townlands. And for tenant farmers and agricultural laborers, economic survival was of more immediate concern than national sovereignty. In addition to parochialism and land hunger, deference to landlords also hindered nationalist mobilizations.

Irish Catholics brought local and family allegiances with them to the United States, but the common American urban experience and confrontations with Anglo-Protestant nativism forged a larger Irish identity. Immigrants from all parts of Ireland worshipped together in Catholic churches, participated in Democratic party politics, and worked side by side on railroads and building sites and in mines and factories. Anglo-American contempt for things Irish deepened an already festering inferiority complex, compelling a search for pride through a common nationality. Irish Americans soon cultivated their own "racial" myths to match those of their persecutors, rejecting what they considered O'Connell's compromising constitutional patriotism and turning instead to Young Ireland's message. Refugees from the 1848 comic-opera, cabbage-patch revolution left Ireland as dismal failures; they arrived in America as heroes.

Irish nationalism jelled and flourished in the ghettos of urban America as an identity search, a cry of vengeance, and a quest for respectability. Irish Americans furnished hate and passion as well as funds to constitutional and physical force nationalisms in Ireland. Their American experience also reinforced the liberal democratic principles that O'Connell had injected into the blood stream of nationalism in Ireland. Lord Spencer, a British Liberal, understood this when in 1887 he made a case for Irish Home Rule:

> The Irish peasantry still live in poor hovels, often in the same room with animals; they have few modern comforts; and yet they are in close communication with those who live at ease in the cities and

farms of the United States. They are also imbued with the advanced political notions of the American Republic and are sufficiently educated to read the latest political doctrines in the press that circulates among them. Their social condition at home is a hundred years behind their state of mental and political culture.[1]

Nineteenth-century Irish Americans read literature and newspapers that nourished their love for Ireland and antipathy toward Britain. In the immediate post-Famine period, Thomas Davis, Charles Gavan Duffy, James Clarence Mangan, and John Mitchel were the evangelists of cultural nationalism. Late in the century, T. D. Sullivan's edited *Speeches from the Dock* inspired the American Irish with the eloquence so many Irish rebels have expressed on their way to the gallows. Many a second-generation Irish American (dubbed a "narrowback" by native Irishmen) listened in awe, reverence, and pulsing anger as Irish-born fathers or grandfathers recited Robert Emmet's defiance of Lord Norbury.

Irish-American Catholics organized Irish language societies and attended parish hall concerts featuring Moore's "Irish Melodies." They read and memorized passages from Charles Kickham's *Knocknagow or the Homes of Tipperary* (1879), a novel that endorsed their romantic image of Ireland and the courage, generosity, spirituality, and purity of its people. They cheered Kickham's noble Gael, Matt "the Thrasher" Donovan, when he threw the sledge farther than Captain French, a representative and champion of the Protestant Ascendancy, and they wept when beautiful Nora Lacy faced a painful death with saintly joy and stoicism. In another Kickham novel, *Sally Cavanagh* (1869), Neddy Shea expressed an Irish-American messianic determination to liberate Ireland from British oppression. As a one-armed veteran of the American Civil War, Neddy returned to Ireland to mark the grave of his mother, evicted from her farm and cottage by a cruel and greedy landlord. With anger-flashing eyes, he shouted out his hatred of British rule and its landlord agents, promising that although he had been maimed in helping to preserve the American Union, he still had an "arm left for Ireland."

Irish-American nationalism was saturated with bitterness; many of its advocates harbored a deeper hatred of England than a love for Ireland. Despising the English was cathartic for Irish-American tensions and frustrations, a way of expressing and explaining Irish failure, a means of striking out at real and imaginary enemies. Britain had to be punished and humiliated, not only as a step toward Irish freedom but as an atonement for its sins against the Irish. British laws, cruelty, religious bigotry, insensitivity, and indifference to Irish needs had contributed to the deaths and banishment of millions of Irish Catholics.

For Irish-American Catholics, suffering the miseries of urban ghettoes and the scorn of Anglo-American Protestants, Britain was the source of poverty, disgrace, and humiliation at home and abroad. In one of his poems, "Remorse for Intemperate Speech," William Butler Yeats described how the Irish left home with maimed personalities, full of "great hatred," carrying from their "mother's womb a fanatic heart." And during his exile, John Mitchel, the most passionate and unforgiving of the Young Irelanders, analyzed the motives underlying his nationalism:

> I have found that there was perhaps less of love in it than of hate— less of filial affection to my country than of scornful impatience at the thought that I had the misfortune, I and my children, to be born in a country which suffered itself to be oppressed and humiliated by another . . . And hatred being the thing I chiefly cherished and cultivated, the thing which I specially hated was the British system . . . wishing always that I could strike it between wind and water, and shiver its timbers.[2]

There were those who never reconciled themselves to physical or spiritual separation from Ireland nor lost the need for a scapegoat to explain their lack of success in the United States.

But other Irish Americans, who eventually achieved upper-working-class or middle-class incomes and status, tied the success of Irish nationalism to Irish-American acceptability and respectability. They believed as long as Ireland wore the British collar and leash, Anglo Americans would look down on them as a subject people. But when Ireland became a nation state, they would be liberated from the oppression of American nativism. They took seriously the words of Michael Davitt, the founder of the National Land League, who told an 1880 Irish-American audience: "You want to be honored among the elements that constitute this nation. . . . You want to be regarded with the respect due to you; that you may thus be looked on, aid us in Ireland to remove the stain of degradation from your birth . . . and (you) will get the respect you deserve."[3]

Irish Catholics may have been the first but certainly not the last minority in the United States to link their American destiny with the sovereignty of the homeland. Contemporary Jews, African Americans, and Slavs insist on the continued existence of Israel, African freedom, and the independence of Poland and other countries in eastern Europe for the same reasons that nineteenth-century Irish Americans became involved in Irish nationalism.

Because respectability was such a strong motivation in late nineteenth-century Irish-American nationalism, the middle class tended to be more active in Irish freedom movements than workers, who were more involved in bread-and-butter issues of American politics. With the tremendous improvement in the quality of Irish immigrants after 1870, and the rapid occupational and economic mobility of first- , second- , and third-generation Irish Americans, increasing psychological needs for recognition and social status aided the forces of nationalism.

Beginnings of Irish-American nationalism were evident during the Catholic Emancipation agitation in the 1820s, when

Irish Catholics in the United States, with some Protestant support, endorsed Catholic civil rights in Ireland. But repeal in the 1840s actually initiated organized Irish-American commitments to Ireland's freedom. Almost every Irish community in the United States had a local repeal club which sent dollars to swell the treasury of the Dublin organization. In his speeches, O'Connell emphasized that the Irish of the Diaspora had joined with their kinsmen at home in demanding a restoration of the Irish Parliament, warning the British that Irish nationalism had international implications.[4] Pro-repeal speeches and statements from such prominent Americans as Governor William Seward of New York and President John Tyler indicated the potential importance of Irish nationalism as a factor in American politics.

In order to consolidate and publicize Irish-American nationalism, its leaders held two national repeal conventions in the 1840s, but these revealed dissension in the ranks. Many friends of repeal, particularly from the South, denounced O'Connell's attacks on slavery and his demands that Irish Americans remain true to Irish nationalism's liberal, democratic tenets that also were embodied in the American Declaration of Independence. O'Connell told Irish Americans that the Irish historical experience should endow them with a natural empathy for Blacks and persuade them to join the abolitionist cause, and then demand full citizenship for emancipated slaves. He went so far in denouncing Black slavery that he would not accept donations from repeal clubs in the South or those in the North opposed to abolition, insisting that dollars stained with the blood of Black bondage could never be used to free the Irish from British oppression. Irish-American rejection of O'Connell's stand on slavery revealed commitments to American institutions and values and a defensive sensitivity to outside attacks, even from Ireland, on American ways.

The 1840s in Ireland escalated the growth and intensified

the passion of Irish-American nationalism. Famine deaths and emigration convinced many Irish at home and abroad that the British had decided on extermination as a solution to the Irish Question. The failed 1848 rebellion sent Young Ireland refugees to the United States where they provided an ideology and leadership for mobilizing Irish-American discontent and concentrating it on efforts to liberate the homeland.

In developing a rationale for a war on British rule in Ireland, nationalist propaganda emphasized Americanism, praising the United States as the cradle of human liberty, in contrast to aristocratic and imperialistic Britain. It insisted that the United States had a moral obligation to lift the burden of oppression from Ireland. The Irish were the first Americans to use ethnicity as a political tool to manipulate American foreign policy in support of a European freedom movement, a precedent followed later by other minorities.

Following the revolutionary fiasco of 1848, the tide of nationalism flowed back into the constitutional stream. Charles Gavan Duffy melded the conflicting agrarian and political strategies debated in the Irish Confederation into one movement. Along with two other prominent journalists, Dr. John Gray and Frederick Lucas—proprietors and editors of the *Freeman's Journal* and *Tablet*—and with William Sharman Crawford—Ulster Protestant MP and champion of tenant right—Duffy created an independent Irish party dedicated to the achievement of secure tenures at fair rents for Irish tenant farmers. Duffy and his friends hoped that a tenant farmer coalition of Protestants from Ulster and Catholics from throughout the country would eventually undermine sectarianism and lead to an inclusive nationalism.

Unfortunately, the Independent Irish party that emerged from the general election of 1852 with forty-eight seats in the British House of Commons was more than an agrarian "League of the North and South." Duffy, Gray, Lucas, and Crawford also had accepted the collaboration of the Irish Brigade. George

Henry Moore, MP, had organized the Brigade to mobilize Catholic opinion in the United Kingdom against the Whig government's anti-Catholic Ecclesiastical Titles Bill that threatened to prosecute Catholic clergy who took territorial titles derived from the United Kingdom. Duffy admired Moore and respected his integrity, but he suspected that many members of the "Pope's Brass Band"—a popular nickname for the Brigade—were unscrupulous opportunists using popular issues to get elected to Parliament, where they could then satisfy ambitions for place and preferment.

Duffy's suspicions were quickly confirmed when, after the general election, two Brigade members of the Irish party, John Sadleir and William Keogh, accepted positions in Lord Aberdeen's Peelite–Whig coalition government. Some Catholic bishops, including Archbishop Cullen, approved of Keogh and Sadleir breaking their pledges of independent opposition, arguing that it was good for the church to have friends and champions in high places. The conflict between the principle of independent opposition and the machinations of clerical politics led to bitter words and feelings between Duffy and Cullen, who considered the *Nation*'s editor an Irish Giuseppe Mazzini, the Italian nationalist who in 1848 temporarily drove Pius IX out of Rome. In disgust, Duffy sold the paper and left Ireland for a successful career in Australian politics.

While clericalism played an important part in the 1859 collapse of the Irish party, it was not the only factor in its dissolution. From O'Connell's entry into the British House of Commons in 1829 until Charles Stewart Parnell took over the helm of constitutional nationalism in the 1880s, the Irish cause at Westminster suffered from shabby and shady parliamentary representation. Since candidates for the House of Commons paid their own election expenses and, if victorious, served without salary, British politics was a hobby for the aristocracy and gentry. In Ireland landlords were, with few exceptions, committed to the British connection as a guarantee of Protestant property, political and social influence, and religious ascendancy. Many parliamentary candidates who ran as nationalists were adventurers. Once seated at Westminster, they quickly betrayed constituents. People like Sadleir and Keough were symptomatic of the malaise undermining parliamentary nationalism.

In addition to the animosity between Duffy and Cullen, and the undistinguished quality of many Irish nationalist MPs, a shift in tenant-right opinion in the 1850s also damaged the Irish party. Famine times and their immediate aftermath had encouraged a coalition between Protestant and Catholic tenant farmers, but the relative agricultural prosperity of the 1850s, 1860s, and early 1870s resurrected sectarianism and undermined solidarity. It was always difficult for Ulster Protestants of any class to remain in long association with Catholics or accept an Irish over a British nationality. In Ireland, religion, symbolic of cultural identities and loyalties, has for centuries superseded class.

In 1864, after the independent Irish party disappeared, Cullen gave support to the National Association, which George Henry Moore, John Francis Maguire, and John Blake Dillon had organized to agitate for the disestablishment of the Protestant Church in Ireland and to promote tenant rights. Cullen and other Irish bishops were far from social or economic reactionaries. They were interested in the economic security of farmers as a way of improving the rural economy so that young people would not have to emigrate to spiritually dangerous British and American cities. The National Association allied itself to the British Liberation Society, which agitated for complete separation of church and state in the United Kingdom. Radical and Nonconformist BLS members wanted to launch their attack on the established church where it was most vulnerable, Catholic Ireland. While the alliance between Irish Catholicism and British nonconformity was not always ideologically harmonious, it did succeed in impressing W. E. Gladstone and other Liberal politicians with the need to solve the religious dimensions of the Irish Question.

In 1869, Gladstone and the Liberal majority in the House of Commons disestablished the Protestant Church in Ireland. Pope Pius IX, a staunch foe of church–state separation, preferred a dual establishment of Catholicism and Protestantism rather than the disestablishment of the latter. But Cullen despised Protestantism and agreed with the separation of church and state principle that O'Connell had attached to Irish nationalism. He and other Irish bishops knew from the Catholic experience in Ireland that a church free from entanglements with the state was more likely to be a healthy institution. Irish Catholicism was certainly more vital than either Irish or British Protestantism or many forms of Continental Catholicism. A year after disestablishment, Liberals passed an Irish Land Act preventing evictions except for non-payment of rent, and offering government loans for tenants to purchase their farms. Landlords found an escape hatch in the bill, permitting them to raise rents and then evict when a tenant could not pay, and high interest rates discouraged farmers from becoming peasant proprietors. Although it was flawed, the Land Act established an important precedent, a harbinger of things to come: for the first time, a British government had subordinated property rights to social and economic justice, commencing a legislative journey that would lead to Britain's modern welfare state.

The collapse of the independent Irish party confirmed Irish-American nationalist convictions that physical force rather than Westminster speeches would capture the attention of British governments. Irish-American nationalists decided to provide money and guns for freedom movements in Ireland, and to pressure American foreign policy to move in an anti-British direction. During the 1844–1846 dispute between the United States and Britain over the Oregon boundary, Irish-American Catholics were war hawks. After that they constantly tried to promote armed conflicts between Britain and her Continental enemies, emphasizing the slogan "England's difficulty is Ireland's opportunity." For example, during the Crimean War of 1853–1856, Irish-American agents tried to persuade the czar to ally Russia with the forces of Irish nationalism. And they offered support to Spanish efforts to recover Gibraltar, hoping to win a Madrid pledge to aid revolution in Ireland. Throughout the 1850s and 1860s, Irish Americans hoped and prayed that Napoleon III would dispatch an army of liberation to Ireland.

While there was a fantasy quality to much of Irish-American nationalism, Fenianism was a tough, hard-nosed commitment to revolutionary republicanism. It emerged in 1858 from the New York–based Emmet Monument Association, dedicated to fulfilling Robert Emmet's epitaph by establishing an Irish nation-state. Two Young Ireland veterans of 1848, John O'Mahony and Michael Doheny—the author of *The Felon's Track* (1849)—were directors of the Association. They, along with another rebel, James Stephens, escaped a British dragnet in 1848 and managed to reach Paris. Doheny then crossed over to New York, but O'Mahony and Stephens, working as a translator and an English teacher respectively, stayed on in the French capital, absorbing revolutionary conspiracy tactics from a variety of political refugees. In 1851 they both manned the barricades in a futile effort to resist Louis Napoleon's coup d'etat against the Second Republic.

In Paris, Stephens and O'Mahony formulated plans for an Irish revolutionary movement designed to achieve a democratic republic. Ideologically they were socialists, but decided to play down economic issues, still entertaining the Irish-nationalist daydream that Protestant property owners could be persuaded to abandon their loyalty to the British connection. As a result of this unrealistic concept, Stephens and O'Mahony, like earlier and later Irish patriots, deprived their movement of significant economic content.

In 1854 O'Mahony left Paris for New York to work with Doheny in enlisting Irish Americans for revolutionary conspiracy. Stephens concentrated on the United Kingdom Irish. In 1858 he formed the Irish Republican Brotherhood (IRB), absorbing Jeremiah O'Donovan Rossa's Cork-based, literary-political Phoenix Society. O'Donovan Rossa, a dashing, romantic, Gaelic-speaking nationalist, like many other Irish patriots ended his days in New York. He used the legendary phoenix as a symbol of his country's determination to rise from the ashes of British conquest. The same year that Stephens organized the IRB in the United Kingdom, O'Mahony transformed the Emmet Monument Association into its American wing. But since he was a Gaelic scholar who admired the "Fianna" sagas of ancient Irish folklore, O'Mahony decided to name the American organization the Fenian Brotherhood. Because of its romantic allusions to the Gaelic past, Fenianism became the popular designation for republicanism in Ireland, Britain, Canada, and America.

In order to preserve a maximum of secrecy and security, O'Mahony and Stephens employed Continental conspiracy tactics, organizing Fenians into "circles" commanded by a "centre." Each circle was then divided into smaller cells led by "captains," who had authority over "sergeants," who supervised the work of "privates." Lower rank republicans knew only their immediate cell comrades. Stephens was head centre for the United Kingdom; O'Mahony held that post in the United States. Recruits took oaths of secrecy, obedience to officers, and loyalty to the Irish Republic. To avoid offending the American Catholic hierarchy, in the United States Fenians took a pledge rather than an oath of secrecy. Fenian John Devoy enlisted Irish soldiers in the British army, hoping to create a fifth column in the ranks of the enemy.

Like Young Irelanders, many IRB leaders were journalists. Wanting a place in the sun of Irish nationalism, but blocked by O'Connellite and Young Ireland establishments, they made their mark by moving beyond parliamentarianism. Fenianism in the United States and the IRB in Ireland each enlisted about fifty thousand members, but many other emigrants and their offspring were sympathetic and helped fund revolutionary republicanism. In 1865 Irish Americans donated 228,000 dollars to the cause. The next year they increased it to almost 500,000 dollars. In Ireland and America Republicanism had important social aspects that attracted attention and members. In Ireland's Catholic puritan oppressiveness, the IRB sponsored athletic events, reading rooms, discussion groups, and hiking clubs. In the United States, they hosted picnics with food, beer, and speeches.

Most 1848 survivors refused to endorse revolutionary republicanism, and next to the British government, the Catholic Church in Ireland was the leading foe of Fenianism. Bishops denounced the IRB as a secret, oath-bound society, and denied the sacraments to its known members. Dr. David Moriarty, bishop of Kerry, called Fenians "swindlers" and "criminals" deserving damnation, pronouncing that "eternity is not long enough, nor hell hot enough" for their kind. But oaths and secrecy were only minor issues in the confrontation between bishops and Fenians; political considerations were far more important. Revolutionary conspiracy threatened the prospects for an alliance that Cardinal Cullen, through the National Association, was negotiating with British Liberals, a compact that promised the disestablishment of the Protestant Church and government money for Catholic education. Cullen and his fellow prelates were also frightened by the violent rhetoric and strategy of the IRB, believing that the group's inspiration came from Giuseppe Garibaldi-style Continental, anti-Catholic, radical nationalism and the egalitarian and violent mood of urban America. Irish bishops worried that Fenianism might produce a revolution that would destroy Irish lives and property without bringing either freedom or prosperity to compensate for the sacrifice.

In opposing the IRB, bishops contributed to an element of anti-clericalism in Irish nationalism. In their newspaper, *The Irish People,* Fenian journalists Charles Kickham, John O'Leary, and Thomas Clark Luby responded to Cullen and Moriarity. They did not reject their spiritual authority but insisted that the church stay out of politics. In 1861 Fenians challenged Cullen with a patriotic funeral. Terence Bellew McManus, Young Ireland veteran of 1848 and a Van Dieman's land escapee, settled in San Francisco and died there in poverty. American Fenians decided to ship his body back to Ireland for proper tribute and burial. The New York Irish paid homage to McManus's memory before returning him to his native turf. Placing loyalty to a fellow Ulsterman and empathy for nationalist sentiments above episcopal solidarity, Archbishop John Hughes said a funeral Mass in St. Patrick's Cathedral. But while the coffin was crossing the Atlantic on the last stage of McManus's voyage home, Cardinal Cullen decreed that no Catholic church in his archdiocese could be used for any religious ceremony that might be construed as an honor to revolutionary nationalism.

Insisting on public honors rather than a private religious service, the IRB waked McManus in the Mechanic's Institute (later the Abbey Theatre). Fifty thousand people followed the coffin through the streets of Dublin to Glasnevin Cemetery, while hundreds of thousands lined the route. At the graveside, Stephens and other IRB leaders eulogized McManus with fiery speeches, and Father Patrick Lavelle (a radical cleric from Mayo) under the patronage of Cullen's episcopal enemy, Archbishop John MacHale of Tuam, defied the Dublin prelate by blessing the coffin before it was lowered into Irish soil.

No doubt McManus's funeral was a psychological boost for Fenianism, perhaps its high point. But then the American Civil War disrupted republican activities. Fearing that it would divert Irish America's attention from nationalism, Fenians emotionally divided over the conflict between North and South. But most in the former enthusiastically supported the Union because they wanted a strong, unified American foe of Britain. A number of Irish Americans hoped, even believed, that pro-Southern, British opinion and policies would result in a military confrontation between the United Kingdom and the United States, with an independent Ireland the result. Many Irish Americans enlisted in either Union or Confederate armies to acquire military training for future use against Britain. In addition, Fenian agents were active in both camps recruiting for republicanism. During national Fenian conventions, a large number of delegates attended in uniforms of Union blue.

Post–Civil War Fenian planning had Irish Americans participating, financing, and equipping an Irish insurrection. The strategy assumed that once the fighting started, IRB members in the British army would mutiny, paralyzing British efforts to crush the rising. Combat-tested Irish Americans began to train IRB cells in Ireland for military action. But factionalism split American republicanism, postponing rebellion in Ireland. At their 1865 convention in Philadelphia, Fenians adopted a new constitution to adapt their organization to the American political system. It abolished the head centre, substituting a president responsible to a general congress divided into a senate and house of delegates.

Disagreement over this change was only one aspect of Fenian dissension. Colonel William R. Roberts, the senate's dominant personality, rejected the Stephens–O'Mahony strategy for revolution. He insisted that Irish Americans strike at Britain closer to home rather than in Ireland. Roberts reasoned that a Fenian incursion into Canada could provoke conflict between the United States and Britain, resulting in a successful revolt in Ireland. Strife between O'Mahony and the senate prevented an adequate shipment of guns and ammunition to Ireland, persuading Stephens that it would be folly to re-enact the farce of 1848.

While Fenians quarreled, British spies infiltrated the movement on both sides of the Atlantic. After an informer in the

Dublin office of *The Irish People* provided the government with incriminating documents, officials shut it down and arrested the staff, along with Stephens. While British spies were penetrating IRB security, Fenians were establishing contacts within the Royal Irish Constabulary and the Dublin Metropolitan Police. Through the efforts of John Devoy and IRB policemen, Stephens managed to escape from prison and immediately left for the United States to patch up the quarrel between O'Mahony and Roberts. But by the time he landed in New York, the senate had already deposed the former, and Stephens's abrasive personality stirred rather than smoothed the troubled waters of Irish-American nationalism.

In May 1866 about six hundred Fenians invaded Canada, defeated a company of Canadian volunteers and then retreated before the regular army. Instead of discouraging raids across the borders of a friendly neighbor, the United States government used the Fenian menace as a diplomatic weapon in negotiations with Britain. At the time, Washington was insisting that London pay millions of dollars in reparations for damages that the Alabama, a Confederate cruiser built in Britain, inflicted on Union shipping. The United States also wanted Britain to accept the American naturalization of former United Kingdom citizens. Because the British had captured and imprisoned a number of naturalized American Fenians, the last demand had a strong relevance for Irish-American nationalism. Since Fenians invading Canada carried American army surplus weapons and ammunition and the American government arranged transportation home for those who retreated south of the border after the 1866 invasion, it was clear that there were strong links between Washington officials and Irish-American nationalists.

With Fenians focusing on Canada and increasingly reluctant to commit supplies to Ireland, Stephens again decided to delay an Irish rebellion. For this prudent decision, American Fenians branded him a coward and deposed him as international head centre. Early in 1867, a humiliated and frustrated Stephens sailed from New York on his way to a second Paris exile. Never again would he play a decisive role in Irish nationalism.

While Stephens was busy conspiring in the United States, the British government again caught the IRB napping. It transferred Irish soldiers stationed in their own country to other parts of the United Kingdom and empire, suspended habeas corpus, and arrested prominent Fenians. In a futile gesture of defiance, outnumbered, poorly-trained and equipped IRB companies in Kerry, Cork, Tipperary, Limerick, Dublin, and Clare attacked the barracks of the Royal Irish Constabulary and other symbols of British rule. During the snowy months of February and March 1867, the constabulary, assisted by the army, easily smashed and routed small bands of brave but incompetent rebels.

Fenian violence in the United Kingdom was not restricted to Ireland. In September 1867, an IRB rescue party attacked a police van in Manchester, England, freeing two Irish Americans—Colonel Thomas J. Kelly, successor to Stephens as head centre, and Captain Timothy Deasy—but in doing so accidentally killed a police sergeant. British authorities arrested and charged W. P. Allen, Michael Larkin, Michael O'Brien, and Edward Condon with murder. Though they were in the rescue party, no evidence linked them to the fatal bullet. After a trial held in an atmosphere of anti-Irish hatred, a jury found the accused guilty and a judge sentenced them to death by hanging. Since he was a citizen of the United States, the government reprieved Condon. O'Brien claimed the same privilege, but he had earlier avoided a stiff sentence because he was an American, and British officials had no intention of repeating such leniency.

Another incident of Fenian violence in England occurred later in 1867 when the IRB, attempting to free comrades in Clerkenwell Prison by dynamiting a wall, killed twelve and wounded more than a hundred innocent people. This slaughter magnified anti-Irish prejudices in Britain, but the disintegration of the republican movement and the incarceration of many of its members brought the IRB a large measure of public respect and sympathy in Ireland. Prominent people, including Catholic bishops and priests and nationalist politicians, joined an Amnesty Association which petitioned the British government for the release of jailed Fenians. Irish newspapers referred to Allen, Larkin, and O'Brien as the Manchester Martyrs, victims of British injustice. T. D. Sullivan of the *Nation*, inspired by Allen's last words, wrote "God Save Ireland" to the tune of an American Union army song, "Tramp, Tramp, Tramp the Boys Are Marching." It became the anthem of Irish nationalism until "The Soldier's Song" replaced it during the 1919–1921 Anglo–Irish War. It went in part:

> God save Ireland cried the heroes,
> God save Ireland said they all,
> Whether on the scaffold high
> Or on the battlefield we die,
> Oh what matter where for Ireland dear we fall.

With Fenians enshrined as martyrs, Cardinal Cullen found it difficult to sustain clerical animosity to the IRB. Prayers for the souls of Allen, Larkin, and O'Brien, and for the pardon of Fenian prisoners, ascended from Catholic altars. Some bishops and priests justified empathy for republicans by arguing that the split between Irish and American Fenianism purged the former of secularism and violence. In 1870 Irish Catholic opinion resented Pope Pius IX's condemnation of the IRB as a dangerous, anti-Catholic secret society.

Perhaps Fenians became popular in Catholic Ireland when they were no longer a serious threat to either clerical authority or law and order, and when constitutional nationalism revived in the form of Home Rule. In 1870 Isaac Butt, a former Protestant champion of the Union who had become an active Irish nationalist and served as president of the Amnesty Association, established the Home Government Association to persuade British and Irish Protestants that a federal contract between Ireland and Britain would be a conservative and lasting solution to the Irish Question. Irish electors endorsed Home Rule and its candidates at by- and general elections. In 1874 they elected fifty-nine Home Rule MPs who then formed the Irish parliamentary party with Butt as chair. Respecting Butt for his courtroom defense of Fenians and work in the Amnesty Association, the Irish in Britain, including ex-Fenians, formed the Home Rule Confederation of Great Britain, with branches in many cities. The Confederation organized the Irish vote in England and Scotland to support parliamentary candidates in favor of Irish self-government.

In the United States, the hysteria of revived nativism negated some of the efforts of Catholic Americanizers and sustained Irish-American nationalism as an expression of ethnic identity. But by the mid-1870s, Fenianism no longer best represented Irish-American nationalism. In 1870, after the British government conceded the Alabama claims and recognized the validity of American naturalization, President Ulysses S. Grant made it clear that his administration would no longer tolerate an Irish government-in-exile attacking Canada.

Following Grant's statement, a large number of the American Irish abandoned Fenianism for the Clan na Gael. Jerome J. Collins founded the Clan in 1867, but John Devoy, following his 1871 parole from a British prison, arrived in the United States and quickly dominated the new organization. In 1877 the Clan concluded a formal alliance with the IRB, establishing a joint Revolutionary Directory. More disciplined and secretive than Fenianism, it enlisted politicians, businessmen, and professionals. Terence V. Powderly, grand master workman of the Knights of Labor and former mayor of Scranton, Pennsylvania; S. B. Conover, U.S. senator from Florida; and John W. Goff, who became a New York Supreme Court justice, were Clan notables. Local government politicians were also clansmen, and from 1876 through 1881, the Clan's central executive spent sixty thousand dollars financing the efforts of fellow Irishman John Holland to invent a submarine to sweep the British navy from the seas. Holland's invention eventually became the model for the first successful U.S. Navy submarine.

Meanwhile, by the summer of 1876, the Home Rule movement in Ireland, which began with so much promise, was in a near state of collapse. The Home Rule League, modeled on the Catholic and Repeal Associations, which replaced the Home Government Association, had a disappointing membership. And the Irish parliamentary party, mired in lethargy and ineptitude, refused to address agrarian and religious issues dear to various segments of its constituency. In 1877 a large portion of Irish nationalists in both Ireland and Britain deserted Isaac Butt, president of the Home Rule League and chair of the Irish party, to follow Charles Stewart Parnell, a young Protestant landlord from Wicklow who had rejected Butt's policy of conciliation in the House of Commons in favor of one of obstruction. It antagonized British politicians and journalists but captured the enthusiasm of many Irish newspapers and their readers.

Despite his increasing popularity, Parnell preferred not to challenge for the leadership of the bankrupt Home Rule League or the demoralized Irish party. Instead, he ousted Butt as president of the Home Rule Confederation of Great Britain and continued to build constituent support in Ireland, waiting for a new general election to return a braver, bolder body of Irish MPs to Westminster. Parnell was also interested in enlisting the enthusiasm and dollars of the most important wing of the Diaspora, the American Irish.

While Parnell emerged from the back benches of the Irish party, agrarian Ireland experienced a massive economic depression. In 1877, after years of abundant harvests and rising agricultural prices, bad weather destroyed the potato crop, recalling memories of the Great Famine. And in the late 1870s, inexpensively cultivated and harvested American and Canadian grain began to flood the United Kingdom, bringing a sharp reduction in agricultural prices.

Because of their narrow focus on revolutionary republicanism to the neglect of economic and social issues, the Clan na Gael in America and the IRB in Ireland were not in a strong position to exploit Irish discontent. Patrick Ford, populist editor of Irish America's most influential newspaper, the *Irish World*, kept telling the Clan that the land question could arouse the passion of Irish nationalism. He defined agrarian capitalism in Ireland and industrial capitalism in the United States as twin evils degrading and oppressing the Irish. Ford advised Devoy to mobilize the Irish at home and abroad for a war on landlordism as a prelude to rebellion against British colonialism. He predicted that agrarian agitation would energize nationalism in the same way as the Catholic Emancipation agitation did in the 1820s.

Collaborating with Ford and others, Devoy wove the strands of agrarian radicalism and revolutionary nationalism into a New Departure strategy. It called on Parnell and his colleagues in the "active wing" of the parliamentary party to press Home Rule in the House of Commons, and while public attention was focused on Westminster, republicans would quietly prepare the Irish masses for a war of liberation. They would recruit and radicalize the peasantry by agitating for secure tenures at fair rents and for the rights of tenants to sell their interest in farms on leaving by choice or eviction. Tenant right was intended as prologue to an even more radical demand: the substitution of peasant proprietorship for landlordism.[5] When the people were emotionally aroused and disciplined for combat, Parnell would then issue an ultimatum in Parliament: Home Rule or else. If British leaders rejected it, he and his associates would withdraw from Westminster and establish an Irish legislature in Dublin, defended by American armed Irish rebels. Calling on the traditions and mythology of Irish nationalism, the New

Departure projected that by 1882 (the centenary of Henry Grattan's victory), its strategy would result in an Irish nation-state.

When the Clan wired Parnell New Departure alliance terms, his response was cautious and vague. He desired and needed Irish-American financial support, but not at the price of his independence. Parnell also feared that an open alliance with revolutionary republicanism would antagonize the Catholic hierarchy, hurting his chances to become the acknowledged leader of constitutional nationalism. Parnell was always polite to Clan envoys, indicating his interest in an American alliance, but he kept his options open by avoiding firm commitments. He did, however, identify with the agrarian phase of the New Departure, cooperating with its emissary, Michael Davitt.

After serving seven years in a British prison for Fenian activities, Davitt became a New Departure disciple while visiting in the United States. In 1879, under instructions from Ford and Devoy, he returned to Ireland to mobilize the Irish peasantry. Davitt created the Land League of Mayo, which evolved into the National Land League. Demanding the end of the landlord system, it attracted massive support, absorbing the secret terrorist societies that had resurfaced during the depression of the late 1870s. Parnell, Joseph Biggar, O'Connor Power, and other obstructionist MPs appeared on Land League platforms reiterating James Fintan Lalor's "The Land of Ireland for the people of Ireland." Parnell was most impressive when he told an Ennis, County Clare, audience "to keep a firm grip on their homesteads," and to shun and socially ostracize agents of landlordism. Land Leaguers applied his advice to a Mayo estate managed by Captain Charles Cunningham Boycott, and "boycotting" became both a successful tactic in the war against landlordism and a new word in the English language. Immigrant veterans of the Irish land war introduced boycotting into America's working-class conflicts with industrial capitalism.[6]

Collected and distributed through a Clan na Gael front, the Irish National and Industrial League of the United States, and the American Land League, Irish-American money financed the land war in Ireland, making it possible for Irish tenant farmers to resist eviction threats. Davitt described Irish America as "the avenging wolfhound of Irish nationalism," and Land League meetings displayed posters praising the American republic as the enemy of British tyranny.

Davitt was a dedicated and unselfish leader. When he realized that Parnell, a Protestant landlord, had more popular appeal, he resigned as president of the National Land League and persuaded the Home Ruler to take his place. In that capacity, Parnell toured the United States in 1880 to meet the leaders of Irish America and to solicit funds for the League. He was in demand as a speaker and even addressed a joint session of Congress. After returning to Ireland, Parnell contested and won three Irish seats in the 1880 general election, finally deciding to represent Cork in the House of Commons. Shortly after the election, a majority of Home Rule MPs chose him as party chair, replacing William Shaw, a Cork banker who had succeeded Butt when he died in 1879.

Although Parnell was Irish party chair, he continued to concentrate his attention on the Land League, directing an agitation on the fringes of revolution. Not since the glorious days of repeal in 1843 had any protest enlisted so much popular enthusiasm. Catholic Irish America continued to contribute dollars to aid evicted tenants, purchase legal aid for embattled farmers, and publicize the anti-landlord cause. Despite passionate rhetoric, League officials tried to restrain and direct dissatisfaction into passive resistance to landlordism and constitutional demands for agrarian reform. But old traditions of secret-society violence and Fenian influences were difficult to restrain. Angry tenant farmers maimed cattle, burned hayricks, and assaulted agents of and peasants who cooperated with landlords. But Parnell and his lieutenants managed to isolate and minimize violence, preventing the situation from deteriorating into a total and bloody class war.

Finally, agrarian agitation forced Prime Minister Gladstone to make concessions to rural discontent in Ireland. In 1881 he steered a Land Act through Parliament that guaranteed Irish farmers stable tenures at fair rents, destroying manorialism and setting the stage for peasant proprietorship. But since Irish Americans supported the agrarian campaign as only one phase of a grand strategy leading to Irish sovereignty, Parnell could not afford to offend them by offering gratitude to British Liberals. Instead, he insisted that the Land Act be expanded to include tenants in arrears, and cautioned the Irish public not to trust the legislation until it had been tested in the land courts. Because he refused to cease the land agitation, the British, applying a coercion bill, confined Parnell and some of his lieutenants in Dublin's Kilmainham jail. At the time, it was a good place for him to be. He feared that extremists would interpret the Land Act as a sign of Liberal weakness and instigate an insurrection. Parnell preferred that a British prime minister, rather than the leader of the Irish party, deal with hotheads. In prison Parnell would wear a martyr's mantle, while Gladstone weeded out dangerous elements in the land war and Home Rule camps.

Parnell, restless in his cell and worried about a sick child that he fathered with Katherine O'Shea, wanted out of prison, and Gladstone, anxious to come to terms with the Irish leader, worked out an informal arrangement, the Kilmainham Treaty. It pledged Parnell to support a Liberal program for Irish reform in exchange for his release and a Land Act amendment that would extend its benefits to tenants in arrears and end coercion.

When Parnell left Kilmainham in May 1882, the Land League had been outlawed and rural Ireland was relatively calm. Since the vast majority of tenant farmers were satisfied with the Land Act, Parnell could transfer Irish energy and

Irish-American money from the agrarian to the national issue. Using American funds to pay the election expenses and living costs of Home Rule MPs, he solved a financial problem troubling parliamentary nationalism since the O'Connell era. Parnell recruited young, fervent, talented nationalists for the Irish party and made it the most effective unit at Westminster. By extending suffrage to rural males, the 1884 Reform Bill increased party strength to eighty-five. With those numbers and a strong constituency organization, the Irish National League, Parnell changed parliamentary strategy from obstruction to balance of power. Applied in 1885, it persuaded Gladstone to lead the Liberals into an alliance with Irish nationalism. Although an 1886 Liberal split doomed the first Home Rule Bill and the Conservative House of Lords vetoed the second in 1893, the Irish and Liberal parties were joined in an often uneasy marriage that could end only by death or divorce.

In the early 1880s, Parnell cleverly outflanked the Clan na Gael. Seizing command of the agrarian phase of the New Departure, he gained control of Irish nationalism and Irish-American financial resources. By the mid-1880s, the vast majority of the Irish at home and abroad were committed to constitutional nationalism in the form of Home Rule. While the Clan was isolated, futilely financing bombing campaigns in Britain and naively hoping to intimidate British politicians into conceding Irish self-government, most Irish Americans were contributing dollars to the Parnell-dominated National League of America.

In early December 1890, however, after a messy uncontested court case in which Captain William O'Shea successfully sued his wife Katharine for divorce, naming Parnell as correspondent, Nonconformist Protestants informed Gladstone that they could no longer support Liberals unless they cut ties with the Irish adulterer. Gladstone then persuaded an Irish party majority, which believed that the Liberal alliance and Home Rule were more important than its leader, to replace Parnell as chair with Justin McCarthy. Refusing to step aside, Parnell appealed to the ultimate source of his strength, the Irish people. This brought Catholic bishops and priests, who could not appear to be more lax on sexual morality than British Protestants, into the leadership dispute. They were the crucial factor in the defeat of Parnellite candidates in a number of Irish by-elections. The strain of campaigning in the cold, damp countryside destroyed Parnell's health. On October 6, he died in Brighton of rheumatic fever.

Parnell's death did not end the division in parliamentary nationalism. Bitter disputes and by-election contests between the Parnellite minority and the anti-Parnellite majority intensified cynicism and apathy initiated by the divorce scandal and perpetuated by feuds within Home Rule circles. Plummeting nationalist morale also affected the Diaspora, reducing its financial contributions to a fragmented party.

Parnell's divorce scandal and the subsequent Irish party split were not the only sources of disillusionment in Irish-American nationalism. The decision of John Devoy and others (who had always complained of corrupt and compromising Irish-American politics) to support Republican presidential candidates in 1884 and 1888 disturbed Irish-American Democrats. Patrick Ford's efforts on behalf of Henry George's bid for the New York mayoralty in 1886, and his anti-capitalism editorials in the *Irish World* offended more conservative Irish-American Catholics. The Clan na Gael itself was divided between Devoy and Alexander Sullivan factions. Sullivan, headquartered in Chicago, dominated the Clan through much of the 1880s. He used a skirmishing fund to finance a dynamite campaign in Britain. When Sullivan's henchmen murdered a Devoy supporter, Dr. Patrick Cronin, and scattered his body parts throughout the Chicago sewer system, the discredited Clan lost members and supporters.

The need to restore Irish nationalist confidence and solidarity, particularly in the affluent American wing, forced a reunification of the parliamentary party. In 1900 John Dillon, who succeeded McCarthy as head of the anti-Parnellite faction, graciously stepped aside and consented to the election of Parnellite leader John Redmond as chair of a united party. Since fund collecting Home Rule MPs disguised the British constitutional character of Home Rule, and tailored their speeches to the militantly anti-British sentiments of Irish-American audiences, Irish Catholics in the United States continued to bankroll parliamentary nationalism as an effective means to Irish freedom.

While the American branch of the United Irish League, successor to the Irish National League, continued to collect funds for the Irish party, Irish-American leaders pressured American politicians to work against British interests. Irish-American opinion and politics aggravated tensions between the United States and Britain. They opposed free trade agreements that might benefit British commerce, and during the 1895–1896 Venezuelan boundary dispute agitated for a showdown between their country and the United Kingdom.

Taking advantage of an even balance between Liberals and Unionists (Conservatives) in the House of Commons, in 1911 the Irish parliamentary party forced the Liberal government to curb the absolute veto power of the House of Lords to a three-session, two-year duration as a prelude to Irish self-government. The next year Herbert Asquith, the British prime minister, introduced the third Home Rule Bill. After almost a century of effort, Irish nationalism, playing the parliamentary game, approached victory. But when it seemed inevitable, the British changed the rules.

While nationalists prepared to inaugurate an Irish parliament in Dublin, Ulster Protestants, supported by British Conservatives, threatened civil war to avoid participation in a Catholic-majority state. They intimidated British Liberals into compromising Home Rule by suggesting partition. Responding to British Liberal pressure to make some concession, Redmond said that he was prepared to accept, at least temporarily, an exclusion of the four northeastern counties (except for the cities of Newry and Derry), where anti-Home Rule Protestants comprised a majority. But Ulster Orangemen, led by Dubliner Sir Edward Carson, and British Unionists demanded that all or at least six of the nine Ulster counties be omitted from the settlement. With the tone of debate becoming shriller and with Protestant Orange and Catholic Green volunteer forces parading with rifles in Belfast and Dublin, World War I rescued the United Kingdom from perhaps an even worse catastrophe, civil war.

Following Britain's decision to join France and Russia in armed conflict against the Central powers, the government attempted to satisfy Irish nationalists by placing Home Rule on the statute books. To please Ulster unionists, it added a Suspensory Bill postponing its operation until there was peace. Redmond divided Irish nationalism by his decision to support Britain in a crusade against German authoritarianism and in defense of the sovereignty of small nations such as Belgium. He also believed that if Irishmen did their duty, then the British might limit the extent of Ulster exclusion from Home Rule after the war. Irish Americans and extreme nationalists in Ireland viewed World War I as nothing more than a contest between militaristic empires and resented Redmond advising Irishmen to shed their blood for British interests. Clan na Gaelers joined German Americans in demanding United States neutrality. In 1916 John Devoy and his associates helped plan the Easter Week rebellion and sought help from Germany.

On Easter Monday, April 24, 1916, a small number of men and a few women, representing the IRB-dominated, anti-Redmond wing of the Irish Volunteers and James Connolly's socialist Citizen Army, initiated a Dublin rebellion and proclaimed an Irish Republic. After six days of fighting, the Patrick Pearse-led republicans and Connolly socialists surrendered. At first Irish opinion opposed the rising as a German-promoted stab in Britain's back, but after authorities brutally executed Easter Week rebel leaders and imprisoned many other Republicans, Irish nationalists celebrated the dead and imprisoned as martyred heroes. Pearse, a poet, had preached that a successful revolution was unnecessary; he wanted a blood sacrifice to wash away the taint and corruption of parliamentary nationalism and to inspire coming generations to throw off British tyranny. He proved a prophet. Easter Week did nurture the spirit of Irish nationalism. British responses to the 1912–1914 Home Rule crisis and to the rising eventually destroyed constitutional nationalism in Ireland and made another rebellion almost inevitable.

Once the United States entered the war in April 1917 on the side of Britain and France, the overwhelming majority of Irish-American Catholics placed loyalty to their country above Irish nationalism. As in previous wars, they rushed to enlist in the armed forces and enthusiastically purchased victory bonds. Irish-American George M. Cohan wrote the songs that best captured the spirit of American patriotism. And regiments such as New York's "Fighting 69th" proved Irish courage on the battlefield. But once the war in Europe was over, Irish-American nationalists resumed efforts to liberate Ireland.

Britain's surrender to Ulster Protestant intimidation and British Conservative demands that northern counties be omitted from Home Rule, the execution of leaders of the Easter Week "blood sacrifice," the imprisonment of thousands of Irish nationalists without due process, and the slaughter of Irish soldiers on the western front and in the ill-fated Gallipoli venture combined to destroy the credibility of the Irish parliamentary party and its brand of constitutional nationalism. In the December 1918 United Kingdom general election, Irish voters returned seventy-three Sinn Féin (we-ourselves) party candidates pledged to an independent Irish republic.[7] They refused to sit at Westminster, and organized an Irish Parliament, the Dáil, in Dublin. In 1919 passive resistance escalated into rebellion as Irish Volunteers, rechristened the Irish Republican Army, fought the first twentieth-century guerrilla war of liberation against the Royal Irish Constabulary, its "Black and Tan" and Auxiliary supplements, and the British army. For the most part, political rather than economic or social agendas motivated Irish republicans. But a small contingent embraced Connolly's socialism. According to historian Joshua B. Freeman, a number of Anglo Irish and subsequent Civil War veterans helped radicalize the American labor movement. For example, they cooperated with Communists in the creation of the New York Transport Workers Union.[8]

Following World War I, Irish-American Catholics supplied money and guns to Sinn Féin in Ireland, and pressured Washington to recognize the Irish Republic. President Wilson's Anglophilia excluded Ireland from his commitment to national self-determination, costing Irish-American support for the League of Nations and Democratic votes in the 1920 presidential election. But Catholic Irish America contributed to an international public opinion that finally pressured the British government in 1921 to sign a treaty with Sinn Féin rebels that conferred dominion status on a twenty-six-county Irish Free State.

In 1920, during the Anglo–Irish War, the British government attempted to solve the Irish Question with a Better Government of Ireland Bill dividing Ireland into twenty-six- and six-county Home Rule territories. It was hypocritical for British politicians to argue that a United Ireland would be unfair to a 25 percent Protestant minority and then create a 33 percent Catholic Northern Ireland, particularly when two of the six counties, Fermanagh and Tyrone, had Catholic majorities. During treaty negotiations with Sinn Féin, Lloyd George, the British prime minister, promised a Boundary Commission, suggesting that it would attach Catholic majority areas (Fermanagh, Tyrone, South Down, South Armagh, and West Derry) to the Free State, making Northern Ireland economically unfeasible and leading to one Ireland. However, when the Boundary Commission met in 1924 it refused to seriously tamper with the border between North and South.

From the start, the Northern Ireland majority economically and politically discriminated against the minority, shaping "a Protestant nation for a Protestant people." Although Northern Ireland was part of and responsible to the United Kingdom, British politicians ignored violations of civil liberties in their Ulster province.

During the Dáil debate over the Treaty, its republican opponents took issue with the Free State oath of allegiance to the British crown, but barely mentioned partition. Refusing to accept pro-Treaty majority decisions by the Dáil or the Irish electorate, republicans rebelled against Free State authority. In many ways the brief Civil War (1922–1923) was more brutal than the longer Anglo–Irish conflict. Defeated republicans continued to argue that the Republic was inviolate and that the majority had no right to be wrong. After the Boundary Commission refused to alter the North–South border, and the Free State government accepted the situation, republicans vigorously condemned partition as well as the oath of allegiance. The IRA engaged in terrorist activities in Northern Ireland and sometimes in Britain, in an attempt to achieve a United Ireland through violence and intimidation.

Following the establishment of the Free State, Irish-American interests in Irish affairs steadily declined. But a small group of fanatics, led by such unreconstructed republicans as Philadelphia's Joseph McGarrity, continued to encourage and finance physical-force nationalism in Ireland. In the late 1960s, the repression of the civil rights movement in Northern Ireland, the subsequent conflict between the IRA and the British army, the internment without trial of Catholic nationalists, and the hunger strikes by nationalist prisoners provided an opportunity for IRA supporters in the United States to refocus Irish-American attention on the Irish Question.

7. From Ghetto to Suburbs: From Someplace to Noplace?

From the Great Famine until the conclusion of the Anglo–Irish War, Irish-American fanaticism and funds sustained Irish nationalism. But after the establishment of the Free State, American concerns took precedence over Irish interests. Many Irish-American Catholics were disgusted and puzzled by the 1922–23 civil war between Free Staters and Republic die-hards. They agreed with Michael Collins, Ireland's leading hero in the 1919–1921 guerrilla war of liberation, that dominion status was a major British concession, and that it provided an opportunity for expanded sovereignty, a prediction finally fulfilled in 1948 when Ireland became a republic outside the British Commonwealth.

Decreasing physical and cultural contacts between Ireland and Irish America have weakened ties between the two. Nativist-inspired immigrant restriction laws in the 1920s, the Great Depression that started in the last years of that decade and lasted through the 1930s, and World War II greatly reduced Irish entry into the United States. Instead, most emigrants have gone to Britain where the emotional and geographic break with Ireland has been less traumatic. Inexpensive boat tickets and air fares have made it convenient for the Irish in British cities to return home for Christmas and summer holidays.

Adding to the decline in numbers of those going to the United States, the decision of post-independence Ireland to cultivate an exclusive Gaelic nationalism and, more recently, its emphasis on the Irish as a European rather than a diasporic people have widened cultural and interest gaps between the Irish in Ireland and those scattered throughout the English-speaking world. The assimilation of the Irish in America and in British Commonwealth countries, as well as contemporary Irish identity with its paradoxical combination of provincial Gaelic and cosmopolitan European community dimensions, has rejected the strategy of pre-1921 Irish nationalism: the unity of purpose between the Irish at home and abroad.

In the course of the twentieth century, much of the anti-British preoccupation of Irish-American Catholics has either faded or disappeared. Soldiers, sailors, and marines from their community have fought alongside British service men and women in two world wars and several smaller engagements since 1917. During the post-1945 Cold War, Britain was the closest and most dependable ally of the United States. Many Irish-American Catholics have become as Anglo-philiac as American Protestants. Until rather recently, Catholic colleges and universities, with student bodies and faculties heavily Irish, emphasized British history and literature while neglecting Irish studies.

Ireland and Irish Catholic America made a mutual rather than a one-sided decision to inhabit separate cultural spheres. In passing through an identity crisis, the latter lost its psychological dependence on Irish nationalism. In "The Bent Twig— A Note on Nationalism," *Foreign Affairs*, October 1972, Isaiah

Berlin defined nationalism as an expression of "the desire of the insufficiently regarded to count for something among the cultures of the world." During the nineteenth and for a good portion of the first half of the twentieth century, Irish-American Catholics certainly were "insufficiently regarded," yearning for respectability and blaming their low economic and social situation on British conquest and oppressive governance that forced their departure to Anglo-Protestant America, where again they encountered poverty and discrimination. They also believed that a liberated Ireland would emancipate them from the humiliation of Anglo-American contempt. However, their commitment to and reliance on Irish nationalism dissipated in proportion to their increasing status in American life.

In World War I, Irish-American Catholics earned respect for courage and patriotism. After it was over they continued their journey toward American prosperity and respectability. By the 1920s most males had become skilled workers; an increasing number entered the middle class; quite a few, men and women, were in the professions—education, medicine, and law; and many were in the lower, middle, and upper levels of the civil service. In the 1920s, 25 percent continued education after secondary school. These were usually women preparing to be nurses and teachers.[1] With advancing incomes and social standing, Irish Catholics migrated from inner-city neighborhoods to those on the fringes of the city; some even settled in suburbs. The Great Depression interrupted their economic and social progress, but because schools, hospitals, city governments, and transportation systems employed so many Irish Americans in jobs that survived hard times, they probably weathered it in better shape than most ethnic groups.

Anti-Catholic nativism, prominent in the 1928 presidential election, was uncomfortable for Irish America, encouraging portions of it to succumb to the temptations of paranoid politics. In the 1930s millions of Catholics and other Americans listened to Father Charles Coughlin, the Royal Oak, Michigan radio priest, as he shifted from a champion of Franklin D. Roosevelt and the New Deal to an anti-semitic sympathizer of fascist regimes in Europe. Catholic pulpit and newspaper voices that endorsed General Francisco Franco in the Spanish Civil War, and referred to such other dictators as Benito Mussolini, Italy; Antonio de Oliveira Salazar, Portugal; and Juan Peron, Argentina, as Christian corporate state bulwarks against atheistic communism, provided additional ammunition for those insisting that Catholics were congenitally reactionary.[2]

While still not entirely relaxed in America and separated from its mainstream culture, the vast majority of Irish Catholics rejected Coughlin when he turned against Roosevelt. Few voted for his Union party candidate, William Lemke, in the 1936 presidential election. Only two Catholic diocesan papers, the *Michigan Catholic* and *Brooklyn Tablet* remained friendly to Coughlin, and except for his own bishop, Michael Gallagher of Detroit, and Archbishop Francis Beckman of Dubuque, members of the American hierarchy distanced themselves from the clerical demagogue. Chicago's auxiliary bishop, Bernard Sheil, and Monsignor John Ryan of the National Catholic Welfare Conference strongly condemned Coughlin's anti-semitism and fascist leanings.

Instead of playing a role on its paranoid fringes, Irish Catholics in the 1930s were prominent on the national stage of American politics. FDR rewarded them for their important part in fashioning the minority group coalition that was the strength of the Democratic party in the urban North. He placed James J. Farley and Frank Walsh in the cabinet and Frank Murphy on the Supreme Court. Farley also was Democratic party chair. In addition, Roosevelt appointed Catholics, usually Irish, to one in four government positions. Although the New Deal opened up political opportunities for Irish Catholics on the national level, Edwin O'Connor's *The Last Hurrah*, in explaining Frank Skeffington's defeat in his final run for Mayor, argued that it undermined their urban machines:

All over the country the bosses have been dying for the last twenty years, thanks to Roosevelt. . . . The old boss was strong simply because he held all the cards. If anybody wanted anything—jobs, favors, cash—he could only go to the boss, the local leader. What Roosevelt did was to take the handouts out of local hands. A few little things like Social Security, Unemployment Insurance, and the like—that's what shifted the gears, sport. No need now to depend on the boss for everything; the Federal Government was getting into the Act. Otherwise known as the social revolution.

In *The Boston Irish: A Political History,* Thomas H. O'Connor agrees that the New Deal undermined Curley's hold on the electorate. But Steven P. Erie in *Rainbow's End* offers evidence that while in some cities federal officials rather than local politicos distributed Washington money, in others it was filtered through urban political machines. Although Curley took risks in supporting Roosevelt over Al Smith at the 1932 Democratic convention, FDR contemptuously ignored his pleas for government financing of Boston public works projects. On the other hand, Works Projects Administration funds and other federal dollars not only sustained but strengthened the Kelly–Nash machine in Chicago. And a year before *The Last Hurrah* appeared in print, Richard J. Daley started his first of five plus terms as Chicago's mayor. Combining that office with chair of the Cook County Democratic Organization and the largess of federal funds, Daley, an organizational genius and financial wizard, constructed the most powerful, efficient, and successful political organization in the history of urban America. He made Chicago the city that works for upper-working-class and middle-class whites, but not for an increasingly large Black population. But as Daley defenders correctly point out, the African-American situation was desperate in all American cities.

Although federal government patronage preserved and energized a number of healthy political machines until the Ronald Reagan presidency in the 1980s cut back federal funds for local projects, their Irish ambience diminished. Richard J. Daley might have been the true "last hurrah," the end of a line of powerful political bosses. As the Irish disappeared into business, the professions, and the suburbs, they gradually began to surrender urban political offices with their fading importance to other white ethnics, African Americans, and Hispanics. Still they did not completely abandon their addiction to and love of politics, displaying both on state and national levels.

Despite continuing anti-Catholic nativism that sometimes provoked neurotic Irish responses, common suffering during the Depression and shared patriotism during World War II and the subsequent Cold War reduced ethnic and religious, if not racial, tensions in the United States. Popular entertainment, especially motion pictures, did much to improve the Irish-Catholic image. During the Depression, Jimmy Cagney, the rough, tough, fast-talking, arrogant film gangster had tremendous appeal for movie-goers disillusioned with the Anglo-Protestant financial establishment. He was the quintessential urban-Irish anti-hero thumbing his nose at big shots. In a 1942 dramatic switch of roles, Cagney was George M. Cohan in *Yankee Doodle Dandy*. Shown in movie theatres throughout the country at the beginning of World War II, Cohan's patriotic songs were a great advertisement for the Americanism of Irish Catholics. Early in the film, before giving the Congressional Medal of Honor to Cohan, Franklin D. Roosevelt (Captain Jack Young) remarked: "That's one thing I've always admired about you Irish Americans. You carry your love of country like a flag, right out in the open. It's a great quality."

Films also made Catholicism, nativism's bête noir, more acceptable to American opinion. Some of the most popular actors played Irish priests. For example, Spencer Tracy was Father Tim Mullin in *San Francisco* (1936) and won a best actor Academy Award as Father Edward Flanagan in *Boy's Town* (1938). He repeated the role in *Men of Boy's Town* (1941). Tracy's fellow Milwaukeean, Pat O'Brien, was Father Jerry Connolly in *Angels*

with Dirty Faces (1938), competing with old pal gone wrong
Rocky Sullivan, played by Cagney, for the respect of New York's
Hell's Kitchen teenagers. O'Brien also was the movie version
of two real-life clerics, Father Francis Duffy in *The Fighting
69th* (1940), and Father Dunne of St. Louis, a protector of
newsboys, in *Fighting Father Dunne* (1948). Bing Crosby, at the
time America's most popular vocalist and biggest movie box
office draw, was Father Chuck O'Malley in the most successful
of the priest movies, *Going My Way* (1944). It won Academy
Awards for best film, leading actor (Crosby), best supporting
actor (the Abbey Theatre's Barry Fitzgerald as Father Fitzgib-
bon), script (Leo McCarey), director (McCarey), and song
("Swinging on a Star"). The following year, Crosby reprised the
O'Malley role in *The Bells of St. Mary's*, costarring with Ingrid
Bergman who, as the principal of a parochial school, made
nuns as attractive, modern, and relevant as priests. Movies emphasized Catholicism as compatible with rather than contradictory to American values. They seldom showed priests saying
Mass or performing other aspects of their religious vocations.
Instead, they depicted them as social workers, instruments of
law and order, healing dysfunctional families, and steering
young people away from troubled into productive lives.

Education was the springboard that launched the Irish
Catholic majority into the ranks of the American middle class.
Hundreds of thousands took advantage of the 1944 Service-
man's Readjustment Act by enrolling in colleges and universities at government expense. After earning B.A. and B.S. degrees, many went on to graduate and professional schools. Compared to other Catholic ethnics, the Irish were well-equipped
by excellent Catholic and public school secondary educations
to take advantage of the G.I. Bill of Rights. Their parents had
taught them to appreciate education as an American mobility
tool, and in many instances had made financial sacrifices to pay
Catholic school tuitions. Catholic secondary education featured college preparatory curricula, but before and during

World War II few graduates could afford to go on to higher education. High school diplomas could propel the children of blue collar workers into white collar desk jobs, but the G.I. Bill meant that ex-servicemen skipped one sometimes two generational rungs—peasant to Ph.D. or M.D.—on the mobility ladder. Although academia, particularly history and social science departments, continued to discriminate against Catholics in faculty appointments until the 1970s, by that time Irish-American Catholic males, products of government-financed education, were highly visible at the highest levels of business and the professions.

Going off to war and then to college had a tremendous impact on the mentality of many Irish Catholics. Both undermined the parish-centered, neighborhood focus of their lives. Theology and philosophy courses and liturgical practices in Catholic higher education environments tended to substitute a cosmopolitan, intellectual for a parochial, unthinking Catholicism. A great number could never be quite happy in parish churches listening to mushy hymns sung by bad choirs, looking at grotesque statues, and painfully enduring boring, meaningless sermons.

Education also generated Irish Catholic economic and social mobility, encouraging residential shifts from cities to suburbs. A massive migration of African Americans from South to North, and the expansion of Black ghettoes hastened their journey as they left impressive Catholic churches in their wake. Sometimes priests attempted to persuade parishioners to stay and make friends with new African-American neighbors, but increasing crime rates and worries about sinking property values sent them scurrying off to hoped-for promised lands on the fringes of or beyond city limits.

Many Irish-American Catholic insecurities survived class mobility. A subculture persisted that tended to isolate Catholics from the American mainstream. Pulpit sermons and Catholic education encouraged aloofness with constant attacks on American materialism and secularism. St. Thomas Aquinas's *Summa Theologiae* was the core of philosophy and theology courses in Catholic colleges and universities. But in this context Thomism was often apologetics, a verification of Catholic doctrine and moral and social values, rather than an instrument of intellectual inquiry. When I was teaching in an otherwise excellent Catholic women's college in the mid-1950s, the nuns and lay people on the faculty were first-rate educators, but Dominican friars in the philosophy and theology departments were preparing students for life in the thirteenth rather than the twentieth century.

In efforts to shield Catholics from the temptations of American secularism, church leaders attacked indecent books and movies, and waged war against contraceptives and the whole concept of "unnatural" family planning. Instead, bishops and priests reluctantly approved of the rhythm system, so ineffective that the laity referred to it as "Roman roulette." Daniel Lord, S.J., and another Irish Catholic, Martin Quigley, authored the Production Code to curtail sex and violence in the movies, and the Catholic Legion of Decency instructed Catholics on what films to see or avoid.

A number of Irish-American Catholic scholars and literary figures complained of the anti-intellectualism of the Catholic subculture. In *American Catholics and the Intellectual Life* (1955), John Tracy Ellis, then the Distinguished Professor of Church History at The Catholic University of America, quoting from a 1941 comment by British American studies scholar, Denis W. Brogan, criticized American Catholics for placing more emphasis on material success than on learning: "In no Western Society is the intellectual prestige of Catholicism lower than in the country where, in such respects as wealth, numbers, and strength of organization, it is so powerful." For all practical purposes, Ellis was indicting the Irish who dominated the educational and administrative structure of American Catholicism.

In explaining the pathetic condition of Catholic intellectualism, Ellis said that it partially resulted from the adoption of general American values—the fascination with wealth rather than knowledge. He also blamed Catholic education that was still geared to meet the needs of a defensive immigrant church. As a result, Catholic schools and colleges substituted apologetics for creative thought. Ellis might also have pointed out a difficulty, not peculiar to the United States, of establishing a twentieth-century intellectual environment in a smug and stodgy Roman Catholic Church committed to an irrelevant medievalism.[3]

Into the 1970s many Irish-American novelists continued to describe Catholic Irish America in the same way as James T. Farrell did in the 1930s: narrow-minded, paranoid, puritan, and anti-intellectual. In *Moon Gaffney* (1947), Harry Sylvester's lace-curtain Brooklyn Irish of the late 1930s were ultraconservative on social and political issues, sexually naive and prudish, contemptuous of other Catholic ethnics, and prejudiced against Blacks and Jews. Irish-American priests were especially thick-headed and reactionary. The Sunday sermons of Father Malone, a member of the Father Coughlin–influenced, anti-semitic Christian Front with a significant following in Boston and New York, praised fascist dictatorships in Catholic countries. Father O'Driscoll, who taught religion in a Catholic women's college, thought it great fun to purposely give false information on the rhythm system so that former students would get pregnant on their honeymoons. O'Driscoll and Father Rhatigan, a parish priest, attempted to persuade bright, sensitive Ellen Doarn to marry an alcoholic lout, Peter Callahan, because he came from a good Irish Catholic family. The love of a good woman would reform him, and there were worse vices than a manly thirst for drink.

Although *Moon Gaffney* was a minor sensation in Catholic intellectual circles during the late 1940s, it was more sociological opinion than first-rate literature. But its stereotyped Irish

Catholic bigots, drunks, and puritans persisted in the work of writers more talented than Sylvester, such as Jimmy Breslin, James Carroll, John Gregory Dunne, Joe Flaherty, Thomas J. Fleming, Edward Hannibal, Pete Hamill, and Tom MacHale. Fascination with priests both inspired and limited J. F. Powers. His highly respected volumes of short stories and his novel *Morte D'Urban* (1962) satirize builder priests who invite money-changers into the temple. They enjoy good food and drink, drive expensive cars, wear tailored clothes, and golf at country clubs. Their font of wisdom is *The Reader's Digest.* Oblivious to papal pronouncements on poverty and social justice, their sermons address fornication, adultery, contraception, indecent films and books, and the evils of communism. Powers's literary examination of Catholic foibles calls for purification rather than drastic theological or liturgical change. He mocks sanctimonious, superficially learned, faddish, smug liberal members of the clergy as well as the rotarian type. Post–Vatican II Catholicism has not pleased him. But much of Powers's anger has subsided, moving from satire to easygoing humor in *The Wheat That Springeth Green* (1988).

Literary and theatre depictors of Irish-American Catholicism have dwelled on sexual frustration as the sources of its neuroses, psychoses, and alcoholism. Eugene O'Neill's work is saturated with sexual tension and guilt. These neuroses and the inability to discuss them severely damage the marriage of John and Nettie Cleary in Frank Gilroy's prize-winning 1965 play, *The Subject Was Roses.* Catholicism is a major subject in Thomas J. Fleming's novels about the Irish in a New Jersey city. Conceding that Catholicism once sheltered and shielded insecure Irish pioneers of the American urban ghetto, Fleming considers it an irrelevant handicap in post–World War II America, obstructing entry into the advantages and opportunities of a culturally diverse society. He insists that Catholic authoritarianism is incompatible with American liberalism, and that the medieval perspective of Catholic education isolates its products from American reality. After leaving college and university campuses, they enter the mental and social ghetto parishes of suburbia. Residents of Irish Catholic, middle-class suburbia, expressing the values of their subculture, smugly condemn the materialism and secularism of other Americans while pursuing the money hunt as greedily as those they stigmatize. They focus on the family, praising its virtues, but Fleming describes their marriages as full of strife, imprisoning husbands and wives in cold and contentious unions, sublimating natural expressions of affection, confining them to the dictates of the thermometer and calendar regime of the rhythm system.[4]

Literary and scholarly critics were perceptive in their analysis of the shallowness of Irish-American Catholic intellectualism, the unmerited complacency of their subculture, and their hesitancy to take advantage of a more fluid American social, economic, and cultural environment. In the late 1940s and early 1950s, many Irish and other American Catholics, including bishops and priests, especially Francis Cardinal Spellman of New York, displayed a continuing defensiveness in their support of Senator Joseph McCarthy's search for phantom security risks in the government. McCarthy did not discover communist traitors but he did cruelly destroy the reputations of some decent Americans. McCarthyism and earlier Coughlinism expressed an inferiority complex as well as fanatic patriotism; a hatred of the Anglo-Protestant, Ivy-League establishment represented by such people as Alger Hiss, who, unlike Irish Catholics, were not true-blue Americans.[5] The Irish Catholic obsession with communism was a key factor in America's Vietnam involvement, a venture that did much to undermine citizen confidence in the integrity of government.

Although there was much to criticize and lament in the early post–World War II phase of the Irish Catholic journey in America, observers failed to realize that under the surface things were changing. In 1960, economic and social mobility and higher education set the stage for a major Irish-American

Catholic breakthrough represented by the election and presidency of John Fitzgerald Kennedy. He symbolized the Irish rise from the murky bogs of ward politics to the heights of national power.

Kennedy caught the presidential bug when he narrowly lost to Senator Estes Kefauver of Tennessee in an open race for the vice-presidential nomination at the 1956 Democratic convention. For the next four years he applied a considerable amount of his family fortune, political skills, charm, and physical appeal in constructing an effective campaign organization and enlisting public approval to win his party's 1960 presidential nomination at the Los Angeles convention. Previous to that event, Eleanor Roosevelt and other supporters of Adlai E. Stevenson, the failed Democratic candidate in 1952 and 1956, opposed Kennedy. Some questioned his liberalism, others said the time was not ripe for a Catholic presidential candidate. Many of them would rather have lost with the former governor of Illinois than have won with the junior senator from Massachusetts. Ex-President Harry S. Truman, a supporter of Missouri Senator Stuart Symington, doubted Kennedy's maturity for the presidential role. He also despised isolationist, conservative Joseph P. Kennedy, and described the issue as "the pop not the pope." Tough, pragmatic Irish Catholic politicians also had reservations about a Kennedy run for the White House. They feared it might trigger a revival of nativism, and with it the defensiveness and insecurity of their people. In the long run, they submitted to Richard J. Daley's insistence that now was the time for a Catholic president and that JFK was the man for the position, considering the strength of Kennedy forces demonstrated by his victories over Minnesota Senator Hubert H. Humphrey in neighboring Wisconsin and in rural, Protestant West Virginia.

After a first-ballot convention victory, Kennedy began a vigorous campaign, insisting that he was the Democratic not the Catholic candidate. Before an Assembly of Protestant clergy in

Houston, Texas, he proclaimed his commitment to the American constitutional system, its separation of church and state, and the equality of all citizens regardless of race, creed or nationality. He promised that he would never permit his private religious convictions to interfere with the obligations of his office.

While Kennedy maintained independence from Catholic pressure groups, he went all out for Catholic votes, concentrating his campaign in states where they could determine victory or defeat—New York, Pennsylvania, Illinois, New Jersey, Massachusetts, Connecticut, California, Michigan, Minnesota, Ohio, Wisconsin, and Maryland. He was successful in all but Wisconsin, Ohio, and California, his opponent Richard Nixon's home base. Altogether, Kennedy attracted somewhere between 61 (IBM computer calculations) and 78 (Gallup Poll) percent of the Catholic vote. According to John T. McGreevey's *Parish Boundaries: The Catholic Encounter with Race in the Twentieth-Century Urban North* (1996), p. 194, Catholics (only about 25 percent of the country's population) gave Kennedy almost half of the vote he gathered. It represented a significant reversal of their drift to Republican Dwight D. Eisenhower in 1956.

In overwhelming numbers, Jewish and African Americans joined Catholics in voting for Kennedy, restoring the effective Democratic urban coalition of the 1930s and 1940s. On the other hand, a substantial majority of Protestants cast ballots against him, often because he was a Catholic, but mostly because he was a Democrat and they were traditionally Republican. But since the Catholic-ethnic, African-American, Jewish alliance could not win a presidential election on its own, a significant number of white Protestants had to have voted for Kennedy. As his vice-presidential running mate, Senate majority leader Lyndon Johnson, a Texan, certainly harvested southern Protestant ballots for JFK. In fact, the Kennedy organization was disappointed with its share of the Catholic vote.

Obviously not all Catholics believed that one of their own in the White House served their best interests. Perhaps only 50 percent of German Catholics cast Kennedy ballots, damaging his Ohio and Wisconsin chances, and a number of middle-class Irish Catholics in the mid-Atlantic states, expressing class interests rather than political genes, voted Republican. A number of priests favored Nixon, thinking that he would be in a better position to promote government subsidies for parochial schools. But Kennedy publicly thanked nuns for their enthusiastic support. The election was uncomfortably close; Kennedy's much disputed victory margin was slightly over a hundred thousand. Apparently residues of nativism and unexpected Catholic Republican votes turned the contest into an early-morning cliff hanger.

Intellectually, religiously, or culturally Kennedy was not the most Irish or Catholic political leader of his time; but this secular, pragmatic, Harvard-educated Irish American was an appropriate first Catholic president of the United States. He was able to appeal to many Protestants still suspicious of the compatibility of Catholicism and Americanism.[6] American Catholics were proud of two Johns: John XXIII, the pope who attempted to revitalize their church and haul it into the twentieth century, and John F. Kennedy, the politician who symbolized their successful American journey. His exuberance and self-deprecating wit lifted the spirits of the nation. While the most important, Kennedy was not the only example of Irish political success. During his presidency, speaker of the House of Representatives John McCormack; Senate majority leader Mike Mansfield; and chair of the Democratic National Committee John Bailey were Irish Catholics, as was George Meany, president of the unified American Federation of Labor-Congress of Industrial Organizations.

Climates of opinion, religion, and politics have changed since the mid-1960s. Paul VI and John Paul II have negated much of the work of John XXIII, disillusioning many Catholics; time, events, and the pens of revisionist historians and journalists have dimmed the luster of the Kennedy years. In retrospect, his administration had more style than substance; his rhetoric promised more than it delivered. Kennedy's reckless, promiscuous life style endangered the prestige of the office he held. His words often encouraged a dangerous American chauvinism and arrogance in tense, Cold War situations. They were a factor in leading to a major American foreign policy and military blunder, Vietnam. But photographs of Kennedy in the homes of Black and ethnic Americans, the terrible sense of loss—especially among the young—following his 1963 assassination, and the large numbers still visiting his grave at Arlington indicate that Kennedy communicated confidence, enthusiasm, and optimism that no subsequent president has been quite able to match. Ronald Reagan's popularity reflected American greed and self-interest; Kennedy's expressed American compassion and idealism.

Kennedy's presidency was more significant for Irish and other Catholics than for Anglo-American Protestants. If he had lost his White House bid, they might have retreated into the bitterness and defensiveness that followed Al Smith's 1928 defeat. Many would have complained that they were doomed to be permanent outsiders. Such a group neurosis would have debilitated the intellectual and creative talents of the Catholic community, leaving the entire nation poorer. But Kennedy's victory and his ensuing popularity, not only in the United States but throughout the world, diminished Catholic insecurities, unleashing a flurry of endeavor, producing an abundant harvest of excellence. John Ford, the great film director, spoke for much of Catholic Irish America when he remarked to a friend following the 1960 election that for the first time he felt like a first-class American.[7]

Generated by the Kennedy presidency, Irish Catholics displayed confidence and energy in a variety of ways and in many aspects of American life. At Vatican II, 1962–1965, Irish-

American bishops made minor contributions to theological discussions, but they did influence the church's acceptance of liberal democracy, separation of church and state, the integrity of private conscience, and ecumenical dialogue with other Christians and with Jews.

Irish-Catholic politicians continued to be highly visible on the national stage. Senator Eugene McCarthy of Minnesota, who as a congressman had the courage to debate and denounce Senator Joseph McCarthy, in 1968 challenged Lyndon Johnson in Democratic primaries on the issue of Vietnam. The many votes he gathered in New Hampshire and his impending victory in Wisconsin factored in the president's decision not to seek another term. Senator Robert F. Kennedy also entered the primaries, and if he had not been assassinated in June 1968, after winning a narrow California victory over McCarthy, he probably would have gone on to win the nomination at the Chicago convention and a victory over Nixon in November. The youngest Kennedy brother, Edward, Massachusetts's senator, has been an effective leader of the Democratic left in Congress, but his messy, scandalous private life has ruined his presidential chances. Jerry Brown, two-term governor of California, has been a powerful voice in Democratic politics and a contestant in presidential primaries. During the conservative Reagan ascendancy, Thomas P. "Tip" O'Neill of Massachusetts, speaker of the House of Representatives, continued to articulate the message of a communal, caring liberalism. Thomas Foley, congressman from Washington State, was speaker of the House during the George Bush and first two years of the Bill Clinton presidencies until he and his party suffered defeat in the 1994 congressional elections. While Foley was speaker, Senator George Mitchell of Maine was Senate majority leader. He retired in 1994.

In the post-Kennedy years, Irish Catholic talent has found routes to power and influence outside politics and religion. Monsignor Ellis's 1950s' complaint that American Catholicism had failed intellectually is certainly not valid today. In terms of curricula and faculty, Catholic colleges and universities have become more intellectually pluralistic. Thomists have become a scarcity on campuses. Some colleges and universities such as Georgetown, Notre Dame, Boston College, Holy Cross, and Santa Clara compete with the most respected private and state institutions in the United States. And Irish Catholics are prominent on faculties and in student bodies of the best non-Catholic universities in the country. Irish and other Catholics have established positive reputations as scholars in the humanities, sciences, and social sciences. And in literature, Irish Catholics can proudly point to the significance of William Kennedy, Thomas Flanagan, Peter Quinn, Elizabeth Cullinan, Maureen Howard, Valerie Sayers, John Gregory Dunne, Ellen Currie, James Carroll, Anna Quindlen, Pete Hamill, Jimmy Breslin, Alice McDermott, Frank McCourt, Thomas Fleming, and Mary Gordon among others.[8]

As their presence in city, state, and federal government has somewhat diminished, Irish Catholics increasingly have employed their considerable political talent in the boardrooms of major businesses and industries that for a long time excluded them. Their names are featured among the executive officers of some of the leading corporations in the United States.

Although present day Irish Catholics are prominent among executives, coaches, and managers of teams, they are not as numerous among participants in the ring or on the playing fields or indoor courts. Since James J. Braddock lost the heavyweight championship to Joe Louis in Chicago's Comiskey Park in June 1937, and Billy Conn narrowly failed to win it back four years later, few Irish Catholics have been boxing standouts. And Notre Dame's "Fighting Irish" are more likely to be Polish, Italian, or African American. Young Irish students enter college with ambitions to be business executives, lawyers, doctors, professors, even poets or novelists, rather than athletes. Probably the most famous Irish American in the recent sports hierarchy has been John McEnroe, the tennis champion, performing in a game traditionally associated with middle-class Anglo America.

In contrast to a time when Irish Catholics were deservedly labeled as racial bigots and obsessive anti-communist proponents of the Cold War, since the 1960s, nuns, priests, and laymen have been prominent in civil-rights movements and marches and in anti-war protests, frequently going to jail for their convictions. Supporting Rome, the American hierarchy has been conservative on theological, gender, and sexual matters, but exceptionally liberal in speaking out on economic, social, racial, and peace issues. Catholic primary and secondary schools, with a large number of Irish lay and religious teachers and administrators, have been quality educational alternatives for African-American (often non-Catholic) and other minorities attempting to escape from the crime, administrative and teaching ineptitude, and disorder existing in many urban public schools.

In a number of articles and books, sociologist Father Andrew Greeley has provided evidence to support his thesis that of all groups Irish Catholics lag only behind Jews in education, family income, and liberal attitudes on such issues as civil rights, religious and racial tolerance, social reform, and peace. Harris and Gallup polls endorse Greeley's findings.[9]

Not all Irish-American Catholics have experienced significant economic, social, or residential mobility. Many who remain in the urban working class have expressed insecurities and resentments in opposing racial integration in housing and education, often with the support of local politicians. Mid-1970s television news showed Charleston and South Boston, Massachusetts, Irish Catholics verbally and physically assaulting frightened African-American students bussed into their neighborhoods from Roxbury and the South End. Cameras focused on Irish Catholic, rosary-praying women beseeching the Blessed Virgin to save their schools from Black intrusion.

Protests in Boston, Chicago, Queens and other places against

neighborhood or school integration has indicated strife within
Catholic Irish America as much as it has antagonism between
Irish and African Americans; a division between the well-
educated, affluent middle class living in up-scale urban neighborhoods or posh suburbs, and those left behind in working-
class areas of the city. The latter have despised reformers and
social engineers who they believe favor Black over White ethnic
interests. They also have been contemptuous of Blacks who demand and get from government what they thought the Irish
have had to earn. But they have reserved a special hatred for
Holy Cross- and Harvard-educated, Newton-dwelling, Federal
Judge W. Arthur Garrity, who ordered integrated schools and
bussing to achieve them, and Mayor Kevin White, Congressman
Thomas P. O'Neill, and Senator Edward Kennedy who supported the court order, as Irishmen who betrayed their own kind.

Class and psychological fissures in Irish Catholic America
were also evident in responses to the crisis in Northern Ireland.
After the British Parliament partitioned Ireland in the 1920
Better Government of Ireland Bill, the Stormont Parliament
turned the northern Six Counties into "a Protestant nation for
a Protestant people." Gerrymandered electoral districts, a
house-occupancy franchise, and extra votes for business prop-
erties denied the one-third Catholic minority a proportionate
share of power in local government even in counties (Fermanagh and Tyrone) and cities (Derry and Newry) where they
were a majority. Protestants also discriminated against Catholics in government and private employment, and access to government financed housing. In response, Catholics psychologically and culturally rejected inclusion in a British Northern
Ireland, remaining loyal to the Irish nation represented by the
Free State and then the Irish Republic. Some unleashed frustrations as members of the outlawed Irish Republican Army,
participating in terrorist attacks on symbols of British authority in the Six Counties and in subversive activities in Britain
during World War II.

By the 1960s many northern Catholics, especially those who had taken advantage of the 1947 British Education Act to earn university degrees only to find their religion a barrier to success, dismissed promises of southern politicians to end partition, and rejected IRA terrorism as a means to remedy their grievances. In an effort to obtain a fair share of the British welfare state, in 1967 they organized the Northern Ireland Civil Rights Association in imitation of African-American tactics in the United States. During 1968, singing "We Shall Overcome," large numbers of Catholics, joined by Catholic and Protestant students from Queen's University, marched for equality and social justice.

Marches and demonstrations confused Northern Ireland officials and members of the Royal Ulster Constabulary. They preferred to deal with the IRA, whose terrorism provided a rationale for the Special Powers Act that permitted the jailing of suspected republican nationalists without trials, and the use of a gestapo-like B-Special police auxiliary to intimidate the Catholic minority. Despite constitutional protests by the Northern Ireland Civil Rights Association, constables either clubbed demonstrators or joined politicians in looking the other way when Protestant mobs assaulted marchers and threatened to invade Catholic residential areas. Peaceful protest failures, the refusal of the Northern Ireland government to take steps to protect Catholic civil liberties, and Protestant brutality revived the then moribund IRA as a Catholic defense force.[10] This meant that nationalism rather than civil rights became the vital issue in the Ulster crisis.

Suppression of civil-rights demonstrations and violent confrontations between Catholics and Protestants, covered by television crews from all over the world, made public the authoritarian, unjust, and oppressive nature of Northern Ireland. When the nasty Ulster skeleton in the British closet was revealed, Westminster politicians pressured Stormont to make civil-rights concessions. Limited by ties with the ultra-Protestant Orange Order, Northern Ireland leaders responded too slowly to prevent the Six Counties from proceeding toward civil war. In August 1969, confronting the probability of a sectarian massacre, Britain dispatched troops to Northern Ireland. Initially, Catholics welcomed the soldiers as protectors. But since the army was in northeast Ulster to preserve law and order as well as to prevent sectarian strife, it supported the existing Protestant Unionist government, disarming Catholics and interning suspected IRA members and sympathizers.

Finally, in March 1972, Britain suspended the Stormont Parliament, ruled the Six Counties from Westminster, and initiated changes that did improve the civil-rights and social-justice climates. But Protestant hostility to Catholic equality, power sharing, and the prospect of a United Ireland; and, on the other hand, Catholic suspicions concerning British integrity, and the continued terrorism of the IRA, the Irish National Liberation Army, and a number of Protestant paramilitary organizations all combined to perpetuate violence that by 1997 has taken over 3,100 lives of soldiers, civilians, and paramilitaries, and wounded and permanently maimed many more.

Representatives of the Irish and British governments met at Sunningdale in England (1973), and at Hillsborough in Northern Ireland (1985), and agreed that the fate of Northern Ireland depended on the will of a majority of its inhabitants. At the latter conference, Britain accepted a consulting role for the Irish Republic in the affairs of the Six Counties. In December, 1993, the prime ministers of Britain and Ireland, John Major and Albert Reynolds, appealed for a truce and negotiations between all parties involved in the Ulster conflict. In their joint declaration, they repeated that Northern Ireland's majority would decide its Irish or British future. Major said that his government had no intention to prevent a United Ireland against the wishes of a Six-County majority; Reynolds promised that his would never force such a result. Finally, at the close of 1994, Sinn Féin (the political wing of the Republican movement) and

Protestant Unionist paramilitaries agreed to a truce as a preliminary to negotiations between them and Irish and British leaders. Unfortunately, the IRA broke the ceasefire in February, 1996.

When Irish-American Catholics first witnessed on television and read about the oppression of their people in Northern Ireland, they naturally responded in anger and frustration. Assuming that the IRA were noble freedom fighters, they generously contributed to its front organizations, particularly the Northern Ireland Aid Committee. NORAID has claimed that it supports the families of imprisoned Republicans in Northern Ireland, but the American, British, and Irish governments insist that it supplies instruments of violence to the IRA.

In time, reflecting their antipathy toward terrorism and following the advice of such politicians as New York's Governor Hugh Carey, Speaker Tip O'Neill, and Senators Kennedy and Moynihan, middle-class, Irish-American Catholics, while continuing to sympathize with the desire of Northern Ireland nationalists for civil rights and a United Ireland, dropped support for the IRA and strongly backed efforts to negotiate Catholic and nationalist claims in the Six Counties. But a fanatic minority of Irish Americans have continued to collect money for and supply arms to the IRA. For the most part, they represent immigrants and their families who left an impoverished Ireland of the 1950s, embittered that it had not provided them with employment or a decent standard of living, and have not quite assimilated into suburban middle-class, Irish Catholic America. IRA supporters also include working-class Irish left behind in urban ghettoes of place and mind. Both groups, insecure in their American situation, have endorsed and supported revolutionary nationalism in Ireland as an identity statement in the United States.

Most contemporary Irish-American friends of the IRA do not understand the complexities of the situation in Northern Ireland or its connection with problems in other parts of the globe, including the United States. Their provincial nationalism lacks humanitarian idealism. Many are conservative, even reactionary, in terms of the American economic, social, and political spectrum. Despite their empathy for the rights of the large Catholic minority in Northern Ireland, they have been fighting school and housing integration in urban America. Irish-American IRA apologists ignore its stated socialist goals and the fact that it has had ties with terrorist groups, often anti-American, in other places.

Although British politicians have probably over-rated the interests of Irish-American Catholics in Northern Ireland, their political pressures did promote progress toward a settlement of the lasting Ulster dimension of the centuries-old Irish Question. Responding to the requests of Irish-American politicians in Congress, Presidents Jimmy Carter, Ronald Reagan, and Bill Clinton have encouraged London to negotiate with Dublin and all parties in the Six Counties. And they have offered American financial investment to encourage the various factions to reach a settlement. Clinton's intervention was particularly effective in leading to the 1994 truce and promise of negotiations. His late 1995 receptions in Belfast, Derry, and Dublin demonstrated the affection of all the people in Ireland for the United States, and their confidence in American leadership.

The Irish Catholic journey in America from urban working-class, inner-city ghettoes to suburban middle-class, melting-pot neighborhoods has been long and arduous and, at the end, rewarding. Nineteenth-century St. Patrick's Day parades were Irish Catholic defiance demonstrations; now almost everyone is Irish on March 17. Once described as an alien, unassimilable menace, Irish Catholics have become America's favorite ethnics. The Paddy and Biddy stereotypes of American fiction and theatre have disappeared. On current television screens and in the advertising sections of newspapers and periodicals, handsome men and beautiful women and children wearing Irish knit sweaters and with such names as Kevin, Brian, Sean, Sheila, Deirdre, Erin, and Patricia peddle cars, beer, soap, toothpaste, and toys. In the last national census some forty million people, most non-Catholic, admitted to an Irish heritage. At times when nativism flourished, Americans with Protestant and Nonconformist backgrounds in Ireland denied associations with Irish Catholics. Those from Ulster insisted on a Scots-Irish identity. But since the Irish have become more than acceptable and respectable, it is now considered a compliment to be numbered among them.

In the passage from reviled to popular, the religious and political features of Irish Catholic America have been altered. As previously mentioned, a number of Irish Catholics changed parties to vote for Republican Dwight D. Eisenhower in the 1956 presidential election. Because of Kennedy, many returned to the Democratic fold in 1960 and remained to support Johnson in 1964 and Humphrey in 1968. But since 1972 there has been a large swing to the Republicans in state and national elections. Although they belong to an essentially Anglo-Protestant party that has shied away from putting Catholics in leadership positions, Republicans have recruited quite a few Irish Catholics as candidates in congressional, state, and local elections. In 1960 probably 70 percent of Catholics voted for Kennedy; at present, according to a Greenberg Research Inc. survey of registered voters, only 27 percent consider themselves Democrats while 24 percent claim to be independents and 22 percent accept the Republican label.[11]

Why are Irish Catholics voting and contesting elections as Republicans? Some are expressing middle-class incomes and values, abandoning communal liberalism for the politics of self-interest. Others, middle and working class, are hostile to the post-1972 Democratic social agenda that seems to cater to homosexual, feminist, and pro-abortion pressure lobbies. Racial tensions and safety fears also explain Irish Catholic Republican ballots. Like many other Whites, a number of Irish Catholics, who once were victims of discrimination, believe that affirmative action programs give Blacks an unfair advantage in hirings and promotions. At a time when crime and violence have become critical issues in cities, many Americans, including Irish Catholics, believe that civil-libertarian Democrats have been more concerned with the rights of criminals than their victims. Irish and other ethnic Catholic defectors from the Democratic party often insist that it left them rather than they left it.

Responses to Catholicism have been more significant in a changing Irish America than shifts in political allegiance. Religion was the essential ingredient in the identity of Irish Catholics. Unlike most other Catholic nationalities, they have not distinguished between their national, religious, even cultural heritages. With the exception of the northern Six Counties, associations between Irish and Catholic have been more crucial in the United States than in Ireland. In addition to Anglo-Saxon and Anglo-Irish Protestant persecution in Ireland, Anglo-American nativism reinforced Catholic loyalties among Irish Americans. Their religion bridged Old- and New-World experiences, consolidating the community, assuaging Irish misery, and disciplining the Irish character. Irish Catholics diligently practiced their religion not only as a sign of faith but also as a symbol of their ethnicity.

In middle-class suburbs and upscale parts of cities, the country club has replaced the parish as the hub of Irish Catholic life. During the Kennedy years, religious loyalties and practices dominated Irish lives. Catholic schools from primary through university levels were flourishing; seminaries and convents were bulging with young men and women determined on serving the church in religious, social, and educational ways; masses were packed on Sundays with worshippers and communicants; and large numbers attended daily. Thirty years later, parishes and schools are closing, there is a massive shortage of nuns and priests, church pews are sparsely filled, and numbers receiving the sacraments have dwindled.

Observers have offered a variety of reasons to explain declining commitments to Catholicism by the Irish and others. Some emphasize that the liturgical changes initiated by Vatican II have offended many in the pews by destroying continuities with the past, depriving Catholicism of the history and mystery that made it both aesthetically and psychologically satisfying. It does seem strange that when millions of people are purchasing Gregorian chant CDs and tapes, new-style, boring, unsingable hymns offend the ears of Catholics attending Mass. Both conservatives and liberals complain of trashy music and boring sermons. The former wanted nothing in the church to change, the latter wished that it had maintained a traditional liturgy and modernized its theology. Most American Catholics, including many in the clergy, took issue with Pope Paul VI's 1968 encyclical *Humanae Vitae*, a reaffirmation of the church's opposition to contraception. This initial challenge to papal authority expanded to include such issues as clerical celibacy, an all-male priesthood, and divorce. Most Catholics share a general American uneasiness with the large number of medically-terminated pregnancies. But while opposed to abortion on demand, they share a general American consensus that it should not be criminalized. And they believe that in some circumstances—rape, incest, and the psychological and physical health of mothers—abortion is an acceptable alternative to unwanted births.

Sexual scandals, especially those involving pedophile priests and the insensitive and irresponsible ways that the hierarchy has dealt with them, have severely damaged confidence in the church and its clergy. The Irish and other American Catholics respect the Holy Father, but 79 percent of them follow the guidance of their private consciences rather than the dictates of Rome. And 80 percent believe that they can disobey the pope and remain good Catholics. In effect, like the British monarch, he reigns but does not rule.[12]

John Paul II, supported by a conservative Catholic minority, attributes cafeteria, pick-and-choose Catholicism to the spirit of American materialism that has corrupted rather than liberated consciences. Americanism has influenced the mind of Catholics, particularly the Irish, but in more subtle ways than the pope suggests. For almost two centuries, Irish Catholics in Ireland and in America have had contradictory loyalties to an authoritarian church and a liberal, democratic political system. They could not forsake a religion that offered them consolation and psychological security in depressing times and situations and was symbolic of their cultural identity; and they could not turn their backs on political values essential to their nationalism, which in America provided them with opportunities to prosper. Once secure in their Americanism, Irish Catholics could psychologically afford to take a more critical look at the church, and to insist that it permit them the same freedom of thought and expression as their government.

In many instances the cultural and social as well as the political Americanization of the Irish has lessened the intensity of their Catholicism. Since there have been strong connections between ethnic and religious Irish identities, the retreat of one often leads to the decline of the other. As a consequence it has become more difficult to define Catholic Irish America religiously or politically. For many the journey from the ghetto to the suburb has been, from a cultural identity perspective, a trip from someplace to noplace.

Many intelligent and sophisticated Irish-American Catholics hold that the retreat of ethnicity and assimilation into the greater American community has been desirable, the closing chapter of a great success story with a promise that other minorities can also make it in the United States. They consider ethnicity emphases culturally, socially, politically, and religiously divisive and insist that their coreligionists should abandon Old-World allegiances and think of themselves as American Catholics.

Without a doubt, parish-centered, urban-ethnic neighborhoods have been over-sentimentalized. As resistance to school integration and open housing has indicated, they often have been reservoirs of bitter memories, frustrated dreams, strangled expectations, and frozen economic mobility that frequently erupt in paranoia and hate. Ethnicity, however, can and does have positive features. It provides sociological and psychological comfort and identity that come from shared experiences, values, and religious faith. These are important when individuals can easily lose a sense of self-worth in an urban, industrial, automated, mass production, and consumption society. And the energy and creativity of the United States owes much to its pluralism. America's genius as well as its dynamism is a product of its ethnic, racial, and religious mosaic. Although a considerable degree of consensus, especially in regard to the liberal democratic political system, is essential to the nation's health, the strength and the vitality of both the United States and the Catholic Church have derived from the tensions between unity and diversity. Vanishing ethnic and racial identities could result in anti-creative conformity rather than productive consensus.

Although active, self-conscious ethnicity among Irish Catholics has diminished in quantity, there are signs that it has persisted and increased in quality. They still vote Democratic more frequently than Protestants, suggesting that for many communal rather than individual liberalism still informs their political and social ethic. According to the Washington Post–ABC exit poll, more of them supported Michael Dukakis than George Bush in 1988. Clinton in two presidential elections proved more popular among Catholics than Bush or Bob Dole. A September, 1995 Time/CNN poll records that while American Catholics are not exactly ecstatic about their religion, 85 percent are comfortable with it and say that it plays an important role in their lives.[13]

Many Irish Americans, some disappointed with Catholicism

and some not, have decided to define their Irishness in cultural rather than religious terms. They know more about Ireland, its history, literature, and geography, than previous generations, even immigrant parents or grandparents. Quite a few are involved in genealogical research tracing family backgrounds. Musicians and singers entertaining enthusiastic audiences indicate that there is far more interest in Irish traditional music in urban America than in Ireland, where the popular music fads seems to be rock and country western.

More significant than genealogical and musical interests are the hordes of students enrolling in college and university Irish history and literature courses, and then pursuing their intellectual interests in graduate school. University and commercial presses find large numbers of purchasers and readers for books on Irish subjects. The American Conference of Irish Studies, with about 1,500 members, is one of the most successful interdisciplinary scholarly organizations in the country. Its annual meetings on American college and university campuses and at University College, Dublin; University College, Galway; and Queen's University, Belfast, have attracted hundreds of participants.

While interests in things Irish seem to be flourishing, appearances can be a bit deceiving. It will be difficult sustaining Irishness without the Catholic dimension and in suburban melting pots, and in frequent situations where Irish-American Catholics marry outside their ethnic and religious community. The health of academic Irish studies is more fragile than it looks. Many of the Anglo-Irish literature scholars now emphasize theoretical issues such as modernism and post-modernism, structuralism and post-structuralism in language incomprehensible to non-specialists. They have deemphasized the contents of Irish poetry and prose and separated them from historical contexts. For different reasons, the future of Irish history is even bleaker than that of Irish literature. Only three prominent American institutions of higher learning have designated Irish history positions—Notre Dame, Boston College, and Fordham. Considering the importance of the Irish in the development of American Catholicism, it is only natural that these institutions would feature Irish studies. But Irish history and literature have had major Protestant dimensions and are too relevant and significant in both American and European contexts to be confined to Catholic campuses. Eminent historians in a number of Catholic and non-Catholic academic settings offer undergraduate and/or graduate courses in Irish history, but their departments appointed them as British historians. When they retire, their replacements most likely will not be trained or interested in Irish history.

If Irish Americans find it essential to preserve their ethnic heritage, they must act quickly to guarantee the presence of Irish history and literature in the curricula of Catholic and non-Catholic colleges and universities, particularly in metropolitan areas where their people are concentrated. Irish-American Catholics cannot retain their identity unless they know who they are and where they came from. To do this they must understand the Irish and Irish-American experiences through the media of history and literature.

If Irishness in the United States is to survive as something more than St. Patrick's Day parties and parades, Irish-American leaders must take steps to increase the number of college and university Irish studies programs and to support those already existing. Wealthy Irish-American Catholics have contributed considerable amounts of money to business, law, and medical schools; now it is time for them to pay attention to the humanities, particularly those aspects dealing with their own people. What is needed is an investment of funds and concerns that would help guarantee the future of Irish studies, provide students with opportunities to study and research Irish and Irish-American history and literature, and indicate that Irish-American Catholics are indeed proud of their past and have confidence in their future.

Endnotes

Notes to Introduction

1. American Jews are one obvious exception to this statement. Although they share some experiences and grievances with the Irish—their literary expressions, for example, are often similar—a number of Jews arrived in the United States with urban backgrounds and with a rich, cultural tradition. On the other hand, Irish peasants in their technological and cultural impoverishment were more typical of European Catholic immigrant groups and of Blacks and Hispanics who later entered American cities.

2. Kerby Miller and Paul Wagner, *Out of Ireland* (Washington, D.C., 1994), p. 125.

3. Malcolm Campbell, "The Other Immigrants: Comparing the Irish in Australia and the United States," *Journal of Ethnic History* 14 (Spring 1995), pp. 3–22.

4. For other Akenson treatments of this subject see *Being Had: Historians, Evidence and the Irish in North America* (Toronto, 1995); *Small Differences: Irish Catholics and Irish Protestants, 1815–1922* (Kingston and Montreal, 1988); and "Data: What is Known about the Irish in North America," in *The Untold Story: The Irish in Canada,* ed. Robert O'Driscoll and Lorna Reynolds (Toronto, 1988), vol. 1, pp. 15–25. Akenson also challenges the commonly held assumption that Irish America was essentially rural, but he misinterpreted 1870 census statistics and falsely assumed if the Irish were not in the largest cities in America they must have been on farms. Although I have no quarrel with the various polls

and studies that indicate that most people now identifying themselves as Irish in the United States are not Catholic, I am unable to fathom that, even though several hundreds of thousands of Irish Protestants and Nonconformists had a multi-generational head start over Irish Catholics in America, they managed to produce more descendents than the four million Irish Catholics who arrived from 1820 to 1920, especially considering the large families of the latter. Although Akenson says no, many Catholics must have abandoned their religion.

5. When Daniel O'Connell, a political foe of Wellington, heard this statement, he countered that such a creature could be an ass.

6. *The Irish Times*, December 7, 1993.

Notes to Chapter 1

1. Irish poets and playwrights have depicted the coming of the English as the fruits of adultery, jealousy, and vengeance. In William Butler Yeats's "Dreaming of the Bones" in *Four Plays for Dancers* (London, 1921), the poet-dramatist relates how MacMurrough seduced Dervorguilla, wife of O'Rourke, king of Brefni, and how the husband gained revenge by aiding Rory O'Connor, high king of Ireland, in crushing the king of Leinster in an Irish civil war. Although MacMurrough did seduce O'Rourke's wife and the king of Brefni was a decisive factor in MacMurrough's 1166 defeat, his motives for opposing the king of Leinster were probably more associated with the politics of Irish clan society than pique against the man who cuckolded him.

2. Gaelic or Celtic Ireland as used here refers to culture not race. Like other Europeans, the Irish are a mixed breed. Celtic invaders in the Bronze Age determined the popular language and institutions, but pre-Celts remained to influence the cultural trappings of the Irish heritage. Christian influences plus Viking, Anglo-Norman, Tudor, Scots-Irish, Cromwellian, and Williamite invaders and settlers then added their contributions to what emerged as Irish culture.

3. According to Poyning's Law, originally passed in 1494 and subsequently modified, the Irish Parliament could not pass legislation without English government approval. In 1720 the British Parliament's Declaratory Act asserted its right to legislate for Ireland. During the eighteenth century, Britain employed the Declaratory Act to force the Irish economy to adhere to British mercantilism.

Notes to Chapter 2

1. Daniel O'Connell to Archbishop John MacHale, July 25, 1840, in W. J. Fitzpatrick, ed., *The Correspondence of Daniel O'Connell*, 2 vols. (London, 1888), p. 246.

2. Many Young Irelanders demonstrated their abilities in exile. Duffy remained in Ireland until the mid-1850s, editing the *Nation* and hoping to create an independent Irish parliamentary party devoted to the tenant's rights issue.

Frustrated by conservative Catholic clerical influences in Irish nationalist politics, he finally left for Australia, where he became prime minister of Victoria. Later, Duffy returned to Ireland and wrote histories of Young Ireland, the Independent Irish party, memoirs of his career, and a biography of Thomas Davis. John Blake Dillon returned from an American exile and became a prominent parliamentary nationalist in the 1860s. His son, John, a Parnell lieutenant, became chair of the anti-Parnellite wing of the Irish Home Rule party. John's brother James edited the *New World*, the archdiocesan newspaper in Chicago and cofounded Loyola University's law school. Thomas D'Arcy McGee was a journalist in the United States before migrating to Canada and settling in Montreal, where he became a founding father of and a cabinet minister in the Dominion of Canada. Fenian sympathizers assassinated McGee in 1868 because he denounced revolutionary republicanism. Thomas Francis Meagher, who led Young Irelanders out of Conciliation Hall, served as a general in the Union army during the American Civil War. He drowned in the Missouri river on his way to become territorial governor of Montana. John Mitchel escaped from Australian exile to the United States, where he functioned as a journalist denouncing abolitionism and defending slavery and the Confederacy during the Civil War. In the 1870s Tipperary nationalists twice voted him their MP (his first victory coming before he left the United States for Ireland), but Parliament refused to seat a convicted felon. Mitchel's brother-in-law, John Martin, was an early leader of the Home Rule movement and a member of the Irish parliamentary party in the 1870s. Thomas O'Hagan became lord chancellor of Ireland. Michael Doheny, James Stephens, and John O'Mahoney created the Irish Republican and Fenian Brotherhoods. Richard O'Gorman became a successful New York lawyer and superior court judge. His early career was tainted by ties with the corrupt Tweed ring in Tammany Hall.

3. Thomas N. Brown, "Nationalism and the Irish Peasant," *Review of Politics* 15 (October 1953), p. 445.

4. Quakers were particularly generous in their relief efforts, but not all Protestant groups were as charitable. A small number demanded that Catholics become Protestants to earn a bowl of soup. Irish Catholics still use the word "souper" to describe someone who betrays convictions or renounces ethnic and religious identity for personal advancement. It rivals "informer" and "land grabber" in the galaxy of Irish insults.

5. The British government's Famine policy would fit the category of ideological murder defined in Albert Camus's *The Rebel* (New York, 1957).

Notes to Chapter 3

1. E. Estyn Evans, *The Personality of Ireland* (Cambridge, 1973), p. 82.

2. Donald Harman Akenson, in the works cited in footnote 4 of the "Introduction," points to the Irish in rural Canada as evidence that they were competent farmers. But the reality of a poor record of agricultural production,

even after the end of landlordism, and the sloppy, badly managed farms that travelers view in Ireland make clear that Irish Catholics are not very good at farming. People that I know in rural Wisconsin who are not Irish have told me that the Irish were warm, congenial neighbors but pitiful farmers.

3. For a discussion of Bishop John Timon's effort to settle Irish immigrants in rural and small town places, see Leonard R. Riforgiato, "Bishop John Timon, Archbishop John Hughes, and Irish Colonization: A Clash of Episcopal Views on the Future of the Irish and the Catholic Church in America," in William Pencak, Selma Berrol and Randall M. Miller, eds., *Immigration to New York* (Cranbury, N.J., 1991), pp. 7–26. Archbishop Ireland's rural settlement project in Minnesota is the topic of James Shannon, *Catholic Colonization on the Frontier* (New York, 1976).

4. Compared to other European immigrants in the 1840s, 1850s, and 1860s, the Irish were a wretched lot. But according to Philip Taylor, *The Distant Magnet* (New York, 1971), pp. 35–36, they were on a higher economic and social level than those who remained in Ireland. Emigration still involved costs high enough to prevent many from finding an American refuge. In "Inland Urban Immigrants: The Detroit Irish, 1850," *Michigan History* 57 (1974), pp. 121–139, Jo Ellen McNergney Vinyard explains that the pre-Famine Detroit Irish, "the largest minority group in the city," experienced significant social mobility: "Among the pre-famine immigrants, forty percent worked as laborers, whereas seventy-nine percent of those who had come after 1846 were in that category" (p. 125). Vinyard expands her examination of the upwardly mobile Irish on the urban frontier in Detroit and Midwest cities in *The Irish on the Urban Frontier: Detroit, 1850–1880* (New York, 1976). In *To the Golden Door* (Westport, Conn., 1974), George W. Potter also emphasized pre-Famine Irish Catholic business and professional successes.

5. Dennis P. Ryan, *Beyond the Ballot Box* (Rutherford, N.J., 1983), p. 23; and Oscar Handlin, *Boston's Immigrants*, paperback (New York, 1968), p. 257.

6. In *The Orange Riots: Irish Political Violence in New York City, 1870 and 1871* (Ithaca, 1993), Michael A. Gordon, influenced by Kerby Miller's vision of Irish Catholics, interprets them as pre-modern, pre-industrial people, confused and overwhelmed in urban industrial America. They viewed American republicanism from collectivist and egalitarian perspectives. Anglo and other Protestant Americans saw it in individualistic, competitive terms. Orange parades not only reminded New York's Irish Catholics of Anglo-Irish Protestant and Ulster Presbyterian oppression in Ireland; they also interpreted them as visible signs of the American Protestant elite's intention to deprive them of a cultural and political role in the city. According to Gordon, in defending the rights of Orangemen to march on July 12, Anglo Americans expressed contempt for Irish Catholics as an inferior species and their religion as alien and subversive. And they associated Irish "barbarism" with Tammany Hall political corruption.

7. Traditional ballad, source unknown.

8. Will and George Millar, *Lament for the Molly Maguires*, Calgary, Alberta, Canada, Antrim Music Ltd., 1971.

9. Traditional ballad, source unknown.

10. Since the 1950s American Catholic intellectuals, demanding reform and relevance in their church, have attacked the Irish as the source of most of its troubles. They have insisted that the Irish have inflicted authoritarianism, puritanism, conservatism, and anti-intellectualism on American Catholicism. In a number of articles and in *The Rise of the Unmeltable Ethnics* (New York, 1973), the once-liberal Catholic intellectual, Michael Novak, an ethnic studies scholar, describes "chill and bleak and death-centered" Irish Catholicism as a "Celtic heresy," an aberration of true Catholicism. He claims that while the Irish were originally "pagans like the Slavs, the Italians, the Greeks, they have allowed their church to make Christianity an agent of order and cleanliness rather than an agent of mystery, ghostliness, fear, terror, and passion, which at best it was." In "The Devotional Revolution in Ireland, 1850–1875," *American Historical Review* 72 (June 1972), pp. 625–52, Emmet Larkin first presented evidence to show that the pietism and authoritarianism, so identified with Irish Catholicism, are really Roman features that Paul Cardinal Cullen brought with him to Ireland. Desmond Fennell, ed., *The Changing Face of Catholic Ireland* (London, 1968), argues that certain things frequently designated as Irish Catholic—authoritarianism, clericalism, puritanism, anti-intellectualism—are not uniquely Irish but post-Council of Trent Romanism mixed with British Protestant Evangelicalism.

11. Stephan Thernstrom, *Poverty and Progress* (Cambridge, Mass., 1964), pp. 179–80.

12. Ibid., pp. 184–85.

13. Throughout this book there is an emphasis on the relationship between Irish-American success and failure and American regionalism. When I was a graduate student at the University of Iowa, Professor James E. Roohan first suggested to me the importance of social and economic diversity among the American Irish and the effect of moving west on that diversity.

14. In *Irish-Americans, Native Rights and National Empires: The Structure, Divisions, and Attitudes of the Catholic Minority in the Decade of Expansion, 1890–1901* (New York, 1976), p. 67, David Noel Doyle offers the following class breakdowns: Upper middle class: native white, 7.4 percent; German American, 5.8 percent; Irish American, 5.7 percent. Lower middle class: native white, 10.5 percent; German American 14.2 percent; Irish American, 14.4 percent. Doyle's class categories are not traditional, but reflect those of today's newspapers and politicians. He classifies people more by income than by vocation, placing skilled laborers in the lower middle class.

Notes to Chapter 4

1. Guy Fawkes, leader of a Catholic conspiracy in England, on November 5, 1605 attempted to annihilate the British Parliament and kill James I with a gunpowder explosion. Authorities uncovered the plot, arrested, and executed Fawkes. Since that time, the British have celebrated November 5, as Guy Fawkes Day, burning him and sometimes the pope in effigy. At present the occasion is more of fun than of malice.

2. The most bitter part of the Americanization quarrel in European Catholicism resulted from the publication of a French translation of Walter Elliott's biography of Isaac Hecker. Abbé Felix Klein, a French, liberal, Catholic cleric, wrote the introduction and in it distorted the positions of Hecker and American progressive Catholics to score debating points against conservative Catholics in his own country. In condemning the "American heresy," Leo XIII cited the French translation of Hecker's life as evidence justifying his decision.

3. William H. A. Williams, "From Lost Land to Emerald Isle: Ireland and the Irish in American Sheet Music, 1800–1920," *Eire-Ireland* 26 (Spring, 1991), p. 45.

4. There were Irish Americans such as Ignatius Donnelly of Minnesota, Patrick Ford of New York, and Denis Kearney of California who also preached populist prejudices. Ford's attacks on capitalism had anti-semitic ingredients, and Kearney led the fight to exclude Chinese labor from California. But on the whole, Irish politicians and labor union leaders were in the vanguard of those opposing restrictions on immigration. Along with many Americans, however, they feared cheap Chinese labor competition. In "Race and Ethnicity in Organized Labor: The Historical Sources for Resistance to Affirmative Action," in *Ethnicity and the Work Force*, ed. Winston A. Van Horne and Thomas V. Tonneson (Madison, Wis., 1985), pp. 1–64, Herbert Hill accuses Irish-Catholic and Jewish leaders of the American Federation of Labor of promoting the interests of White ethnics at the expense of African, Asian, and Hispanic Americans.

5. Both quotes are taken from L. P. Curtis, Jr., *Anglo-Saxons and Celts: A Study of anti-Irish Prejudice in Victorian England* (Bridgeport, Conn., 1968). Freeman is quoted on page 81, the Webbs on page 63. In addition to *Anglo-Saxons and Celts*, Curtis explores British anti-Irish racialism in *Apes and Angels: The Irishman in Victorian Caricature* (Washington, D.C., 1971). In an essay in his *Paddy and Mr. Punch: Connections in Irish and English History* (New York, 1963), R. F. Foster argues, not too convincingly, that Curtis exaggerates British anti-Irishness, stressing the malice but not the fun in *Punch* cartoons.

Notes to Chapter 5

1. John Paul Bocock, "The Irish Conquest of Our Cities," *Forum* 17 (April 1894), p. 195.

2. The Spring-Rice quote can be found in Alan J. Ward, *Ireland and Anglo-American Relations, 1899–1921* (London, 1969), p. 93.

3. Joseph Dinneen, *Ward Eight* (New York, N.Y., 1936); Edwin O'Connor, *The Last Hurrah* (Boston, Mass., 1956); Thomas J. Fleming, *All Good Men* (New York, N.Y., 1961); *King of the Hill* (New York, N.Y., 1965); *Rulers of the City* (New York, N.Y., 1977); Mary Deasy, *O'Shaughessy's Day* (New York, N.Y., 1957); John O'Hara, *Ten North Frederick* (New York, N.Y. 1955); Ramona Stewart, *Casey* (Boston, Mass., 1968). New York Tammany boss Richard Croker is the model for Casey.

4. Bocock, "Irish Conquest," p. 195.

5. Anthony Gronowicz, "Labor's Decline within New York's Democratic Party from 1844 to 1884," in *Immigration to New York*, ed. William Pencak, Selma Berrol, and Randall M. Miller (Philadelphia, Pa., 1991), p. 16.

6. Fleming, *All Good Men*, p. 30.

7. Daniel Patrick Moynihan, "The Irish," in Nathan Glazer and Daniel Patrick Moynihan, *Beyond the Melting Pot: The Negroes, Puerto Ricans, Jews, Italians, and Irish of New York City* (Cambridge, Mass., 1963), p. 229.

8. Joseph Huthmacher, "Urban Liberalism in the Age of Reform," *Mississippi Valley Historical Review* 49 (1962), pp. 231–41; John B. Buenker, *Urban Liberalism and Progressive Reform* (New York, N.Y., 1973); Robert Dahl, *Who Governs? Democracy and Power in American Cities* (New Haven, Conn., 1961); and Elmer E. Cornwell, "Bosses, Machines, and Ethnic Groups," *Annals* 353 (May 1964), pp. 27–39.

9. Dennis P. Ryan, *Beyond the Ballot Box: A Social History of the Boston Irish, 1845–1917* (East Brunswick, N.J., 1983), p. 106.

10. Thomas N. Brown, "The Irish in United States Politics," paper delivered to American Conference for Irish Studies annual meeting, Stonehill College, Easton, Massachusetts, April 1975.

11. Gronowicz, "Labor's Decline in New York City's Democratic Party from 1844 to 1884," p. 18.

12. Edward R. F. Sheehan, *The Governor* (New York, N.Y., 1970), pp. 196–97.

13. Ibid., p. 80.

14. O'Connor, *The Last Hurrah*, p. 67.

15. William V. Shannon, *The American Irish* (New York, N.Y., 1963), p. 231.

16. William M. Riordan, *Plunkitt of Tammany Hall* (New York, N.Y., 1963), pp. 91–93.

17. Jane Addams, "Why the Ward Boss Rules," *Outlook* 58 (1898), pp. 879–82; and Allen F. Davis, "Jane Addams and the Ward Boss," *Journal of the Illinois State Historical Society* 53 (1960), pp. 247–65.

18. To the Irish, "honest graft" refers to taking a little off the top in exchange for services rendered, a kind of fee. It assumes a just compensation for constructive and useful efforts. "Dishonest graft," on the other hand, means

appropriating large sums of public money without compensating the tax payer with services rendered. This distinction between "honest" and "dishonest" graft is so subjective that it becomes a matter of private conscience.

19. Terry Nichols Clark, "The Irish Ethic and the Spirit of Patronage," *Ethnicity* 2 (December 1975), pp. 305–59.

20. In "Urban Liberalism and the Age of Reform," J. Joseph Huthmacher argues that the poverty experience of Catholic ethnics, their religious values, and their welfare-oriented political machines made them the main force challenging *laissez-faire* liberalism. Huthmacher suggests that Anglo Protestant progressivism was much more concerned with conformity, making ethnics 100 percent American, rather than with significant social change. He pointed out that progressive nativism attacked parochial schools as divisive, imposed prohibition and other puritan panaceas as remedies for social disorder, and placed Anglo Saxons above lesser breeds. Naturally, Catholic ethnics responded negatively to such nativist, puritan reform rhetoric. Huthmacher shows how Catholic ethnic politicians in state legislatures sponsored and supported bills to improve the working conditions and social security of the working class. In *Urban Liberalism and Ethnic Reform,* John B. Buenker applies Huthmacher's thesis to urban machine politics in such cities as Providence, Cleveland, Chicago, New York, and Pittsburgh. In *Power and Society: Greater New York at the Turn of the Century* (New York, N.Y., 1982), David C. Hammack discusses the anti-Catholic conformity goals of New York's Anglo Protestant elite reformism. Ethnic Catholic communalism, in contrast with Anglo-American Protestant individualism, and the political, social, economic, and cultural implications of these two conflicting value systems is the main theme of Michael Novak's *The Rise of the Unmeltable Ethnics,* which concentrates on analyses of Italian and Slav attitudes. Although many Catholic bishops, priests, and journalists have advocated extremely conservative positions regarding private property and social change, such conservatism seems to be more eastern than nation-wide. In general, Catholic laymen in the United States, like those in Ireland, do not follow the dictates of bishops and priests on political, economic, or social issues unless the opinions of clerics coincide with theirs on the general interests of the total Catholic community. Irish-American workingmen took their social gospel from labor unionism, not from papal encyclicals.

21. In an article "Thanks to the Irish," *America* (May 1966), Philip Gleason refutes Catholic intellectuals and literati who argue that Irish control over American Catholicism has made it authoritarian and conservative. He insists that it was fortunate that the Irish were the first Catholic ethnics to arrive in the United States because "they were the best equipped among all the immigrating Catholic groups to assist the Church in effecting a positive adjustment to American life." Continental Catholics came from ultraconservative environments where church and state were united, serving as twin agencies of upper-class dominance. In America, they found the separation of church and

state to be strange and hostile. As reluctant citizens of the United Kingdom, the Irish on the other hand had successfully learned to organize and operate within the Anglo-Saxon Protestant political system and to sustain a church dependent on private financial support, free of state money and control. Because of their experience in Ireland, their familiarity with the Anglo Protestant mindset and political system, and their command of English, the Irish could communicate and compete with Anglo Americans. Irish political experience protected Catholic interests and in the process "Americanized" Catholic ethnics.

Notes to Chapter 6

1. Quoted from James Loughlin, *Gladstone, Home Rule and the Ulster Question, 1892–93* (Atlantic Highlands, N.J., 1987), p. 189.

2. Thomas Flanagan, "Rebellion and Style: John Mitchel and the Jail Journal," *Irish University Review* 1 (Autumn 1970), pp. 4–5. Flanagan borrowed this quote from William Dillon's two-volume *Life of John Mitchel* (London, 1888).

3. This speech printed in the *Irish World*, November 13, 1880, appears in this context in Thomas N. Brown, *Irish-American Nationalism* (Philadelphia, Pa., 1966), p. 24.

4. O'Connell was an accurate prophet. He understood that while emigration was a disaster to the Irish, it would eventually haunt the British. In *States of Ireland* (New York, N.Y., 1973), Conor Cruise O'Brien wrote: "The beginnings of the Irish revolution—that is the revolution of the Catholic Irish—are as much in America as in Ireland." (p. 45) He argues that most of the post-Famine emigration came from the least Anglicized regions of Ireland. According to O'Brien, "the original Gaelic stock of Ireland split into two branches, one of which learned English and other American." They did communicate with each other and "those who stayed at home were encouraged to rebel by those who left." (p. 44) O'Brien quotes Sir William Harcourt, British home secretary in the 1880s, on the ties between emigration and Irish nationalism: "In former Irish rebellions the Irish were in Ireland. . . . We could reach their forces, cut off their reserves in men and money and then to subjugate them was comparatively easy. Now there is an Irish nation in the United States, equally hostile, with plenty of money, absolutely beyond our reach and yet within ten days sail of our shores." (p. 45)

5. Patrick Ford and Michael Davitt, both disciples of nineteenth-century, single-tax socialist Henry George, preferred land nationalization to peasant proprietorship. But the conservatism of peasant and Catholic Ireland precluded such a radical solution to the agrarian dimension of the Irish Question.

6. Michael Gordon, "Irish Immigrant Culture and the Labor Boycott in New York City, 1880–1886," in *Immigrants in Industrial America, 1850–1920*, ed. Richard L. Ehrlich (Charlottesville, Va., 1977), pp. 111–22.

7. Sinn Féin's official existence dates back to 1905. Its founder, Arthur

Griffith, a Dublin journalist, advocated a dual monarchy, based on the Austro-Hungarian model, as a solution to the Irish Question. Sinn Féin means "we ourselves," emphasizing the economic self-sufficiency aspects of Griffith's ideology. Shortly after Sinn Féin's beginnings, the IRB infiltrated it, changing the political goal from dual monarchy to complete separation from Britain. After Easter Week, republican opponents of the Irish party identified themselves as Sinn Féiners, and Griffith surrendered the leadership of the organization to Eamon de Valera, the only surviving commandant of the 1916 rising.

8. Joshua B. Freeman, "Catholics, Communists, and Republicans: Irish Workers and the Organization of the Transport Workers Union," in *Working Class America: Essays on Labor, Community, and American Society,* ed. Michael H. Frish and Daniel J. Walkowitz (Urbana, Ill., 1983), pp. 256–83.

Notes to Chapter 7

1. Andrew Greeley, *The Irish-Americans: The Rise to Money and Power* (New York, N.Y., 1981), p. 112.

2. In "Catholics, Neutrality, and the Spanish Embargo, 1937–1939," *Journal of American History* 54 (June 1967), pp. 73–85, J. David Valaik presents evidence that a majority of American Catholics rejected pulpit and Catholic press advice by not supporting Franco's attack on the Spanish Republic.

3. Thomas F. O'Dea, *The American Catholic Dilemma* (New York, N.Y., 1958), offered strong support to Ellis's critique of Catholic intellectuals. Sociologist O'Dea, like Ellis, emphasized the peasant-immigrant character of American Catholicism. And he agreed with the monsignor that Catholic bishops shared the anti-intellectual biases of the working class from which they came. O'Dea also argued that the authoritarianism, clericalism, moralism, and defensiveness that pervaded the Church as a teaching institution frustrated intellectual freedom and the formation of creative imagination, both essential for artistic and scholarly excellence.

4. Thomas J. Fleming's New Jersey Catholic and political novels are *All Good Men* (New York, N.Y., 1961); *The God of Love* (New York, N.Y., 1963); *King of the Hill* (New York, N.Y., 1965); *Romans, Countrymen and Lovers* (New York, N.Y., 1969); *The Sandbox Tree* (New York, N.Y., 1970); *The Good Shepherd* (New York, N.Y., 1974); *Rulers of the City* (New York, N.Y., 1977); and *Promises to Keep* (New York, N.Y., 1978).

5. Novelist Maureen Howard explains her father's pro-McCarthyism as an Irish resentment of upper-class Anglo Americans in *Facts of Life* (Boston, Mass.), pp. 67–68.

6. Many Anglo Americans and a few Irish Americans had some difficulty accepting Harvard-educated, rich Kennedy as truly Irish. However, journalist Benjamin C. Bradlee, in *Conversations with Kennedy* (New York, N.Y., 1975),

made it clear that culturally and emotionally JFK identified himself as Irish and distrusted Anglo America.

7. Joseph M. Curran, *Hibernian Green on the Silver Screen: The Irish and American Movies* (Westport, Conn., 1989), p. 133, n. 4. Curran found Ford's reaction to Kennedy's victory in an interview by James Warner Bellah (typescript), B. 11, F 16, John Ford Papers, Lilly Library, Indiana University, Bloomington.

8. I have no information concerning the Catholic commitments of the writers I refer to, but they were raised in the Irish Catholic tradition and can be thought of as cultural Irish Catholics.

9. Greeley's evidence on the prosperity and high educational attainments of Irish America can be found in his *The Irish-Americans*, p. 118.

10. In the early 1960s, after a failed bombing campaign in the North, which had small support in the Catholic community, the IRA under a Sinn Féin party name abandoned terrorism for socialist politics in the South. During the civil rights phase of the Six-County Catholic protest, the IRA kept a low profile, promoting the civil liberties cause as a mobilizing tactic in Catholic ghettos. In 1969, after the IRA resumed its role as a nationalist guerrilla army, it split into Official and Provisional wings. Officials applied a Marxist interpretation to the Northern Ireland situation, arguing that sectarian conflict results from capitalist divisive tactics and projecting an All-Ireland socialist republic as a solution. Until a truce with the British army in 1974, they directed violence against symbols and agents of British authority, carefully avoiding attacks on Irish Protestant civilians. After the truce, Officials concentrated on politics, North and South, under a Sinn Féin party label. It eventually evolved into the Workers Party that now has a small but still significant following in the Republic. Provisionals also claim to be socialists. While their political party, Provisional Sinn Féin, promotes a workers republic, the fighting corps represents traditional republicanism's attempt to drive Britain out by bombs and bullets. While Provisionals denounce sectarianism and have advocated a Nine-County Ulster province in a federated united Ireland, they do not discriminate in their violence, killing Protestant civilians as well as unionist paramilitaries and British soldiers. In 1975 a Trotskyite faction broke with the Officials to form the Irish Republican Socialist party. Its military expression, the Irish national Liberation Army, became the most promiscuously violent terrorist group operating on the nationalist side.

11. Michael Tackett, "Middle-Class Catholics Shun the Democrats," *Chicago Tribune*, December 27, pp. 1, 13. Since German and Italian Catholics are more likely to vote Republican than the Irish, the Irish Catholic Democratic vote probably exceeds 27 percent.

12. There have been a number of poll results indicating American Catholic disagreements with Rome. A Time/CNN survey of September 27–28, 1995,

Time, October 9, 1995 shows that 70 percent favor married priests, 60 percent approve of ordaining women, 69 percent would allow divorced people to remarry in a Catholic ceremony, only 20 percent think it wrong to have sex before marriage, 79 percent believe it is permissible to make up their own minds concerning contraception, 59 percent practice birth control, and 80 percent said that they could disagree with the pope and remain good Catholics.

13. Ibid.

Recommended Reading

The Irish Experience

There are a number of general histories of Ireland that provide useful information on the religious, political, social, and economic roots of Irish America, including J. C. Beckett, *The Making of Modern Ireland, 1603–1923* (New York, N.Y., 1966); Karl S. Bottigheimer, *Ireland and the Irish: A Short History* (New York, N.Y., 1982); Roy Foster, *Modern Ireland, 1600–1972* (New York, N.Y., 1989); Thomas E. Hachey, Joseph M. Hernon, Jr., and Lawrence J. McCaffrey, *The Irish Experience: A Concise History* (New York, N.Y., 1996); K. Theodore Hoppen, *Ireland since 1800: Conflict and Conformity* (New York, N.Y., 1989); Robert Kee, *Ireland: A History* (London, 1980); F. S. L. Lyons, *Ireland since the Famine* (New York, N.Y., 1979); Nicholas Mansergh, *The Irish Question, 1840–1920* (Toronto, 1964); Lawrence J. McCaffrey, *Ireland from Colony to Nation State* (Englewood Cliffs, N.J., 1979) and *The Irish Question: Two Centuries of Conflict* (Lexington, Ky., 1995); and T. W. Moody and F. X. Martin, eds., *The Course of Irish History* (Cork, 1978). Beckett and Bottigheimer supply much content on the seventeenth and eighteenth centuries, but their material thins out on the nineteenth and twentieth. Hachey's, Hernon's, and McCaffrey's *Irish Experience* and McCaffrey's *Ireland from Colony to Nation State* strengths are in the nineteenth and twentieth centuries. McCaffrey's *Irish Question* emphasizes the interactions between Irish nationalism and British policy in Ireland that established precedents for the welfare state throughout the United Kingdom. He also discusses the complexity of the current Northern Ireland situation and peace prospects in that troubled place. Mansergh was a ground breaker in analyzing Anglo-Irish relations and his work still deserves attention. Moody's and Martin's *Course of Irish History* contains stimulating expert essays. The late F. S. L. Lyons was one of Ireland's most thoughtful historians. His book is a masterpiece of detail and explication. Hoppen offers an excellent combination of good writing, interesting information, and creative and challenging interpretation. For readers who have some knowledge of Irish history, Foster's highly readable *Modern Ireland* is an important example of its current revisionism. On occasion he goes too far in absolving Britain for Ireland's problems (the Famine is a good example), but on balance his judgments are thoughtful and usually sound. Kee writes exceptionally well, and his book is the basis of his popular BBC/RTE series on Irish history. Alan J. Ward, *The Irish Constitutional Tradition: Responsible Government and Modern Ireland, 1782– 1992* (Washington, D.C., 1994), looks at the Irish historical process from constitutional perspectives, emphasizing the British model. W. E. Vaughn, ed., *Ireland under the Union I: 1801–1870* (Oxford, 1989), vol. 5 of *The New History of Ireland*, features significant essays by some of the leading Irish Studies scholars in Ireland, Britain, and the United States. In *The Irish Question and British Politics, 1868–1986* (London, 1988), a short but comprehensive examination of how British politicians reacted to Irish issues, D. G. Boyce says they responded to British rather than Irish opinion.

For Irish Catholics their religion was a cultural bridge between Old and New Worlds and a spiritual and psychological comfort station in urban America. Emmet Larkin is the leading expert on the subject of Irish Catholicism. He has published a number of volumes in his study of the Catholic Church in Ireland during the nineteenth century. His essay, "The Devotional Revolution in Ireland, 1850–1875," *American Historical Review* 77 (June 1972), pp. 625–52, stimulated considerable research on Irish Catholicism. Its description of pre-Famine Irish Catholicism featured an ignorant, superstitious laity lax in the practice of the faith; a poorly educated, frequently rebellious clergy; a quarreling, factionalized hierarchy; and a Church short on clergy and chapels. According to Larkin, the Famine laid the foundation for reform by eliminating through death and emigration the poorest segment of the rural proletariat, thereby diminishing religious ignorance and the shortage of priests and places of worship. Larkin credits Paul Cardinal Cullen for directing a devotional revolution that made the Irish the strongest Catholics in the Western World. "The Devotional Revolution" essay and three others that Larkin published in the *AHR* are combined in *The Historical Dimensions of Irish Catholicism* (Washington, D.C., 1984). Larkin also edited and translated *Alex de Tocqueville's Journey in Ireland, July–August, 1835* (Washington, D.C., 1990). Its contents indicate that pre-Famine Irish Catholics were more devotional than the Continental variety, especially those in France. S. J. Connolly's *Priests and People in Pre-Famine Ireland, 1780–1845* (New York, N.Y., 1982) supports Larkin's analysis of pre-Famine, pre-Cullen Irish Catholicism. Patrick Corish, *The Irish Catholic Experience: A Historical Survey* (Wilmington, Del., 1985); James O'Shea, *Priest, Politics and Society in Post-Famine Ireland: A Study of County Tipperary, 1850–1891* (Atlantic Highlands, N.J., 1983); and K. Theodore Hoppen, *Elections, Politics, and Society in Ireland, 1823–1885* (Oxford, 1984) argue that the condition of pre-Famine Irish Catholicism was related to regional economic and social conditions. For example, in the more advanced Anglicized parts of the country, doctrinal and liturgical Romanization had been advancing since the eighteenth century, while superstition and non-Roman expressions of faith continued in backward, Gaelic portions of Ireland. They and Larkin's Introduction to the 1984 version of *The Historical Dimensions of Irish Catholicism* would describe religious change as more of a devotional evolution than revolution. But Larkin, supported by strong evidence, continues to insist that the Famine and Cullen were the two most important factors in reforming and energizing Irish Catholicism. Two important articles indicate the impact of the Famine on Irish Catholicism: David W. Miller, "Irish Catholicism and the Great Famine," *Journal of Social History* 9 (September 1975), pp. 81–98. and Eugene Hynes, "The Great Hunger and Irish Catholicism," *Societas* 8 (Spring 1978). Miller details weaknesses in pre-Famine Catholicism, Hynes argues that the social consequences of the Famine more than Catholic puritanism initiated Irish celibacy and late marriage. Other important contributions to the history of Irish Catholicism are David W. Miller, *Church, State, and Nation in Modern Ireland, 1898–1921* (Pittsburgh, 1973), and

John Whyte, *Church and State in Modern Ireland* (New York, N.Y., 1971).

Nationalism was another bridge uniting Ireland and Irish America. Robert Kee, *The Green Flag: The Turbulent History of the Irish Nationalist Movement* (New York, N.Y., 1972), is an informative and exceptionally well-written work. It argues that constitutional rather than physical force nationalism best represented Irish opinion until the failure of the Home Rule effort, 1912–1914, and that the Easter Week martyrdom gave dramatic impetus to the revolutionary cause. D. George Boyce, *Nationalism in Ireland* (Baltimore, Md., 1982), is another first rate examination in the Irish struggle for sovereignty. Tom Garvin's *The Evolution of Irish Nationalist Politics* (Dublin, 1981) is an intelligent and imaginative examination of various aspects of Irish nationalism from the eighteenth into the twentieth century. His *Nationalist Revolutionaries in Ireland, 1858–1928* (Oxford, 1987) portrays Irish nationalist leaders as usually lower middle-class Catholics, mostly from Munster. Anti-Protestant and anti-British, they were far more conservative in goals than they were in tactics, and were vague on the nature of the Ireland they were attempting to achieve. Thomas E. Hachey and Lawrence J. McCaffrey, eds., *Perspectives on Irish Nationalism* (Lexington, Ky., 1988) contains essays on the language, folklore, literary, agrarian, and religious aspects of Irish nationalism by R. Vincent Comerford, Mary Helen Thuente, Thomas Flanagan, James S. Donnelly, Jr., and Emmet Larkin. One of the most illuminating essays concerning the character of Irish nationalism is Thomas N. Brown, "Nationalism and the Irish Peasant, 1800–1848," *Review of Politics* 15 (October 1953), pp. 403–45. It has been reprinted in the *American Committee for Irish Studies Reprint Series* (Chicago, Ill., 1971), Emmet Larkin and Lawrence J. McCaffrey, eds., and in *Irish Nationalism and the American Contribution*, ed. Lawrence J. McCaffrey (New York, N.Y., 1976).

Daniel O'Connell's agitations for Catholic Emancipation and Repeal were important in injecting the principles of liberal democracy into Irish nationalism, politically civilizing its Catholicism ally, and forming the Irish political style and values. In two volumes Oliver MacDonagh has produced the best scholarly biography of O'Connell: *The Hereditary Bondsman: Daniel O'Connell, 1775–1829* (New York, N.Y., 1987), and *The Emancipist: Daniel O'Connell, 1830–1847* (New York, N.Y., 1989). MacDonagh acknowledges his debt to Maurice R.

O'Connell, ed., *The Correspondence of Daniel O'Connell*, 8 vols. (New York, N.Y., 1973–1980). Sean O'Faolain's *King of the Beggars: A Life of Daniel O'Connell* (Dublin, 1986) is a literary masterpiece as well as a splendid biography. According to Fergus O'Ferrall, *Catholic Emancipation: Daniel O'Connell and the Birth of Irish Democracy, 1820–1830* (Dublin, 1985), O'Connell along with Andrew Jackson put modern political democracy into action. While O'Connell authored Irish political nationalism, journalists and literary figures supplied the contents of Irish cultural nationalism. There are a number of quality studies of this subject, including Mary Helen Thuente, *The Harp Restrung: The United Irishmen and the Rise of Irish Literary Nationalism* (Syracuse, N.Y., 1994); Thomas Flanagan, *The Irish Novelists, 1800–1850* (New York, N.Y., 1959) and "Literature in English," W. E. Vaughn, ed., *Ireland under the Union, 1: 1801–1870* in vol. 5 of *The New History of Ireland;* R. Vincent Comerford, *Charles Kickham (1828–82): A Study in Irish Nationalism and Literature* (Dublin, 1979); F. S. L. Lyons, *Culture and Anarchy in Ireland 1890–1939* (Oxford, 1979); R. F. Foster, *Paddy and Mr. Punch: Connections in Irish and English History* (London, 1993); Terence Brown, *Ireland: A Social and Cultural History, 1822–79* (Ithaca, N.Y., 1985); Malcolm Brown, *The Politics of Irish Literature from Thomas Davis to W. B. Yeats* (Seattle, Wash., 1972); and John Hutchinson, *The Dynamics of Cultural Nationalism: The Gaelic Revival and the Creation of the Irish Nation State* (London, 1987).

The multi-faceted Irish cultural personality is the subject of Sean O'Faolain's *The Irish* (Harmondsworth, England, 1969), a pioneer work in Irish intellectual history. It presents the contributions of Celts, Normans, and Anglo Saxons as well as poets, priests, writers, and politicians. Patrick O'Farrell's *Ireland's English Question* (New York, N.Y., 1972), and *England and Ireland since 1800* (New York, N.Y., 1975); and Oliver MacDonagh's *States of Mind: A Study of Anglo-Irish Conflict, 1780–1880* (Boston, Mass., 1983) explore the convictions and prejudices that obstruct understanding between two nations geographically close but culturally distant from each other. In *Ireland's English Question*, O'Farrell tends to over-emphasize the Catholic dimension of the Irish mind, but he certainly restores a balance in *England and Ireland since 1800*. I found it one of the most useful books to assign to students in Irish studies courses.

The overwhelming majority of Irish-Catholic emigrants to the United States were from rural Ireland, victims of poverty, hunger, and limited opportunities. Valuable information on the social and economic environment that produced the beginnings of Catholic Irish America can be found in K. H. Connell, *The Population of Ireland, 1750–1845* (Oxford, 1950); James S. Donnelly, Jr., *The Land and People of Nineteenth Century Cork* (London, 1975) and *Landlord and Tenant in Nineteenth-Century Ireland* (Dublin, 1973); W. E. Vaughn, *Landlords and Tenants in Ireland, 1848–1904* (Dublin, 1984); Kevin O'Neill, *Family and Farm in Pre-Famine Ireland* (Madison, Wis., 1984); Daniel J. Casey and Robert E. Rhodes, eds., *Views of the Irish Peasantry, 1800–1916* (Hamden, Conn., 1977); Conrad Arensberg, *The Irish Countryman* (Gloucester, England, 1937), and *Family and Community in Ireland* (Cambridge, Mass., 1968) coauthored with Solon T. Kimball; Henry Glassie, *Irish Folk History* (Philadelphia, Pa., 1982) and *Passing the Time in Ballymenone: Culture and History of an Ulster Community* (Philadelphia, Pa., 1982); L. M. Cullen, *An Economic History of Ireland* (Baltimore, Md., 1972); Mary E. Daly, *Social and Economic History of Ireland since 1800* (Dublin, 1981); and Cormac Ó Grada, *Ireland: A New Economic History 1780–1939* (Oxford, 1995). A major influence on improving the future of Irish Catholics in Ireland and in the United States was the national educational system. It is the subject of Donald H. Akenson, *The Irish Educational Experiment* (Toronto, 1970).

The Famine was the most decisive event in Irish history, creating and/or intensifying economic, social, religious, and demographic change. It also speeded the pace and institutionalized emigration as an economic and social safety valve in Irish life. R. Dudley Edwards and T. Desmond Williams, eds., *The Great Famine: Studies in Irish History, 1845–1942* (New York, N.Y., 1956) was the first serious scholarly examination of the disaster. But it was Cecil Woodham-Smith's *The Great Hunger: Ireland, 1845–1849* (New York, N.Y., 1962) that captured general interest in the subject. Two especially clear and lucid examinations of the Great Hunger are Cormac Ó Grada, *The Great Irish Famine* (Atlantic Highlands, N.J., 1988) and "The Great Hunger, 1845–1851," eight chapters by James S. Donnelly, Jr. in *Ireland under the Union, I (1801–1870)*, vol. 5 of *The New History of Ireland*. The 150th anniversary of the Famine has generated a number of books on the subject. Some are good, a few are excellent, including Christine Kinealy, *This Great Calamity: The Irish Famine, 1845–52* (Dublin, 1994); Robert James Scally, *The End of Hidden Ireland: Rebellion, Famine, and Emigration* (Oxford, 1995); Peter Gray, *The Irish Famine* (London,

1995); and Christopher Morash, *Writing the Irish Famine* (Oxford, 1995). Scally focuses on a small community in County Roscommon to discuss causes and consequences of starvation, fever, and emigration. Taking on revisionist historians, he and Kinealy place considerable blame on Britain for misery in Ireland. In a small, compact, nicely designed volume, Gray provides all the vital information one needs to understand what happened in Ireland during the dreadful 1840s. Morash discusses and analyzes the work of John Mitchel and others who wrote about the Famine. With graceful prose and great insight, Peter Quinn discusses the Famine and its American consequences in "Bridget Such-a-One: The Great Irish Famine and Its Impact on America," *American Heritage* (December 1997).

The Irish-American Experience

There are a number of general interpretations of the Irish-American experience, including John B. Duff, *The Irish in America* (Belmont, Calif., 1971); Dennis Clark, *Hibernia America: The Irish and Regional Cultures* (New York, N.Y., 1986); Marjorie Fallows, *Irish-Americans: Identity and Assimilation* (Englewood Cliffs, N.J., 1977); Andrew M. Greeley, *That Most Distressful Nation* (New York, N.Y., 1973) and *The Irish-Americans: The Rise to Money and Power* (New York, N.Y., 1981); William D. Griffin, *A Portrait of the Irish in America* (New York, N.Y., 1981) and *The Book of Irish-Americans* (New York, N.Y., 1990); Lawrence J. McCaffrey, *Textures of Irish America* (Syracuse, N.Y., 1992); Joseph P. O'Grady, *How the Irish Became American* (New York, N.Y., 1973); William V. Shannon, *The American Irish* (New York, N.Y., 1974); and Carl Wittke, *The Irish in America* (New York, N.Y., 1970). Wittke's study is rich in detail, Shannon provides much more than narrative history. He offers solid and perceptive essays on Irish-America's political style, literary talent, athletic prowess, and religious values. Greeley's efforts combine historical and sociological perspectives. He insists that Irish America has emerged as a progressive, intellectual, affluent, and generally liberal community, and that it still retains a unique ethnic identity. Fallows also combines historical and social science approaches that result in an informative and lively book. O'Grady and Duff present brief but useful examinations of Irish America. Clark attempts to explain how regional environments result in Irish-American diversity. His well-written, ambitious, and usually successful examination of the varieties of Irish America suggests that urban physical and mental ghettoes delayed Irish success and assimilation but, once removed from city neighborhoods, Irish economic and social mobility and the impact of regional influences faded Irish ethnicity. McCaffrey's book emphasizes the three main aspects of Irish America: religion, politics, and nationalism. He agrees with Greeley and others that the Irish journey in America has been full of frustration and insecurity but has been a success story. He also shares Clark's view that education, affluence, and suburbanization has challenged Irish ethnicity. Patrick Blessing's "The Irish," in *The Harvard Encyclopedia of American Ethnic Groups*, ed. Stephan Thernstrom (Cambridge, Mass., 1980), is a succinct, exceptionally intelligent and informative survey of Irish-American history. Blessing has also produced *The Irish in America: A Guide to the Literature and the Manuscript Collections* (Washington, D.C., 1992). It is an essential guide for those researching Irish America. Seamus P. Metress, *The Irish-American Experience: A Guide to the Literature* (Washington, D.C., 1981), also provides bibliographical information. Two volumes containing perceptive examinations of various components of the Irish-American experience are *America and Ireland, 1776–1976*, ed. David Noel Doyle and Owen Dudley Edwards (Westport, Conn., 1980) and *The Irish in America* (New York, N.Y., 1985), P. J. Drudy, ed.

Terry Coleman's *Going to America* (New York, N.Y., 1972) and Philip Taylor's *The Distant Magnet* (New York, N.Y., 1971) deal with emigration. Coleman focuses on Liverpool departures and the arduous transatlantic crossing. Most of his travelers were Irish. Taylor discusses the entire scope of European emigration, describing the voyage to America and the problems newcomers faced there. In *Irish Emigration, 1801–1921* (Dundalk, Ireland, 1984), David Fitzpatrick examines the economic and social factors that encouraged and/or forced young people to leave Ireland. His "Irish Emigration in the Later Nineteenth Century," *Irish Historical Studies* 22 (September 1980), pp. 126–43, contains interesting and useful information on the class and gender component of Irish emigrants to Australia, Canada, New Zealand, and the United States, the places they settled in, and their New World occupations. In his prize-winning *Emigrants and Exiles: Ireland and the Exodus to North America* (New York, N.Y., 1985), Kerby A. Miller discusses Ulster Presbyterian and Irish Catholic reasons for leaving Ireland, and describes their American fortunes. His reading of emigrant letters persuades him that religious and Gaelic influences rendered pre-modern Irish Catholic peasants psychologically unfit to cope with Protestant, industrial, urban America. Consequently they felt alienated, exiles from their native turf, strangers in a new land. Their loneliness and discontent were expressed in Irish nationalism. In response to Miller's alienation and exile thesis, Donald H. Akenson's *The Irish Diaspora: A Primer* (Toronto, 1994) argues that Irish Catholic religious and Gaelic cultural values were not obstacles to relatively quick economic and social mobility in the United States, Canada, Australia, and New Zealand. Miller's and Paul Wagner's coauthored *Out of Ireland* (Washington, D.C., 1995), the basis of a quality Public Broadcasting System documentary, qualifies the *Emigrant and Exile* alienation-exile thesis, pointing out that the Irish were far less likely to return home than other European immigrants in the United States, and some that did go back were highly disappointed in what they found there and realized that America was truly their home. Previous to Miller's *Emigrants and Exiles,* Arnold Shrier's *Ireland and the American Emigration* (New York, N.Y., 1970) made good use of letters back home to analyze aspects of the Irish-American experience. Eighteenth-century Irish emigration to North America was largely Ulster Protestant, but Audrey Lockhart's *Some Aspects of Emigration from Ireland to North America between 1660 and 1775* (New York, N.Y., 1976) identifies a significant number of indentured servants and transported convicts in eighteenth-century America who were Irish Catholics. A small American Catholic Church, limited in personnel and resources, could not meet their spiritual needs and, after serving sentences or completing indentures, they melded into Evangelical Protestant communities on the Appalachian frontier. W. F. Adams's *Ireland and Irish Immigration to the New World from 1815 to the Famine* (New York, N.Y., 1967) reveals his Anglo Protestant antipathies to Irish Catholic culture, but it is an excellent study of the character of pre-Famine Irish emigration. Like the Adams book, *To the Golden Door* by George W. Potter (Westport, Conn., 1974) deals with pre-Famine immigrants. It is a gold mine of information, but Potter was too concerned with and probably exaggerated Irish economic and social advances. Unfortunately, the author died before the completion of his work and the reader is left in the dark concerning the sources for much of his information and conclusions.

Irish emigration to the United States is not only unique in the many unmarrieds but also in the large number of women who left home.

Robert E. Kennedy, Jr., *The Irish: Emigration, Marriage, and Fertility* (Berkeley, Calif., 1973), uses documentary evidence gathered by British and Irish governments to indicate that the Irish people (Catholic and Protestant) used emigration along with permanent celibacy and late marriages as economic and social safety valves to improve and then sustain post-Famine rising standards of living. Kennedy explains that a lack of marriage opportunities and declining status persuaded women, more than men, to set off for America. In *Ourselves Alone: Women's Emigration from Ireland, 1855–1920* (Lexington, Ky., 1989), Janet A. Nolan intelligently and interestingly explains how the Great Famine so altered Irish marriage patterns and the place of women in Irish society that they had more reason than men to emigrate. This thesis is reinforced in an exceptionally well written essay " 'She Never Then After that Forgot Him': Irishwomen and Emigration to the United States in Irish Folklore," by Grace Neville, *Mid-America* 74 (October 1992), pp. 217–90. In *Women and the Family in Post-Famine Ireland: Status and Opportunity in a Patriarchal Society* (New York, N.Y., 1992), Rita M. Rhodes discusses the gender discrimination problems that compelled women to cross the Atlantic and what awaited them on the other side. Ide O'Carroll's *Models for Movers: Irish Women's Emigration to America* (Dublin, 1989) contends that an oppressive patriarchy and a rigid, male chauvinist Catholicism have forced women out of Ireland. But oral interviews, her main source material, do not sustain her thesis.

Short on the skills and temperament to farm successfully in the United States, the overwhelming majority of Irish immigrants chose to live in cities and towns that thrived off industrial and transportation economies. This decision was lamented by Irish journalists and many Irish and Irish-American prelates and priests. In 1851 Reverend John O'Hanlon, an Irish cleric who had served on the American mission in St. Louis, authored a guide for Irish immigrants that told them what to carry with them and what to expect from life in the United States. Worried that the American urban environment was a threat to their Catholic loyalty and values, O'Hanlon advised them to avoid cities and to settle in rural areas. Portions of O'Hanlon's counsel to immigrants and other information about the immigrant experience is in Edward J. Maguire, ed., *Reverend John O'Hanlon's The Irish Emigrant Guide for the United States* (New York, N.Y., 1976). John F. Maguire was the proprietor of the *Cork Examiner* and a prominent nationalist MP in the British House of Commons. His *The Irish in America* (New York, N.Y., 1974), originally published in 1868, also presents a bleak picture of Irish urban life. One of the early advocates of rural settlement for Irish immigrants was Buffalo's Catholic bishop, John Timon. His efforts to resettle the urban Irish on farms or small towns, and his dispute with New York's Archbishop John Hughes, who believed that the Church could best serve immigrants if they were huddled in cities, is the subject of Leonard R. Riforgiato, "Bishop John Timon, Archbishop John Hughes, and Irish Colonization: A Clash of Episcopal Views on the Future of the Irish and the Catholic Church in America," *Immigration to New York* (Cranbury, N.J., 1991), ed. William Pencak, Selma Berrol, and Randall M. Miller, pp. 27–55. In *Catholic Colonization on the Western Frontier* (New Haven, Conn., 1957), James P. Shannon discusses the failed effort of St. Paul's Archbishop John Ireland to plant a colony of Connacht Irish Catholics in rural Minnesota.

Oscar Handlin's *Boston's Immigrants: A Study in Acculturation* (1941 rpt. New York, N.Y., 1968) is a highly regarded case study of the first Irish-American urban ghetto. Dennis P. Ryan's *Beyond the Ballot Box: A Social History of the Boston Irish, 1845–1917* (Rutherford, N.J., 1983) is a judicious and informative study of the Boston Irish beyond their politics. Stephan Thernstrom's *Poverty and Progress* (Cambridge, Mass., 1964) discusses sluggish Irish economic and social mobility (they invested in property rather than education) in Newburyport, Massachusetts from 1850 to 1880. In a later publication, *The Other Bostonians: Poverty and Progress in the American Metropolis, 1860–1970* (Cambridge, Mass., 1973), Thernstrom discovers that the Irish in Boston were no more successful in moving up the American success ladder than those in Newburyport. Instead of defining an Irish-American stereotype, which some claim he does, Thernstrom's findings indicate that the New England Irish were exceptions to the general success of Irish Americans. As Dennis Clark's *Hibernia America: The Irish and Regional Cultures* and Lawrence J. McCaffrey's *Textures of Irish America* indicate, there was and is great diversity in Irish America. It responds and adjusts to local situations. Recommended local studies are Robert Ernst, *Immigrant Life in New York City, 1825–1863* (Syracuse, N.Y., 1994); Ronald H. Bayor and Timothy J. Meagher, eds., *The New York Irish* (Baltimore, Md., 1996); Ann M. Shea and Marion R. Casey, *The Irish Experience in New York City: A Select Bibliography* (Syracuse, N.Y., 1995);

R. A. Burchell, *The San Francisco Irish, 1848–1880* (Berkeley, Calif., 1980); Dennis Clark, *The Irish in Philadelphia* (Philadelphia, Pa., 1973) and *Erin's Heirs: Irish Bonds of Community* (Lexington, Ky., 1991); David N. Emmons, *The Butte Irish: Class and Ethnicity in an American Mining Town, 1875–1925* (Urbana, 1989); Lawrence J. McCaffrey, Ellen Skerrett, Michael Funchion, and Charles Fanning, *The Irish in Chicago* (Urbana, Ill., 1987); Grace McDonald, *History of the Irish in Wisconsin in the Nineteenth Century* (New York, N.Y., 1976); Brian C. Mitchell, *The Paddy Camps: The Irish of Lowell, 1821–61* (Urbana, Ill., 1988); Earl F. Niehaus, *The Irish in New Orleans* (New York, N.Y., 1976); Jo Ellen McNergney Vinyard, *The Irish on the Urban Frontier: Detroit, 1850–1880* (New York, N.Y., 1976); and Douglas V. Shaw, *The Making of an Immigrant City: Ethnic and Cultural Conflict in New Jersey, 1850–1877* (New York, N.Y., 1976). Many of the leading historians of Irish America contribute essays to *The New York Irish*. Emmons's study of the Irish in Butte, Montana, where they were owners and bosses as well as copper miners, indicates how much can be discovered about an ethnic group by studying them in a small, compact urban area. Vinyard presents solid evidence that Irish Catholics on the urban frontier, Buffalo west, achieved more social and economic progress than those on the Atlantic seaboard. Local studies, such as Emmons's as well as the essays in Timothy J. Meagher, ed., *From Paddy to Studs: Irish Communities at the Turn of the Century Era, 1880–1920* (Westport, Conn., 1986) conclude that Western and Midwestern Irish Americans came closer to achieving the American dream than those in the East. Irish success in the West is the subject of a number of articles in *The Irish in the West* (Manhattan, Kans., 1993), eds. Timothy J. Sarbaugh and James P. Walsh. With two exceptions, these articles originally appeared in *Journal of the West* 31 (April 1992).

Hasia Diner's *Erin's Daughters in America: Irish American Women in the Nineteenth Century* (Baltimore, Md., 1983) makes a strong case that Irish-American Catholic progress has gender as well as regional variations, and that for a long period more women achieved middle-class and professional status than men. Other valuable glimpses at Irish-American Catholic women are Eileen Brewer, *Beyond Utility: The Role of Nuns in the Education of American Catholic Girls, 1860–1920* (Chicago, Ill., 1987), and Janet A. Nolan, *Ourselves Alone* and "A Patrick Henry in the Classroom: Margaret Haley and the Chicago Teacher's Federation," *Eire-Ireland* 30 (Summer 1995), pp. 104–17. In "Charity,

Poverty, and Child Welfare," *Harvard Divinity Bulletin* 25:4 (1996), pp. 12–17, Maureen Fitzgerald credits social work by nineteenth-century New York City nuns among women and children with doing much to preserve families of the poor and setting patterns for the welfare state. Another creative look at the significance of nuns in improving the nineteenth-century urban social milieu is Sue Ellen Hoy's "Walking Nuns: Chicago's Irish Sisters of Mercy," in *At the Crossroads: Old Saint Patrick's and the Chicago Irish,* Ellen Skerrett, ed. (Chicago, Ill., 1997), pp. 39–52. Hoy convincingly argues that Chicago's Mercy nuns were in the social work field earlier and on a larger scale than Jane Addams's Hull House group.

For a considerable period of time, Catholics had to struggle with the prejudices of American nativism as well as a poverty of skills and social dysfunctionalism resulting from the trauma of transferring from a rural Irish to an American urban environment. The leading studies of American anti-Catholicism are Ray Allen Billington, *The Protestant Crusade, 1800–1860* (1938 rpt. Chicago, Ill., 1964) and John Higham, *Strangers in the Land: Patterns of American Nativism, 1860–1925* (1955 rpt. Chicago, Ill., 1965). Dale T. Knobel, *Paddy and the Republic: Ethnicity and Nationality in Antebellum America* (Middletown, Conn., 1986), insists that prejudice against the Irish was more ethnic than religious. His book is full of important material, but he underestimates the anti-Catholic quotient in American nativism. Other informative studies of American nativism and its religious dimension are Donald L. Kinzer, *An Episode in Anti-Catholicism: The American Protective Association* (Seattle, Wash., 1964); and Kenneth Jackson, *The Ku Klux Klan in the City* (New York, N.Y., 1967). Anglo-Saxon racism that affected both British and American hostility to the Irish is the subject of L. P. Curtis, Jr., *Anglo-Saxons and Celts: A Study in Anti-Catholic Prejudice in Victorian England* (Bridgeport, Conn., 1968) and *Apes and Angels: The Irishman in Victorian Caricature* (Washington, D.C., 1997); and Richard Ned Lebow, *White Britain and Black Ireland: The Influence of Stereotypes on Colonial Policy* (Philadelphia, Pa., 1976). The simian featured, brutal Irish in British magazine and newspaper cartoons also appeared in American counterparts. They are presented and analyzed in John J. and Selma Appel, "The Distorted Image" (Anti-Defamation League of New York), a slide collection.

A good number of Irish Catholics responded to prejudice with their own biases against African Americans, Jews, and even other

Catholic ethnics. They displayed their racial bigotry in the 1863 New York draft riot when Blacks fell victim to their rage. For information on the draft riot see Adrian Cook, *The Armies of the Street: The New York Draft Riots of 1863* (Lexington, Ky., 1974). The draft riot provides the backdrop of Peter Quinn's excellent novel, *The Banished Children of Eve* (New York, N.Y., 1994). In clear and graceful prose Quinn provides great insight into the varieties of life among the New York Irish in the 1860s and their relationship with other races, nationalities and creeds. Iver Bernstein's *The New York City Draft Riots: Their Significance for American Society and Politics in the Age of the Civil War* (New York, N.Y., 1990) sees more than racism and hostility to Anglo-American unfairness in Irish conduct during the riots. To him, Irish Catholics were engaged in a class war against an oppressive Protestant elite. Joseph M. Hernon, Jr. discusses Irish reaction in Ireland and in the United States to the War between the States in *Celts, Catholics & Copperheads* (Columbus, Ohio, 1968). Irish Catholics in New York rioted again in July 1870 and 1871. Their targets were July 12 Orange parades. In his *The Orange Riots: Irish Political Violence in New York City, 1870 and 1871* (Ithaca, N.Y., 1993), Michael A. Gordon, like Iver Bernstein, explains Irish Catholic conduct in terms of lower–working-class resentment against nativist elites frustrating their political, economic, and social ambitions. He underestimates the significance of Old Country feuds exported across the Atlantic. Ronald H. Bayor, *Neighbors in Conflict: The Irish, Germans, Jews, and Italians of New York, 1921–1941* (Baltimore, Md., 1978), details Depression-generated Irish anti-semitism in the 1930s and 1940s in New York. Since the 1940s, especially after World War II, there has been much tension, often leading to violence, between African Americans and Catholic ethnics, including the Irish, over housing and education. Arnold R. Hirsch's *Making the Second Ghetto: Race and Housing in Chicago, 1940–1960* (New York, N.Y., 1983) discusses Irish efforts in Chicago to prevent the migration of Blacks to ethnic neighborhoods. The most interesting, and exceptionally well-written study of Irish and Black conflict is Anthony J. Lukas's *Common Ground: A Turbulent Decade in the Lives of Three Families* (New York, N.Y., 1985). Lukas understands that the effort to integrate schools in the Boston area through bussing imposed a heavy burden on two insecure, defensive groups, Irish and Blacks, and also involved conflict between working-class Irish Catholics in the neighborhoods and affluent Irish Catholics downtown or in the suburbs. An important new book on conflict and tensions between African Americans and the Irish and other Catholic ethnics is John T. McGreevy, *Parish Boundaries: The Catholic Encounter with Race in the Twentieth-Century Urban North* (Chicago, Ill., 1996). McGreevy respects the role of ethnic parishes in forming bonds of community for Catholic groups insecure in the United States. But he observes that these parishes evolved from ethnic to White, anti-Black "fortresses" resistant to neighborhood and school integration.

Until quite recently, Irish Catholics in the United States shared with their coreligionists in Ireland a view that their religion symbolized their culture and nationality. Much of their power and influence came from their control of American Catholicism. The two best surveys of the Church in the United States are Jay P. Dolan, *The American Catholic Experience* (New York, N.Y., 1985); and James Hennesey, S.J., *American Catholics: A History of the American Catholic Community in the United States* (New York, N.Y., 1981). Three shorter but good histories of American Catholicism are John Cogley, *Catholic America* (New York, N.Y., 1973); John Tracy Ellis, *American Catholicism* (Chicago, Ill., 1956); and Andrew M. Greeley, *The Catholic Experience* (New York, N.Y., 1967). Specific information about the Irish dimension of Catholicism in the United States can be found in Thomas N. Brown and Thomas McAvoy, *The United States of America*, vol. 6 of *A History of Irish Catholicism*, ed. Patrick Corish (Dublin, 1970). Jay P. Dolan, *The Immigrant Church, New York's Irish and German Catholics, 1815–1865* (Baltimore, Md., 1975); and Ellen Skerrett, "The Catholic Dimension," in McCaffrey, Skerrett, Funchion, and Fanning, *The Irish in Chicago* (Urbana, Ill., 1987). Skerrett is particularly good on parishes as the religious, social, and educational focal point of Irish neighborhoods. She also emphasizes this point in *Chicago: A City of Neighborhoods* (Chicago, Ill., 1986), which she coauthored with Dominic Pacyga; and in Ellen Skerrett, Edward R. Kantowicz, and Steven M. Avella, *Catholicism, Chicago Style* (Chicago, Ill., 1993). Skerrett has also contributed to and edited the earlier mentioned *At the Crossroads: Old Saint Patrick's and the Chicago Irish*, which contains a number of essays on the mother parish of the Chicago Irish. Eileen McMahon's *What Parish Are You From? A Chicago Irish Community and Race Relations* (Lexington, Ky., 1995) tells the interesting and highly relevant story of Chicago's St. Sabina's parish in transition from Irish to Black. The previously discussed *Parish Boundaries* by John T. McGreevy also is concerned with

relations between Catholic ethnics and African Americans. Lawrence S. Connor retired as managing editor of *The Indianapolis Star.*
His autobiography, *Hampton Court: Growing Up Catholic in Indianapolis
Between the Wars* (Indianapolis, Ind., 1995), validates the parish as the
center and glue of Irish-American Catholic urban life.

An exceptionally important and thorough biography of an Irish
member of the American Catholic hierarchy is Marvin O'Connell's
John Ireland and the American Catholic Church (St. Paul, Minn., 1988).
New York's conservative Archbishop Corrigan competed with St.
Paul's liberal Archbishop Ireland for American Catholic leadership.
His life is the subject of Robert Emmet Curran, *Michael Augustine Corrigan and the Shaping of Conservative Catholicism in America, 1878–1902*
(New York, N.Y., 1978). William Henry O'Connell, cardinal archbishop of Boston, for most of the first half of the twentieth century,
was one of the most conservative forces in American Catholicism.
James M. O'Toole's *Militant and Triumphant: William Henry O'Connell
and the Catholic Church in Boston, 1859–1944* (Notre Dame, Ind., 1992)
reveals that O'Connell was not the efficient, completely in control administrator that he appeared to be, that he antagonized members of
the hierarchy in New England and other parts of the country, and
that scandal involving his nephew, the chancellor of the archdiocese,
plagued his administration and damaged his standing in Rome. Other
important profiles of Irish-American bishops are Peter Guilday, *The
Life and Times of John England: First Bishop of Charleston, 1786–1842*
(New York, N.Y., 1927); John Tracy Ellis, *The Life of James Cardinal
Gibbons, Archbishop of Baltimore, 1834–1921,* 2 vols. (Milwaukee, Wis.,
1952); Richard Shaw, *Dagger John: The Unquiet Life and Times of Archbishop John Hughes of New York* (New York, N.Y., 1977); and James P.
Gaffey, *Citizen of No Mean City: Archbishop Patrick Reardon of San Francisco, 1841–1914* (Wilmington, N.C., 1976).

O'Connell's biography of Ireland thoroughly discusses relations
between Irish-American bishops and Rome, as does Gerald P. Fogar-
ty's *The Vatican and the American Hierarchy from 1870 to 1965* (Wilmington, Del., 1985). O'Connell is quite good on the Americanist
issue that divided the hierarchy in the United States and provoked
Roman intervention. This subject is also well treated in Robert D.
Cross, *The Emergence of Catholic Liberalism in America* (1958 rpt. Chicago, Ill., 1967). In *American Catholics and the Social Question, 1865–
1900* (New York, N.Y., 1976), James Edward Roohan discusses the

social conservativism and intellectual defensiveness of the Catholic hierarchy in the East, indicating the regional differences that existed in Irish America. Those variations are a major emphasis in David Noel Doyle's *Irish-Americans, Native Rights, and National Empires: The Structure, Divisions, and Attitudes of the Catholic Minority in the Decade of Expansion, 1890–1901* (New York, N.Y., 1976). Monsignor John Ryan of St. Paul played a major part in defining a liberal Catholic approach to social and economic problems, one that preceded and helped inspire the New Deal. His role is the subject of Francis L. Broderick, *Right Reverend New Dealer John A. Ryan* (New York, N.Y., 1963). David J. O'Brien's *American Catholics and Social Reform: The New Deal Years* (New York, N.Y., 1968) is also an excellent discussion of American Catholic efforts in the direction of social justice. Until quite recently there was a distinct Catholic subculture in the United States, condemning materialism and secularism, promoting a neo-Thomistic view of the world, influencing legislative and entertainment attitudes toward cultural values, but at the same time digesting general American capitalistic attitudes. This subculture is treated in Philip Gleason, *Catholicism in America* (New York, N.Y., 1970) and *Keeping the Faith: American Catholicism Past and Present* (Notre Dame, Ind., 1987); James Terence Fisher, *The Catholic Counter Culture in America, 1933–1962* (Chapel Hill, N.C., 1987); and Paula M. Kane, *Separatism and Subculture: Boston Catholicism, 1900–1920* (Chapel Hill, N.C., 1994). Gary Will's fascinating *Bare Ruined Choirs* (Garden City, N.Y., 1972) probes the values and worship of pre– and post–Vatican II American Catholicism. His critique of the Church's position on contraception is devastating. John Tracy Ellis's *American Catholics and the Intellectual Life* (Chicago, Ill., 1956), endorsed by Thomas O'Dea's *American Catholic Dilemma* (1958 rpt. New York, N.Y., 1962), touched off a passionate discussion concerning the quality of Catholic education and intellectualism. Ellis blamed inadequacies in both to an Irish-led immigrant Church focusing on the survival and respectability needs of its flocks at the expense of intellectual life and to Catholic acceptance of American materialism and pragmatism. O'Dea added an indictment of the Irish-American Catholic authoritarianism that squelched creativity and imagination. In *Religion, Culture, and Values: A Cross-Cultural Analysis of Motivational Factors in Native Irish and American Irish Catholicism* (New York, N.Y., 1976), Bruce Francis Biever, employing a quantitative method of research, decides that although Irish-American Catholicism is much like the Irish variety, it is much less likely to accept clerical authoritarianism in non-religious matters. Like their non-Catholic fellow citizens, American Catholics are suspicious of institutionalized religion, respect individual conscience, and insist on democratic and pluralistic controls over the Church. Biever's book originated as a 1965 University of Pennsylvania Ph.D. dissertation. Since that time, Irish-American Catholic enthusiasm for the Church has lessened, and dissent has spread to religious as well as secular issues. In *Once a Catholic* (New York, N.Y., 1987), Peter Occhiogrosso interviews present and former Catholics, many Irish, concerning the permanent impact of that religious experience on their lives.

James P. Walsh, ed., *The Irish: America's Political Class* (New York, N.Y., 1976), presents a variety of interpretations of the Irish-American political style and influence. In "The Irish" essay in Nathan Glazier's and Daniel Patrick Moynihan's *Beyond the Melting Pot: Jews, Italians, and Irish of New York City* (Cambridge, Mass., 1963), Moynihan praises the Irish skill at acquiring political power but laments their inability to use it to solve urban problems. He blames this on a conservative, Catholic peasant, parish pump mentality. Dissenters, such as John B. Buenker, *Urban Liberalism and Progressive Reform* (New York, N.Y., 1973) and Robert Dahl, *Who Governs? Democracy and Power in an American City* (New Haven, Conn., 1961) argue that Irish political power speeded their social mobility and alleviated the poverty and misery of other ethnics and integrated them into the mainstream of American politics.

Steven P. Erie's *Rainbow's End: Irish-Americans and the Dilemmas of Urban Machine Politics, 1840–1885* (Berkeley, Calif., 1988) is the most comprehensive look at Irish-American politics. It rejects the claim that politics accelerated Irish-American mobility or that Irish Americans generously included others in the economic or power spoils of politics. Erie argues that jobs that stemmed from politics locked the Irish into blue-collar and lower-middle-class occupations, and that the principal benefits stemming from Irish politics went to the Irish while other ethnics got the leavings. His book is a needed corrective to exaggerations about Irish-American politics. But it also assumes that despite nativist prejudices, nineteenth- and early-twentieth-century Irish Catholics had better alternatives than the employment offered by politics or its connections, and it undervalues Irish political services to others. Like Anglo-Protestant politicians, the Irish variety catered to members of their own community, but they were more generous in dispensing favors and services and more concerned about non-Irish ethnics than were Anglo-Protestant moral reformers.

Alfred Connable and Edward Silberfarb, *Tigers of Tammany* (New York, N.Y., 1967), studies the first, powerful Irish-American urban machine, as does Oliver E. Allen, *The Tiger: The Rise and Fall of Tammany Hall* (New York, N.Y., 1993). A great deal of information about New York's Irish Catholic politics and its opposing forces can be found in David C. Hammack, *Power and Society: Greater New York at the Turn of the Century* (New York, N.Y., 1982). In "Labor's Decline within New York City's Democratic Party from 1844 to 1884," *Immigration to New York*, pp. 7–26, Anthony Gronowicz claims that the influence of the Irish over Tammany's leadership actually declined during the nineteenth century. A recent paperback edition of *Plunkett of Tammany Hall: A Series of Very Plain Talks on Very Practical Matters*, recorded by William L. Riordan, is an entertaining and instructive guide to the techniques of a Tammany Irish politician (New York, N.Y., 1995). It has an intelligent and perceptive introduction by Peter Quinn, author of *The Banished Children of Eve*. Quinn's essay is an excellent survey of the history of Tammany Hall, discussing the motivation and tactics of its Irish bosses, and indicating that their strength lay in their closeness to constituents. He points out that, contrary to the Moynihan thesis, the Irish did know what to do with power, both for themselves and for others. The leadership of Charles Francis Murphy had much to do with Tammany finally moving beyond the quest for power to addressing the social and economic issues that troubled its important working class constituency. He is the subject of Nancy Joan Weiss, *Charles Francis Murphy, 1858–1924: Respectability and Responsibility in Tammany Politics* (Northampton, Mass., 1968). Thomas McLean Henderson in *Tammany Hall and the New Immigrants: The Progressive Years* (New York, N.Y., 1976) explains how Jewish and Italian challenges forced Irish politicians in New York to deal with social issues, but in doing so they directed their efforts at Jews while ignoring Italians. Italian reactions to neglect led to the anti-Irish power coalition, which included some Irish, that elected Fiorello La Guardia mayor and lessened Irish significance in Tammany and the politics of the city.

The career of James Michael Curley and his fictional clone, Frank Skeffington, in Edwin O'Connor's *The Last Hurrah* (Boston, Mass., 1956), has centered much attention on Boston's Irish Catholic politics.

Jack Beatty's *The Rascal King: The Life and Times of James Michael Curley (1874–1958)* (Reading, Mass., 1992) is a magnificent biography, rich in detail, honest and perceptive in interpretation, and exceptionally well written. Beatty manages to reveal the scoundrel in Curley while at the same time conveying the charm and skill that appealed to a defensive Boston Irish electorate. Another important contribution to the historiography of the Boston Irish and their politics is Thomas H. O'Connor's *The Boston Irish: A Political History* (Boston, Mass., 1995). O'Connor's narrative takes readers from the period when Hugh O'Brien, Patrick Collins, Patrick O'Connor, and John Boyle O'Reilly attempted to build bridges of understanding between Irish Catholics and Anglo-Protestants, through the times when James Martin Lomasney, Patrick J. Kennedy, John F. "Honey" Fitzgerald, and Curley catered to and instigated the passions of a paranoid ghetto, to the present where there are conflicts of interest between the Irish stuck in neighborhoods and the affluent, well-educated Irish downtown or in the suburbs. O'Connor buys *The Last Hurrah* thesis that the New Deal welfare state killed off Irish political machines. Steven P. Erie says that in the case of Boston and New York, Washington usurped the welfare role of the machine, but in other places federal funds flowed through machines strengthening their hold on voters. Chicago's democratic machine thrived on WPA and other federal money. Roger Biles describes that situation in *Big City Boss in Depression and War: Mayor Edward J. Kelly of Chicago* (De Kalb, Ill., 1984). Kelly winked at graft and corruption, but he was a tough and effective administrator who beautified the city and did much to bring African Americans into the Democratic camp. The machine that Kelly and Patrick Nash controlled, Mayor Richard J. Daley perfected. He probably was the true "last hurrah" of urban-Irish machine politics. There have been a number of biographical studies of Daley. I particularly appreciate William F. Gleason, *Daley of Chicago: The Man, the Mayor, and the Limits of Conventional Politics* (New York, N.Y., 1970). Other recommendations are Mike Royko, *Boss* (New York, N.Y., 1970); Eugene Kennedy, *Himself: The Life and Times of Richard J. Daley* (New York, N.Y., 1978); and Roger Biles, *Richard J. Daley: Politics, Race, and the Governing of Chicago* (De Kalb, Ill., 1995). Biles includes the latest research material. He credits Daley with managerial genius, taking care of the needs of White constituents, but avoiding and/or neglecting the problems of African Americans. But that could be said for administrations in most

American cities in the 1950s, 1960s, and 1970s. Milton Rakove's *Don't Make No Waves—Don't Back No Losers* (Bloomington, Ind., 1975) and *We Don't Want Nobody that Nobody Sent* (Bloomington, Ind., 1979) are interesting and entertaining discussions of Daley's machine in operation. Three informative studies of Chicago Irish politics are Michael Funchion, "The Political and Nationalist Dimensions," in *The Irish in Chicago;* Edward M. Levine, *The Irish and Irish Politicians* (South Bend, Ind., 1966); and Paul Michael Green, "Irish Chicago: The Multiethnic Road to Machine Success," *Ethnic Chicago*, ed. Peter d'A. Jones and Melvin Holli (Grand Rapids, Mich., 1981). George Q. Flynn, *American Catholics and the Roosevelt Presidency* (Lexington, Ky., 1968), discusses the Irish contribution to the New Deal.

Catholic Irish America produced political villains as well as heroes. The ideas and tactics of Father Charles Coughlin in the 1930s and early 1940s, and Senator Joseph R. McCarthy in the 1950s, threatened American liberal democracy. Alan Brinkley's *Voices of Protest: Huey Long, Father Coughlin, and the Great Depression* (New York, N.Y., 1982) presents a perceptive analysis of Coughlin. Charles J. Tull's *Father Coughlin and the New Deal* (Syracuse, N.Y., 1965) and Donald Warren's *Radio Priest: Charles Coughlin, the Father of Hate Radio* (New York, N.Y., 1995) offer valuable information on the clerical radio demagogue. Thomas C. Reeves, *The Life and Times of Joe McCarthy* (New York, N.Y., 1982), is the most comprehensive biography of "Tail Gunner" Joe. Donald F. Crosby, *God, Church, and Flag: Senator Joseph R. McCarthy and the Catholic Church, 1950–57* (Chapel Hill, N.C., 1978), discusses American Catholic responses to the senator from Wisconsin.

The presidency of John F. Kennedy did much to end Irish Catholic defensiveness and make them feel like first-class citizens. Herbert S. Parmet's *Jack: The Struggles of John F. Kennedy* (New York, N.Y., 1980), and *JFK: The Presidency of John F. Kennedy* (New York, N.Y., 1983) is an exceptionally good two-volume study of the first American Catholic president. In a carefully considered *A Question of Character: A Life of John F. Kennedy* (New York, N.Y., 1991), Thomas C. Reeves concludes that character flaws prevented John F. Kennedy from achieving his promise, but that his administration improved with experience. Garry Wills, *The Kennedy Imprisonment* (Boston, Mass., 1982) a critical study, describes Joe Kennedy and his sons as far more impressed with upperclass Anglo-Protestant than Irish Catholic values. Irish Catholic communal values did influence the political creed and conduct of Speaker of the House, Thomas P. O'Neill. They are the theme of Thomas P. O'Neill with William Novak, *Man of the House: The Life and Political Memoirs of Speaker Tip O'Neill* (New York, N.Y., 1987). In *What I Saw at the Revolution: A Political Life in the Reagan Era* (New York, N.Y., 1990), Peggy Noonan, a speechwriter for Presidents Ronald Reagan and George Bush, explains her defection from the party of her ancestors. Her position that the Democrats left her rather than that she left them reveals the feelings of many Irish and other Catholic ethnics now voting Republican.

Irish nationalism held the passionate allegiance of many Irish Americans. Without their enthusiasm and financial generosity, both constitutional and physical force nationalisms might have perished in Ireland. *Irish Nationalism and the American Contribution*, ed. Lawrence J. McCaffrey (New York, N.Y., 1976), includes two brilliant essays by Thomas N. Brown, the leading expert on Irish-American nationalism: "Nationalism and the Irish Peasant, 1800–1848" (reprinted from *Review of Politics* 15 (October 1953), and "The Origins and Character of Irish-American Nationalism" (reprinted from *Review of Politics* 18 (July 1956). Brown argues that the local allegiances of peasants in Ireland and their focus on land and their deference to landlords were obstacles to nationalist mobilizations. In America their loneliness, victimization by nativism, and their search for respectability through the instrument of an emancipated homeland initiated and nourished strong nationalist activities and sentiments. In *The United States and Ireland* (Cambridge, Mass., 1973), Donald H. Akenson discusses the Irish-American contribution to freedom efforts in Ireland. In *Emigrants and Exiles*, Kerby Miller sees alienation as the key source of Irish-American nationalism. R. V. Comerford, *The Fenians in Context: Irish Politics and Society 1848–82* (Atlantic Highlands, N.J., 1985) is the best and most up-to-date study of the Irish Republican Brotherhood and its American counterpart, the Fenian Brotherhood. Comerford describes IRB leaders as bright, lower-middle-class young men, often journalists, whose leadership potential was blocked by O'Connellite and Young Ireland establishments. Through advocating a revolutionary-republican alternative to constitutional methods they acquired an audience and gained status. Comerford also points out that in a repressive Catholic rural environment, Fenianism provided social and recreational outlets. This thesis is developed in Brian Griffin's "Social Aspects of Fenianism in Connacht and Leinster, 1858–1870," *Eire-*

Ireland 12 (Spring 1986), pp. 16–38. Nationalist picnics and clambakes with food, drink, and gushing patriotic oratory also gave Irish Americans recreational opportunities and pleasures. Other interesting studies of Fenianism are Leon Ó Broin, *Fenian Fever* (New York, N.Y., 1971); Maurice Harmon, ed., *Fenians and Fenianism* (Seattle, Wash., 1970); and T. W. Moody, *The Fenian Movement* (Cork, 1968). William D'Arcy presents a detailed examination of the American wing of the IRB in *The Fenian Movement in the United States, 1858–1886* (New York, N.Y., 1971).

In *Fenians and Anglo-American Relations during Reconstruction* (Ithaca, N.Y., 1969), Brian Jenkins describes how the United States government patronized Fenianism to pressure Britain into paying reparations for damages to Union shipping by British built blockade runners during the Civil War, and into accepting the American naturalization of former British citizens. After winning a diplomatic victory by this tactic, Washington withdrew support from Irish-American revolutionary nationalism. Thomas N. Brown's *Irish-American Nationalism* (Philadelphia, Pa., 1976), no doubt the leading study of the subject, credits the Irish-American Clan na Gael for formulating the New Departure strategy in Irish nationalism that mobilized rural Ireland around a war on landlordism. Brown repeats his thesis that late nineteenth-century Irish-American nationalism was motivated more by the quest for respectability by liberating Ireland than by an alienated Irish-American hatred for Britain as the source of its economic failures in the United States. He relates how Clan na Gael factionalism, the Parnell–Kitty O'Shea scandal, the Dr. Cronin murder in Chicago, and political activities by Clan leaders diminished the unity and intensity of Irish-American nationalism in the 1890s. The Cronin murder that resulted from conflict in the Clan between John Devoy and A. M. Sullivan is the subject of Michael F. Funchion, *Chicago's Irish Nationalists, 1881–1890* (New York, N.Y., 1976). John Devoy was the most influential of Clan na Gael leaders. *Devoy's Post Bag, 1871–1928*, 2 vols., ed. William O'Brien and Desmond Ryan contains his correspondence.

Journalists were important recruiters and propagandists for Irish-American nationalism. Two of the most important were Patrick Ford and John Boyle O'Reilly. Ford coupled American populism with Irish nationalism, denouncing American industrial capitalists and Irish landlords as twin scourges of Irish peasants and Irish-American laborers. Industrial violence eventually moved him from left to a bit right of center. He stopped attacking Catholic clericalism and capitalism and advised his readers to achieve success by embracing thrift and the middle-class work ethic. His life is the subject of James Paul Rodechko's *Patrick Ford and His Search for America: A Case Study of Irish-American Journalism, 1870–1913* (New York, N.Y., 1976). In *The American Years of John Boyle O'Reilly, 1870–1890* (New York, N.Y., 1976), Francis G. McManamin describes how the former IRB member switched to constitutional nationalism in the United States. As editor of the *Boston Pilot*, O'Reilly also advocated Catholic interests, promoted social reform, championed other religious and ethnic minorities, and tried to improve relations between Irish Catholics and Anglo-Protestants. In *Editors and Ethnicity: A History of the Irish-American Press, 1848–1883* (New York, N.Y., 1976), William Joyce Leonard explains the role of Irish-American newspapers in preserving Irish-American ethnicity while at the same time encouraging their accommodation to American ways, building bridges between the Irish "retrospect" and the American "prospect." He believes that O'Reilly's *Boston Pilot* best represented this effort.

In *America and the Fight for Irish Freedom, 1886–1922* (New York, N.Y., 1957), C. C. Tansill details Irish America's financial contributions to freedom efforts in Ireland. Studies of the Irish-American factor in Anglo-American relations include Joseph Patrick O'Grady, *Irish-Americans and Anglo-American Relations, 1880–1888* (New York, N.Y., 1976); Joseph Edward Cuddy, *Irish-America and National Isolationism, 1914–1920* (New York, N.Y., 1976); Alan J. Ward, *Ireland and Anglo-American Relations, 1899–1921* (London, 1969); John Patrick Buckley, *The New York Irish: Their View of American Foreign Policy, 1914–1921* (New York, N.Y., 1976); and Francis M. Carroll, *American Opinion and the Irish Question, 1910–1923* (New York, N.Y., 1978). After the 1922 Anglo-Irish Treaty, Philadelphia's Joseph McGarrity was the leading Irish American supporting the IRA's effort to abolish the border between the Free State and Northern Ireland. His activities are featured in Marie Veronica Tarpley, *The Role of Joseph McGarrity in the Struggle for Irish Independence* (New York, N.Y., 1976). There are a number of books that deal with Irish-American involvement in the current Northern Ireland situation, including Jack Holland, *The American Connection: U.S. Guns, Money, and Influence in Northern Ireland* (New York, N.Y., 1987); Dennis Clark, *Irish Blood: Northern Ireland and the American Conscience* (Port Washington, N.Y., 1977); Sean Cronin, *Washington's Irish Policy, 1916–1986: Independence, Partition, and Neutrality* (Dublin, 1986); and Andrew M. Wilson, *Irish America and the Ulster Conflict, 1968–1995* (Washington, D.C., 1995). The Wilson book is the most comprehensive, thoroughly researched, and perceptive analysis of the Irish-American role in the Northern Ireland crisis. It is also exceptionally well written.

More than Irish political or Catholic values, Irish nationalism inspired Irish-American labor radicalism. Boycotting, a feature of the 1880s land war in Ireland, was transported to America as a tactic in the struggle for just wages, an eight hour day, and decent working conditions. According to Steven P. Erie in *Rainbow's End*, "Cautious and conservative in local politics, the Irish controlled building trades set a record for industrial conflict, generating nearly three times as many strikes, boycotts, and sympathy strikes as other industries such as mining" (p. 50). Michael Gordon, "Irish Immigrant Culture and the Labor Boycott in New York City, 1880–1886," in *Immigrants in Industrial America, 1850–1920,* ed. Richard L. Ehrlich (Charlottesville, N.C., 1977), pp. 111–22, discusses the Irish contribution to boycotting in the United States. According to Joshua B. Freeman, "Catholics, Communists, and Republicans: Irish Workers and the Organization of the Transport Workers Union," in *Working Class America: Essays on Labor, Community, and American Society,* ed. Michael H. Frish and Daniel J. Walkowitz (Urbana, Ill., 1983), Irish immigrant veterans of the Anglo-Irish and Civil Wars cooperated with Communists in the creation of the New York Transport Workers Union.

The Molly Maguires were the most famous and most romanticized of Irish-American labor radicals. In *The Molly Maguires* (Cambridge, Mass., 1964), Wayne G. Broehl makes it clear that they were as much motivated by hatred of English and Welsh mine bosses and foremen as by a determination to better their working and living conditions. William A. Gudelunas, Jr., and William G. Shade, *Before the Molly Maguires: The Emergence of the Ethno-Religious Factor in the Politics of the Lower Anthracite Region, 1844–1872* (New York, N.Y., 1976) argue that ethnic antagonisms and loyalties rather than economic conditions or social issues decided political affiliations in the Schuylkill County, Pennsylvania coal region. *America and Ireland, 1776–1976,* ed. Doyle and Edwards, contains a significant essay by David Montgomery, "The Irish and the American Labor Movement." Henry J. Browne, *The*

Catholic Church and the Knights of Labor (New York, N.Y., 1976) discusses the conflict between liberals such as James Cardinal Gibbons and Archbishop John Ireland and conservative Archbishop Michael Corrigan over the rights of the working class. In "Race and Ethnicity in Organized Labor: The Historical Source for Resistance to Affirmative Action," in *Ethnicity and the Work Force*, ed. Winston A. Van Horne and Thomas V. Tonneson (Madison, Wis., 1985), Herbert Hill insists that Irish and Jewish American Federation of Labor leaders did much for White ethnic workers but little or nothing for African or Hispanic Americans.

Throughout this book I have used novels as a source and an insight into the Irish-American mind and character. The beginnings of Irish-American literature were closely associated with journalism. A school of writers gathered around John Boyle O'Reilly at the *Boston Globe*. They were inspired by Young Ireland romanticism and the idealism of the New England literary establishment. According to Charles Fanning, *Finley Peter Dunne and Mr. Dooley: The Chicago Years* (Lexington, Ky., 1978), Finley Peter Dunne, a Chicago journalist, created the first realistic ethnic community in American literature in his Mr. Dooley essays about Chicago's Bridgeport Irish. Fanning continues his discussion of Dunne and moves on to James T. Farrell (whose second and third generation Chicago Irish achieve social and residential mobility, migrating farther and farther south, away from the central city in advance of an expanding Black ghetto) in "The Literary Dimension," McCaffrey et al., *The Irish in Chicago*. This essay also includes information on some interesting women writers, Kate McPhelim Cleary and Clara E. Laughlin. Fanning, the leading scholar of Irish-American literature, sums up its history in the perceptive and elegantly written *The Irish Voice in America: Irish-American Fiction from the 1760s to the 1880s* (Lexington, Ky., 1990). In addition, he has edited two important anthologies: *Mr. Dooley and the Chicago Irish: The Autobiography of a Nineteenth-Century Ethnic Group* (Washington, D.C., 1987) and the *Exiles of Erin: Nineteenth-Century Irish-American Fiction* (Notre Dame, Ind., 1987). Daniel J. Casey and Robert E. Rhodes, eds., *Irish-American Fiction: Essays in Criticism* (New York, N.Y., 1979) includes contributions by prominent scholars on a number of Irish-American literary figures. Casey and Rhodes also have edited an anthology: *Modern Irish-American Fiction: A Reader* (Syracuse, N.Y., 1989).

Irish America has made its mark in the theatre as well as the written page. Maureen Murphy's "Irish-American Theatre," *Ethnic Theatre in America*, ed. Maxine Schwartz Seller (Westport, Conn., 1983) describes the presentation of the Irish in early American plays. To many experts, Eugene O'Neill is America's greatest playwright. In *Eugene O'Neill, Irish and American: A Study in Cultural Context* (New York, N.Y., 1976), Henry Cornelius Cronin insists that O'Neill viewed life from an Irish Catholic original sin and guilt perspective even though he formally rejected Catholicism.

Sports and popular entertainment in the United States—comedy, singing, dancing—have had a strong Irish presence. Stephen A. Reis, *Touching Base: Professional Baseball and American Culture in the Progressive Era* (Westport, Conn., 1980), pp. 184–87, mentions the disproportionately large numbers of Irish and German players in baseball's early period. In *The Bill James Historical Baseball Abstract* (New York, N.Y., 1986), pp. 8–59, the author credits the Irish with dominating the game from 1870 to 1900, especially in the 1890s, as does Peter C. Bjarkman in "Forgotten Americans and the National Pastime: Literature on Baseball's Ethnic Religious, and Racial Diversity," *Multi-Cultural Review* 1 (April 1992), pp. 46–48. In an exceptionally interesting and well-written journey into American popular culture, *'Twas Only an Irishman's Dream: The Image of Ireland and the Irish in American Popular Song Lyrics, 1800–1920s* (Urbana & Chicago, Ill., 1996), William H. A. Williams argues that the changing and improving image of the Irish and their homeland in American popular music was significant in their march to acceptability and respectability.

Early movies expressed the negative, nativist image of the brawling, feckless Irish. But starting in the 1930s, favorable portraits of the Irish, especially priests, and the popularity of stars such as Jimmy Cagney, Spencer Tracy, Bing Crosby, Grace Kelly, and Gene Kelly, and the genius of director John Ford elevated the Irish into "America's favorite ethnics." This story is told with intelligence, humor, style, and vigor in Joseph M. Curran, *Hibernian Green on the Silver Screen* (Westport, Conn., 1989).

In *The Irish Diaspora: A Primer* and in other places such as *Being Had: Historians, Evidence and the Irish in North America* (Toronto, 1995) and "Data: What Is Known about the Irish in North America," in *The Untold Story: The Irish in Canada*, ed. Robert O'Driscoll and Lorna Reynolds (Toronto, 1988), vol. 1, pp. 15–25, Donald Harmon Akenson criticizes me and other historians of Irish America for failing to make essential comparisons with the Irish Diaspora in other places such as Australia, Canada, and New Zealand. Malcolm Campbell supports Akenson's point in "The Other Immigrants: Comparing the Irish in Australia and the United States," *Journal of Ethnic History* 14 (Spring 1995), pp. 3–22. No doubt it is important to understand how the loyalties and values that Irish immigrants carried with them from Ireland to other countries are altered or stay the same in a variety of environments. But it is doubtful that we can significantly enlarge our understanding of the Irish-American Catholic experience by comparing it to that of their co-ethnics in various parts of the British Commonwealth. Life for American-Irish Catholics was so much different. They were more attached to urban communities and an industrial economy; they were required to interact with a wider variety of other religions, races, and nationalities; and increasingly they were more influenced by regional climates, interests, and values than were Irish Catholics in New Zealand, Canada, Britain, and Australia. Nevertheless, there are a number of first-rate studies of the non-American Irish Diaspora that deserve examination, including: John Archer Jackson, *The Irish in Britain* (London, 1963); Graham Davis, *The Irish in Britain, 1815–1914* (Dublin, 1991); Lynn Lees, *Exiles of Erin: Irish Migrants in Victorian London* (Ithaca, N.Y., 1979); Kevin O'Connor, *The Irish in Britain* (London, 1972); John Hickey, *Urban Catholics: Urban Catholicism in England and Wales from 1829 to the Present Day* (London, 1967); Robert O'Driscoll and Lorna Reynolds, eds., *The Untold Story: The History of the Irish in Canada*, 2 vols.; Patrick O'Farrell, *The Irish in Australia* (Notre Dame, Ind., 1989); and David Fitzpatrick, *Oceans of Consolation: Personal Accounts of Irish Migration to Australia* (Ithaca, N.Y., 1994). The O'Farrell and Fitzpatrick volumes are especially impressive in style and content. Fitzpatrick's effort is a model for the use of immigrant letters to construct a moving and informative story of a traumatic experience. Despite my criticism of *The Irish Diaspora: A Primer,* Akenson provides valuable comparative information on the Irish throughout the English-speaking world that contradicts the Kerby Miller *Emigrants and Exiles* contention that religious and Gaelic cultural elements were obstacles to the progress of Irish Catholic emigrants in the United States and other places. In this, he provides a good example of the positive aspects of comparing experiences.

Index

Abbey Theatre, 88, 151
Aberdeen, Lord (Prime Minister), 145
Abolitionist movement: Irish opposition to, 73–74, 143
Abortion controversy, 95, 195
Act of Union, 31–32, 34
Act of Supremacy (Ireland), 19
Adams, Henry, 113
Addams, Jane, 128
Adrian IV (Pope), 14
African Americans: Irish-American prejudices against, 73–74, 143, 187–88, 192, 193–94, 206 n. 4; part of Irish led urban Democratic coalition, 129–30, 182; support for Kennedy, 182, 184; receive Irish Catholic support for civil rights, 187; take advantage of urban Catholic schools, 187; inspire civil rights movement in Northern Ireland, 189
Agrarian Secret Societies (Ireland), 27–28, 55, 64, 161
Aisling Poems, 55
Akenson, Donald H., 3–5, 201–2n.4
Alabama claims, 156
Alcoholism, Irish Catholic, 82, 83
Alexander VIII (Pope), 23
Alien and Sedition Acts, 95, 120
All Good Men (Fleming), 133
Allen, W. P., 154, 155
American Catholicism: target of nativism, 94–95, 98–102, 110–11, 114; pre-Irish character of, 96–97; Irish influences on, 82, 97–98, 114, 184–85; anti-intellectualism

of, 177–78, 210n.3; literary criticisms of, 178–80; intellectual and cultural improvements in, 185–86; support for social justice, 187; schools intellectually nourish African-American youngsters, 187; current crisis in, 194–96
American Conference for Irish Studies, 198
American Enlightenment: and nativism, 93
American Federation of Labor, 85, 206n.4
American Irish (Shannon), 125
American Land League, 160
American Minute Men, 114
American nativism, 71, 75, 86, 91–115
American Party (Know Nothings), 101–2
American Protective Association, 114
American Revolution, 29, 95
American wake, 78
Americanist controversy: in Catholic Church, 104–8
Amnesty Association, 155
Ancient Order of Hibernians, 75
Anglo-American moral and laissez faire reformism, 132, 135–36
Anglo-American patriotism, 28–29
Anglo-Irish agreement (Dec., 1993), 190
Anglo-Irish patriotism, 28–29
Anglo-Irish Protestants, 4–5, 24–32, 42–43, 47, 88
Anglo-Irish Treaty (1921), 167, 168

242   *Index*

The Irish Catholic Diaspora in America was composed in Baskerville by Brevis Press, Bethany, Connecticut; printed on 60-pound Glatfelter B-31 and bound by Cushing-Malloy, Inc., Ann Arbor, Michigan; and designed and produced by Kachergis Book Design, Pittsboro, North Carolina.